Qumran Questions

Qumran Questions

Collected Essays

Sidnie White Crawford

CASCADE *Books* • Eugene, Oregon

QUMRAN QUESTIONS
Collected Essays

Copyright © 2025 Sidnie White Crawford. All rights reserved. Except for brief quotations in critical publications or reviews, no part of this book may be reproduced in any manner without prior written permission from the publisher. Write: Permissions, Wipf and Stock Publishers, 199 W. 8th Ave., Suite 3, Eugene, OR 97401.

Cascade Books
An Imprint of Wipf and Stock Publishers
199 W. 8th Ave., Suite 3
Eugene, OR 97401

www.wipfandstock.com

PAPERBACK ISBN: 979-8-3852-1844-8
HARDCOVER ISBN: 979-8-3852-1845-5
EBOOK ISBN: 979-8-3852-1846-2

Cataloguing-in-Publication data:

Names: Crawford, Sidnie White, author.

Title: Qumran questions : collected essays / Sidnie White Crawford.

Description: Eugene, OR: Cascade Books, 2025. | Includes bibliographical references and index.

Identifiers: ISBN 979-8-3852-1844-8 (paperback). | ISBN 979-8-3852-1845-5 (hardcover). | ISBN 979-8-3852-1846-2 (ebook).

Subjects: LCSH: Dead Sea Scrolls. | Qumran community. | Qumran site (West Bank).

Classification: BM487 C73 2025 (print). | BM487 (epub).

VERSION NUMBER 07/17/25

In Loving Memory of M. Ottilie White Bulakites

1927–2024

"What a lioness was your mother among lions!"
—Ezekiel 19:2

Contents

Preface | ix
Acknowledgments | xi
Abbreviations | xiii
Introduction | xv

Part 1: Questions of Archaeology

1. Qumran: Caves, Scrolls and Buildings | 3
2. Qumran Cave 4Q: Its Archaeology and its Manuscript Collection | 24
3. The Inscriptional Evidence from Qumran and Its Relationship to the Cave 4Q Documents | 38
4. Economic Activity, Trade, and Manufacture at Qumran, with a Special Look at the Inscriptions and Documentary Texts | 50

Part 2: Questions Concerning Women

5. Not According to Rule: Women, the Dead Sea Scrolls, and Qumran | 71
6. Mothers, Sisters, and Elders: Titles for Women in Second Temple Jewish and Early Christian Communities | 94
7. "There Is Much Wisdom in Her": The Matriarchs in the Qumran Library | 107
8. Traditions about Miriam in the Qumran Scrolls | 126
9. Lady Wisdom and Dame Folly at Qumran | 137
10. The Meaning of the Phrase עיר המקדש in the Temple Scroll | 149

Bibliography | 161

Preface

It is my pleasusre to thank everyone who has helped me with this project. At Cascade Books (Wipf and Stock Publishers), I would like to thank Michael Thomson for his enthusiastic support of my proposal, and K. C. Hanson for his patient shepherding of the manuscript through the publication process. Princeton Theological Seminary's library was invaluable for tracking down obscure references.

I have had many conversation partners over the years. Jodi Magness, Marcello Fidanzio, Dennis Mizzi, and Joan Taylor are my mentors in all things archaeological. Eileen Schuller, Devorah Dimant, and Carol Newsom were the pioneering female scholars and my role models in Dead Sea Scrolls research. Cecilia Wassén, Jutta Jokiranta, Charlotte Hempel, Sarianna Metso, Judith Newman, George Brooke, Lawrence Schiffman, James VanderKam, and Benjamin G. Wright III have been colleagues for many years, and I thank them for their support and friendship.

My husband Dan as always gave unstinting support to my scholarly work. This volume is dedicated to the memory of my mother, M. Ottilie White Bulakites, who sacrificed to put me through college and enabled me to pursue my dreams.

Acknowledgments

All previously published works are listed here with the gracious permission of the original publishers.

"Economic Activity, Trade, and Manufacture at Qumran, with a Special Look at the Inscriptions and Documentary Texts." In *Pushing Sacred Boundaries in Early Judaism and the Ancient Mediterranean*, edited by Dennis Mizzi et al., 326–48. JSJSup 208. Leiden: Brill, 2023.

"The Inscriptional Evidence from Qumran and its Relationship to the Cave 4Q Documents." In *The Caves of Qumran: Proceedings of the International Conference, Lugano 2014*, edited by Marcello Fidanzio, 213–20. STDJ 118. Leiden: Brill, 2016.

"Lady Wisdom and Dame Folly at Qumran." *Dead Sea Discoveries* 5 (1997) 355–66.

"The Meaning of the Phrase עיר המקדש in the Temple Scroll." *Dead Sea Discoveries* 8 (2001) 1–13.

"Mothers, Sisters, and Elders: Titles for Women in Second Temple Jewish and Early Christian Communities." In *The Dead Sea Scrolls as Background to Postbiblical Judaism and Early Christianity*, edited by James R. Davila, 177–91. STDJ 46. Leiden: Brill, 2003.

"Not According to Rule: Women, the Dead Sea Scrolls and Qumran." In *Emanuel: Studies in the Hebrew Bible, Septuagint and Dead Sea Scrolls in Honor of Emanuel Tov*, edited by Shalom Paul et al., 127–50. VTSup 94. Leiden: Brill, 2003.

Acknowledgments

"Qumran Cave 4: Its Archaeology and Its Manuscript Collection." In *Is There a Text in This Cave? Studies in the Textuality of the Dead Sea Scrolls in Honour of George J. Brooke*, edited by Ariel Feldman et al., 105–21. STDJ 119. Leiden: Brill, 2017.

"Qumran: Caves, Scrolls, and Buildings." In *A Teacher for All Generations: Essays in Honor of James C. VanderKam*. Edited by Eric Mason, et al. JSJSup 153.1, 253–74. Leiden: Brill, 2011.

"'There Is Much Wisdom in Her': The Matriarchs in the Qumran Library." In *Celebrate Her for the Fruit of Her Hands: Essays in Honor of Carol L. Meyers*, edited by Susan Ackerman et al., 133–52. Winona Lake, IN: Eisenbrauns, 2015.

"Traditions about Miriam in the Qumran Scrolls." In *Women and Judaism*, edited by Leonard J. Greenspoon, Ronald A. Simkins, Jean Axelrad Cahan, 33–44. Studies in Jewish Civilization 14. Omaha: Creighton University Press, 2003.

Abbreviations

AB	Anchor Bible
ANESSup	Ancient Near Eastern Studies Supplement Series
BA	*Biblical Archaeologist*
BAIAS	*Bulletin of the Anglo-Israel Archaeological Society*
BAR	*Biblical Archaeology Review*
BAR	British Archaeological Reports
BASOR	*Bulletin of the American Schools of Oriental Research*
BZAW	Beihefte zur Zeitschrift für die alttestamentliche Wissenschaft
CBQ	*Catholic Biblical Quarterly*
DJD	Discoveries in the Judaean Desert
DSD	*Dead Sea Discoveries*
EC	*Early Christianity*
EDSS	*Encyclopedia of the Dead Sea Scrolls*. Edited by Lawrence H. Schiffman and James C. VanderKam. 2 vols. Oxford: Oxford University Press, 2000
FAT	Forschungen zum Alten Testament
HAR	*Hebrew Annual Review*
HTR	*Harvard Theological Review*
IEJ	*Israel Exploration Journal*
ISACR	Interdisciplinary Studies in Ancient Culture and Religion
JAJ	*Journal of Ancient Judaism*
JBL	*Journal of Biblical Literature*
JJS	*Journal of Jewish Studies*

JQR	*Jewish Quarterly Review*
JSJ	*Journal for the Study of Judaism in the Persian, Hellenistic, and Roman Periods*
JSJSup	Journal for the Study of Judaism in the Persian, Hellenistic, and Roman Periods Supplements
JSOT	*Journal for the Study of the Old Testament*
JSP	Judea and Samaria Publications
LSTS	Library of Second Temple Studies
NTOASA	Novum Testamentum et Orbis Antiquus Series Archaeologica
PEQ	*Palestine Exploration Quarterly*
QC	*Qumran Chronicle*
RB	*Revue Biblique*
Res	*Res: Anthropology and Aesthetics*
RevQ	*Revue de Qumran*
SBL	Society of Biblical Literature
SBT	Studies in Biblical Theology
SDSSRL	Studies in the Dead Sea Scrolls and Related Literature
SJOT	*Scandinavian Journal of the Old Testament*
STDJ	Studies on the Texts of the Desert of Judah
TSAJ	Texte und Studien zum antiken Judentum
VTSup	Vetus Testamentum Supplements
WUNT	Wissenschaftliche Untersuchungen zum Neuen Testament
ZAW	*Zeitschrift für die alttestamentliche Wissenschaft*

Introduction

THIS VOLUME OF ESSAYS chronicles my work in two related areas of Dead Sea Scrolls research: studies in the archaeology of the broader archaeological site of Qumran, in particular the manuscript caves, and the question of the presence or absence of women in the Qumran sectarian texts and at the settlement of Qumran. As such, it forms a companion volume to my 2022 collection, *The Text of the Pentateuch: Textual Criticism and the Dead Sea Scrolls*, which represented my work in the textual criticism of the Hebrew Bible that was deeply informed by the Qumran biblical manuscripts.

These essays range in date from 1997 to 2023 and thus were written mostly after the completed publication of the Qumran scrolls in the Discoveries in the Judaean Desert series (DJD). The essays are lightly edited, mainly by bringing the bibliography up-to-date. In one article, "Qumran: Caves, Scrolls, and Buildings," I have added an appendix to reflect changes in my thinking since its publication.

The first section, Questions of Archaeology, consists of four essays. The first, "Qumran: Caves, Scrolls, and Buildings," is a broad investigation of the archaeological site of Qumran, located on the northwestern shore of the Dead Sea. The site of Qumran includes the buildings, cemeteries, and related structures located on the marl plateau near the shore of the Dead Sea, the humanmade caves dug out of the marl plateau, some of which were manuscript caves, the natural caves (some of which were also manuscript caves) located in the limestone cliffs within a five-kilometer radius of the Qumran settlement, and the satellite settlement of 'Ein Feshkha, located to the south of Qumran. The most important question I consider in this section is the relationship between the manuscript caves and the settlement. Does the archaeological evidence indicate that the Jewish group that lived

Introduction

there during the second phase of the settlement (c. 100–75 BCE to 68 CE) was the same group that deposited the manuscripts in the marl terrace and limestone cliff caves? If the answer to that question is affirmative (which I argue to be the case), then the corollary question arises: when and why did they deposit those manuscripts in the caves?

The second essay, "Qumran Cave 4Q: Its Archaeology and Manuscript Collection," takes a deeper dive into the archaeology and manuscript collection of the marl terrace cave 4Q. Cave 4Q contained by far the largest manuscript collection of the eleven manuscript caves (c. 75% of the recovered manuscripts) and the other cave collections are inevitably compared to it. The essay explores the archaeology of the cave with a special concern for the deposition of the manuscripts. It then presents an overview of the 4Q manuscript collection, highlighting certain special features that set it apart.

Skin and papyrus manuscripts are not the only written artefacts recovered from Qumran and its caves. Chapter 3, "The Inscriptional Evidence from Qumran and its Relation to the Cave 4Q Documents," surveys the inscriptional evidence from Qumran found both in the ruins and the caves. Most of this evidence, mainly consisting of inscriptions on pottery, written in Hebrew/Aramaic, Greek, and perhaps Latin, is extremely fragmentary and difficult to decipher. It is mostly economic, i.e., weights and measures, lists, and receipts, giving a glimpse into the economic life of the settlement. A few, however, are scribal exercises, an independent attestation of a scribal presence at Qumran. I then compare that corpus to similar finds among the manuscripts of cave 4Q, in particular scribal exercises, lists of names, and documentary texts.

The last essay in this section, "Economic Activity, Trade, and Manufacture at Qumran, with a Special Look at the Inscriptions and Documentary Texts," concerns the quotidian life of the Qumran settlement apart from the preparation, copying, repair, and storage of scrolls. Did the inhabitants farm, raise animals, or manufacture goods? How did the settlement survive for 150 years in such an inhospitable climate? The essay demonstrates that the Qumran inhabitants did engage in small-scale agriculture (especially at nearby 'Ein Feshkha) and raising animals such as sheep and goats, and they manufactured much of their own pottery, including their signature "scroll jars." Further, although Qumran was not on a major road or shipping route, it was connected by a network of paths to nearby cities and towns, enabliing the inhabitants to conduct trade and barter for goods.

Introduction

Part 2, Questions Concerning Women, consists, as its title suggests, of essays that deal in one way or another with the role and status of women in the Qumran sect, and their presence or absence at the site of Qumran. These inquiries were greatly advanced by the publication in the 1990s of the more fragmentary Qumran manuscripts and, in the 2000s and continuing, the complete archaeological data from the site.

The first essay in this section, "'Not According to Rule': Women, the Dead Sea Scrolls, and Qumran," inquires into both of these questions. The first half of the article looks at the textual evidence from the caves that directly concerns women. This evidence revolves mainly around the intertwined issues of ritual purity, sexuality, and marriage. The inescapable conclusion from these texts is that women were part of the Qumran sect, although under the authority of men. The archaeological evidence, presented in the second half, is much more ambiguous. While there is a small amount of evidence for the presence of women there, mainly from the cemeteries, overall the archaeological picture is that of a site inhabited by adult males living a communal, not family-oriented, lifestyle. In the article's conclusion, I attempt to reconcile these conflicting bodies of evidence.

Chapter 6, "Mothers, Sisters, and Elders: Titles for Women in Second Temple Jewish and Early Christian Communities," looks at two fragmentary texts, the 4Q remains of the Damascus Document, and 4Q502, a very fragmentary text that contains a community ritual of some kind. Both of these texts contain honorary titles for women (e.g., "mothers," "female elders," etc.) in sectarian contexts. I then place these titles within the broader context of Second Temple Judaism and early Christianity, utilizing inscriptional evidence from early synagogues, churches, and cemeteries throughout the Mediterranean world, as well as textual evidence from Second Temple and Rabbinic Judaism and the New Testament.

The next two chapters, "'There is Much Wisdom in Her': The Matriarchs in the Qumran Library," and "Traditions about Miriam in the Dead Sea Scrolls," discuss traditions concerning prominent women from Israel's pre-monarchic past. In Second Temple literature as a whole, traditions about figures such as Sarah, Rebekah, Rachel and Leah, and Miriam were greatly expanded beyond the biblical material. These traditions were often recorded in books of the so-called Apocrypha and Pseudepigrapha, such as Jubilees and 1 Enoch. The Qumran caves yielded more traditional information about Israel's matriarchs, which I present here.

Introduction

The figures of "Lady Wisdom" and "Dame Folly," well-known from Proverbs 1–9, are the subject of chapter 9, "Lady Wisdom and Dame Folly at Qumran." While the role and character of Lady Wisdom does not change much in the hitherto unknown Qumran texts 4Q184, 185, and 525, the figure of Dame Folly, or the "Strange Woman," is portrayed not only as a sexual temptress, but also as a dark, cthonic figure, leading her unwitting dupes into the depths of the underworld.

The final chapter, "The Meaning of the Phrase עיר המקדש in the Temple Scroll," draws together the two parts of the volume. It considers the meaning of the phrase עיר המקדש, "the city of the sanctuary," in the context of the geography and architecture of the Temple Scroll. It then asks why sexual intercourse appears to be banned in עיר המקדש, and whether or not that ban results in the complete exile of women from the Temple Scroll's ideal temple.

Part 1

Questions of Archaeology

1

Qumran
Caves, Scrolls and Buildings

THE CAVES IN THE vicinity of Khirbet Qumran and their contents have been the subjects of many questions since their discovery. Who owned the hundreds of ancient Jewish manuscripts found in the caves, and who put them there? The answers to those questions depend on how one interprets the archaeological data from Khirbet Qumran and its surrounding caves.

There is broad agreement on the following matters: The first archaeological phase at Qumran dates to the Iron II period. There followed a long period of abandonment; then the site was resettled in the first quarter of the first century BCE and continued, perhaps with interruption, perhaps not, until it was destroyed by a fire in the middle to late first century CE. There was a very short period of habitation as a Roman army encampment after the first century CE destruction, followed by some ephemeral squatting, then the site was permanently abandoned until it was excavated by Roland de Vaux of the École Biblique et Archeologique Francaise in the 1950s. All archaeologists agree that the inhabitants of the site during that long period of settlement in the last century BCE and first century CE were Jews, owing to the presence of stepped pools and Hebrew inscriptions found at the site. After that broad agreement, however, archaeologists part company.[1]

---

[1]. De Vaux, *Archaeology*, 1–45. De Vaux argued that the site was first settled in the mid-second century BCE (4), but the archaeological evidence for that date is doubtful. I follow the dating proposed by Magness, *Archaeology*^{2}, 64–72. See also Broshi, "Qumran Archaeology;" Galor and Zangenberg, "Qumran Archaeology," 1–9. For a discussion of

Part 1: Questions of Archaeology

Two competing positions currently exist on what Khirbet Qumran was and who lived there. The first position, originally articulated by de Vaux and today championed in the archaeological community by Magness, Mizzi, the late Magen Broshi and the late Hanan Eshel, states that Qumran was a sectarian settlement, most probably Essene, one of the three main Jewish movements in the Greco-Roman period described by Josephus, with secondary support from Philo and Pliny.[2] The Essenes who lived at Qumran owned the scrolls, and hid them in caves in proximity to the ruins, in which they were found. The Qumran manuscripts are therefore the remnants of an Essene library and open a window onto the thought world of a major Jewish movement of the Second Temple period. This is popularly known as the Qumran-Essene hypothesis.[3]

The second position is not so much a position as an anti-position, arguing against the Qumran-Essene hypothesis. Those who hold this position do not agree on the particulars, but do agree that Qumran was not a Jewish sectarian settlement, and that the manuscripts found in the caves are not related to the site of Qumran. The most well-known proponents of this position are Robert Donceel and Pauline Donceel-Voûte, the late Norman Golb, the late Yizhar Hirshfeld, Yitzhak Magen and Yuval Peleg, and the late David Stacey. The Donceels have argued that Qumran was a "villa rustica," with wealthy inhabitants. Golb argued that Qumran was a Hasmonean/Herodian fortress, and that the scrolls were part of the Jerusalem Temple library, hidden in the caves before the siege and destruction of the Temple in 70 CE. Hirshfeld held that Qumran was a rural estate complex; the scrolls were brought for concealment in the caves from some public library, probably in Jerusalem. Magen and Peleg contend that Qumran was at first a fortress and then became an important pottery production center.[4] The scrolls, meanwhile, were hidden by fleeing refugees during the Great Jewish Revolt. Finally, Stacey argued that Qumran was a seasonal industrial center connected to Jericho, and the scrolls were brought to the caves from Jerusalem and were unconnected to the site.[5] What all these

---

the army encampment of Period III, see Taylor, "Kh. Qumran," 139–42.

2. VanderKam has been one of the most articulate proponents of this view in general Dead Sea Scrolls scholarship. See his case for the Essene Hypothesis in *Dead Sea Scrolls Today*, 71–87. See also my arguments in Crawford, *Scribes and Scrolls*, 269–308.

3. For an interesting discussion of the entire Qumran-Essene hypothesis, see Ullmann-Margalit, *Out of the Cave*.

4. Magen and Peleg, *Back to Qumran*, 110.

5. Donceel and Donceel-Voûte, "Archaeology." Norman Golb, *Who Wrote*. Hirshfeld,

hypotheses have in common (while differing widely in their particulars) is that the scrolls were brought from Jerusalem and hidden in the caves as a consequence of the revolt in 66–73 CE.

What we may characterize as the "anti-de Vaux" interpretations are united by the way that they each reinterpret the archaeological data using only the ruins of the buildings of Khirbet Qumran. What they do not do, or at best do only superficially, is to take into account the archaeological data from the caves, which were excavated by de Vaux in the 1950s at the same time that he excavated the site of Qumran. That archaeological data, written up by de Vaux in DJD 1, 3 and 6 and presented in English in his Schweich Lectures, sheds much light on the question of who put the scrolls in the caves, and why.[6] But it is also important, when making a historical reconstruction of the events that led to the deposit of the scrolls in the caves, to take into account the contents of the scrolls themselves and the nature of the collection. In what follows I attempt to do both.

Archaeological Evidence

The Caves

Cave 1Q, discovered accidentally in 1947 by Ta'amireh Bedouin, famously contained seven scrolls, two of which, the Serekh ha-Yaḥad and the Pesher Habakkuk, were found wrapped in linen and stored in a jar. Another, the Great Isaiah Scroll (1QIsaiaha), was found in the same jar without wrappings. It is not clear whether the other four scrolls retrieved by the Bedouin, the Genesis Apocryphon, 1QIsaiahb, the Hodayot, and the War Scroll, were either stored in jars or wrapped in linen.[7] The jar in which the first three scrolls were found is a tall storage jar, hole-mouthed, with a cylindrical

---

"Qumran." Magen and Peleg, "Back to Qumran," 66–68, 92–94, 99–101. Stacey, "Seasonal Industries." Humbert offers a modification of de Vaux's theory, arguing that Qumran originally was built as a fortress, but became "a religious center for a Jewish sect living around the Dead Sea." Humbert, "Some Remarks," 37. Taylor, *Essenes*, 251–61, follows that line of reasoning, arguing that the Essenes were permitted to settle and expand Qumran in the reign of Herod the Great. She believes that the scrolls did belong to the inhabitants of the settlement, whom she identifies with the Essenes (275–77).

6. Harding, "Introductory," and de Vaux, "La Poterie," in DJD 1. De Vaux, "Archéologie^1," in DJD 3. De Vaux, "Archéologie^2," in DJD 6.

7. The possibility has been raised by Weston Fields that the Bedouin actually found two caves, only one of which was subsequently located by Harding and de Vaux. Fields, *History*, 111–13.

Part 1: Questions of Archaeology

body, a well-marked (carinated) shoulder, and a flat base. It was fitted with a bowl-shaped lid. Since scrolls were found stored inside, this type of jar became known as a "scroll jar." However, it is important to recognize that only one jar from Cave 1Q was found by the Bedouin with scrolls inside. Other empty whole jars were also found by the Bedouin, lined up in a row against the wall of the cave.[8]

1Q was excavated by the Jordanian Department of Antiquities and the École Biblique, under the direction of G. Lankester Harding and de Vaux, in 1949. During the excavation, fragments of seventy-two scrolls were found, some linen wrappings,[9] and sherds from at least fifty cylindrical jars and their bowl-shaped lids. One scroll, in its wrapping, was found adhering to the mouth of its broken jar.[10] 1Q also contained phylactery cases and other pottery, e.g., three bowls, a pot, a juglet, two Hellenistic period lamps, and two Roman period lamps.[11]

Cave 2Q, a natural cave found by the Bedouin in 1952, yielded only six jars, one lid, and three bowls, but thirty-three fragmentary manuscripts.[12] The discovery of 2Q prompted de Vaux to undertake a survey of the caves in the limestone cliffs overlooking Qumran. In a race with the Bedouin, archaeologists discovered Cave 3Q in 1952, which had collapsed in antiquity. 3Q yielded fragments of fourteen skin manuscripts, sherds of thirty-five cylindrical jars, more than twenty lids, two jugs, and a lamp. The Copper Scroll was also found in 3Q, deposited not in the back of the collapsed cave with the other finds, but set against the north wall at the front of the cave.[13]

---

8. Magness, *Archaeology*^{2}, 92.

9. An analysis of the linen cloths from Cave 1Q was done by Crowfoot. She states that some of these cloths "were certainly scroll wrappers," but some were "covers once tied over the jar tops," and some may have been used as packing material in the jars. "Linen Textiles," 19, 20. For a complete analysis of all the textiles found at Qumran, see Bélis, "Des textiles," 207–76.

10. See DJD 1, Pl. 1, 8–10.

11. De Vaux, *Archaeology*, 49.

12. De Vaux, *Archaeology*, 50. Mizzi lists nine jars or fragments, a count taken from de Vaux's handwritten inventory. "Miscellaneous Finds," 140n14. The statistics for the manuscript finds are all taken from the tables found in Tov, *Revised Lists*, 29–114.

13. De Vaux, "Archéologie^1," 7. The Copper Scroll is anomalous in several ways. As its name implies, it is engraved on thin copper sheets, the only composition from antiquity found on copper. Its language is an early form of Mishnaic Hebrew, not the (archaizing) Biblical Hebrew of the rest of the Qumran scrolls. It is not in any sense a literary composition, but instead is a listing of treasure deposits and their hiding places. Whether or not these treasures (which were enormous) were real was the subject of great controversy.

The Bedouin discovered Cave 6Q,[14] which contained skin and papyrus fragments of thirty-one manuscripts, including one account or contract,[15] one jar, and a bowl. Until 1956, these four caves were the only caves in the limestone cliffs in which manuscripts were uncovered. In 1956, the Bedouin discovered Cave 11Q. 11Q contained thirty manuscripts or fragments of manuscripts (including the Temple Scroll, 11Q19), as well as one jar and other pottery sherds. 11Q19, according to its discoverers, was found wrapped in linen in a scroll jar.[16]

The context of the limestone cliff manuscript caves must be kept in mind when considering how and when the manuscripts were placed in those caves. In the 1952 survey of the limestone cliffs, de Vaux and his team made soundings in 270 caves in a section of the cliffs eight kilometers long, with Khirbet Qumran approximately in the center. 230 of the caves had nothing in them, but forty contained pottery and other objects. Some were as old as the Chalcolithic period, some as late as the modern period, but twenty-six contained remains from the Greco-Roman period that were similar to the finds from 1Q, 2Q, 3Q, 6Q, and 11Q. De Vaux gives a complete list of these finds in DJD 3.[17] The list includes, over and over, storage jars (cylindrical and ovoid), bowl-shaped lids, lamps, juglets, and bowls. The pottery types uncovered in the caves are the same types that were excavated at Qumran. Further, as de Vaux notes, the density of occupation increases as one gets closer to Qumran. Later surveys underscore de Vaux's findings. Patrich conducted surveys in the limestone cliffs in the 1980s. While no new scrolls were discovered, Patrich basically confirmed de Vaux's conclusions.[18] In the 1990s, Broshi and Eshel excavated two caves (C and F) 200 meters north of Qumran and discovered pottery sherds from the first century BCE and the first century CE.[19]

Given the Copper Scroll's unique characteristics, and the fact that it was deposited in another area of 3Q, away from the main deposit, I believe that the Copper Scroll was deposited in 3Q separately, by a different group or individual (possibly from the Jerusalem Temple) than the rest of the Qumran scrolls. Crawford, *Scribes and Scrolls*, 126-27. See the recent article by Høgenhaven, "Copper Scroll."

14. There is uncertainty concerning the actual location of 6Q. Two possible candidates present themselves, according to de Vaux's notes. See Fidanzio, "Searching."

15. Baillet, "Textes," 138-39.

16. Crawford, *Temple Scroll*, 12; Taylor, "Buried Manuscripts," 7. The wrapper has been published by Sukenik in Elgvin et al., *Gleanings*, 339-49.

17. De Vaux, "Archéologie¹," 6-13.

18. Patrich, "Khirbet Qumran," 73-96.

19. Broshi and Eshel, "Residential," 328.

Part 1: Questions of Archaeology

The conclusion is inescapable. The caves in the limestone cliffs saw a density of human habitation at the same time as Khirbet Qumran, and the same types of pottery were in use in both places. In only a few of those caves, however, were manuscripts discovered, although they may have been used for manuscript storage in antiquity, given the presence of cylindrical jars in some of them.[20] It is unlikely that the caves in the limestone cliffs were used for long-term occupancy, since they are small, not well ventilated or lit, and with uneven floors and ceilings. Long-term storage, therefore, is the best possibility. The situation is different, however, for the second group of caves to be discovered.

In 1952, the Bedouin discovered what is probably the most famous of the Qumran caves, Cave 4Q. 4Q, which actually was two caves in antiquity, 4a and 4b, was dug into the southwest spur of the marl plateau on which Qumran sits. It is well ventilated and lit, with level floors and humanmade niches. Pottery fragments of storage, cooking and serving vessels were found in the cave. It was, according to de Vaux, meant to be used as a living space.[21] However, when the Bedouin entered it for the first time, they discovered it was packed with scroll fragments. When the archaeologists followed the Bedouin into 4a, they found that the fragments went right down to the floor of the cave.[22] Over 10,000 fragments coming from over 500 manuscripts were eventually recovered. Cross, who made preliminary identifications of the excavated 4Q materials, reports, "I was struck with the fact that the relatively small quantity of fragments from the deepest levels of the cave nevertheless represented a fair cross section of the whole deposit in the cave, which suggests . . . that deterioration of the manuscripts must have begun even before time sealed the manuscripts in the stratified soil, and that the manuscripts may have been in great disorder when originally abandoned in the cave. The paucity of sherds in the cave certainly indicates that the scrolls of Cave IV were not left stored away in jars."[23] In other words, according to Cross, the scrolls were placed in the cave in haste and all at once. Based on Cross's observations and the pottery found in

20. There are records from the late Roman and medieval periods of manuscripts being found in Judean Desert caves. Reports of scrolls discovered in caves are found in Eusebeius concerning Origen (Eusebius, *Hist. Eccles.* 6:16:3), Epiphanius (*De Mens. et Pond.* 17–18;), Pseudo-Athanasius (*Synopsis* PG 28), and in a letter from Patriarch Timotheus of Seleucia to Sergius, Metropolitan of Elam (Taylor, *Essenes*, 280).

21. De Vaux, *Archaeology*, 56.

22. De Vaux, *Archaeology*, 100.

23. Cross, *Ancient Library*², 27n32.

the cave, we can conclude that the original purpose of 4Q may not have been as a storage space or hiding place for scrolls, but may have been, as de Vaux originally hypothesized, a dwelling space. However, if it was used as a dwelling space at all, that phase did not last long; 4Q's primary function, as we shall see, was scroll storage.

An exploration of the marl terrace followed. Caves 5Q and 10Q were located in the southwest spur near 4Q; caves 7Q–9Q were found on the southern spur, on the same terrace of the plateau on which the settlement sits. All are artificial caves, well lit and ventilated, and evidently originally made for daily use, perhaps as workshops or dwelling places. Pottery fragments, all from the same period and type, including lamps, bowls, and cooking vessels, were recovered in all caves. 5Q contained fifteen identified manuscripts; 7Q contained nineteen; 8Q contained five; 9Q contained one unidentified papyrus fragment; and 10Q contained only one inscribed ostracon. 7Q–10Q were not used to store scrolls, but evidently were used as living quarters or workshops. 7Q, whose pottery finds included a lamp, contained only Greek manuscripts. 8Q's finds included a Genesis manuscript, a Psalms manuscript, a manuscript containing a hymn or a prayer, a phylactery, and (possibly) a mezuzah.[24] Further, 8Q also contained over 100 leather tabs used for fastening scrolls.[25] The idiosyncratic nature of the finds in 7Q and 8Q show that these caves had users with particular interests. Whoever used 8Q probably manufactured the scroll fasteners or attached them to scrolls, which leads to the assumption that there must have been scrolls nearby on which the fasteners were meant to be used.

Caves 9Q and 10Q revealed almost no inscribed material, but 10Q did contain a lamp, a reed mat, and date pits. Again, this is evidence for use as living quarters. In addition, during their excavations at Qumran in the 1990s, Broshi and Eshel discovered Cave H to the east of 9Q, which had been occupied in antiquity, as well as several more collapsed artificial caves in the marl terrace. They estimate there may have been between twenty and forty artificial caves dug into the plateau surrounding Qumran at the time of its Second Temple period occupation.[26] Finally, and very tellingly, they

---

24. On the tefillin and mezuzot found at Qumran, see Feldman, *Tefillin*, and Adler, "Distribution."

25. Carswell, "Fastenings," 23–28. According to Carswell, Milik first made the suggestion for "a specialized worker who made tags, phylactery fastenings and cases, either localized in Cave 8, or whose material was stored there when the library scrolls were stored away before the Roman attack." "Fastenings," 24n1.

26. Broshi and Eshel, "Three Seasons," 325; "Residential," 328, 335.

discovered an "intricate network of trails" leading from Qumran to both the marl terrace caves and the caves in the limestone cliffs, with staircases cut into the cliffs leading to the marl caves.[27] If one considers these findings from the perspective of landscape archaeology, the ruins of the buildings and the marl terrace caves are all one archaeological site, or one occupation area.[28] In other words, while today these caves are more difficult to access, at the time of the Qumran settlement there would have been easy traffic between the buildings and the marl caves, and at least occasional traffic to the limestone cliff caves. These facts argue against the notion that the scrolls were abandoned in caves by fleeing Jerusalemites, who were simply looking for a remote hiding place.

The Pottery

Let us turn to the pottery. De Vaux's published remarks on the pottery from the caves and Qumran can be found in several places, most especially DJD 3 and 6, along with drawings. In his Schweich lectures de Vaux states concerning the pottery: "The pottery from the caves is identical with that of the Khirbeh. The same pastes have been used and the same forms recur here, particularly in the case of the many cylindrical jars..."[29] Since the time of de Vaux's statement, the Judean Desert region has been extensively excavated, and much more comparative material is available. Rachel Bar-Nathan has made an extensive survey of pottery types in the Jericho region, including Qumran. She notes that the pottery types found at Qumran are also found throughout the region, most notably the pottery from the palaces at Jericho.[30] Therefore, she concludes that the pottery at Qumran for the most part is not unique, but part of the larger regional repertoire of the period. However, Magness, relying on de Vaux's preliminary publications and his field notes, has made several studies of the particular pottery repertoire found at Qumran.[31] Magness agrees with Bar-Nathan's general conclusion, but argues that the "peculiarities" of the Qumran assemblage have to be taken into account.[32] Most important for our purposes is the ubiquity of

27. Broshi and Eshel, "Residential," 328, 335.
28. Taylor, "Buried Manuscripts," 4.
29. De Vaux, *Archaeology*, 54.
30. Bar Nathan, "Hasmonaean and Herodian," 263–64.
31. Magness, *Archaeology*^{2}, 84–102; see also her "Community."
32. Magness, *Archaeology*, 75–77.

the hole-mouthed cylindrical storage jar type at the site of Qumran and in the Qumran caves.

We have already noted the number of cylindrical jars or their fragments and their bowl-shaped lids, which were found in the caves, particularly the natural caves in the limestone cliffs. These same type of storage jars, along with two other similar types, "ovoid" and "bag-shaped," were also found in the ruins of Qumran. In addition, "wasters" of these jars were found in the eastern garbage dump, indicating that they were produced on site.[33] The jars are, therefore, an important material connection between the caves and the khirbeh. Now, it is true that two of these types of storage jars (ovoid and bag-shaped) appear in other sites in Judea in the same period. But the cylindrical jars are almost entirely absent outside of Qumran. Why were these hole-mouthed cylindrical jars so ubiquitous at and unique to Qumran?

Bar-Nathan connects the function of the jars to the scrolls. She claims that most of the cave pottery comes only from the first century CE (*contra* de Vaux), and that the cylindrical jar only appears (at all sites) in the late first century BCE. She argues that the cylindrical jar was in fact created in this period to hold scrolls, and that the scroll jars should be narrowly dated to the Great Jewish Revolt against Rome, when they were manufactured to hide scrolls in caves. Her term for these jars is "archival," and she argues that they do not point to any necessary connection between the caves and the site of Qumran. Their presence in both locations is just evidence of the broad regional repertoire of which Qumran is a part.[34] Her argument might be an attractive solution to the question posed above, but it contains several weaknesses. First, as Bar-Nathan herself admits, this type of jar is so far absent from other sites, in particular Jerusalem, which might be expected to house several archives. Second, the jars in the Qumran caves do not seem to have been used only for scroll storage. The majority of the whole jars discovered (primarily in 1Q) were empty or contained organic material, while most of the scrolls were discovered lying unprotected on the cave floors. Although the shape of this jar, and its close-fitting lid, works very well for storing scrolls, this would seem to be a secondary usage, and not what the jars were *created* to do. This conclusion is reinforced by the evidence from the buildings; examples of these jars were found sunk into the floor at Qumran, which is certainly not optimal for scroll storage, but

---

33. Bar-Nathan, "Hasmonaean and Herodian," 275.
34. Bar-Nathan, "Hasmonaean and Herodian," 275, 277.

rather suggests food storage. Therefore, the cylindrical jars must have had multiple uses.³⁵

To sum up thus far, the following facts argue for a connection between the caves and Khirbet Qumran: 1) The caves in the marl terrace fall within the parameters of the Qumran archaeological site; they were deliberately constructed for human use, and they are connected to the Qumran buildings by paths and staircases. 2) There are also paths leading from Qumran to the natural caves in the limestone cliffs. 3) An identical pottery repertoire, from the same time period, was found in the limestone cliff caves, the marl caves, and the buildings. The ubiquity of the hole-mouthed cylindrical storage jars in all three locations indicates use by the same group. Thus, there is good archaeological evidence, independent of the scrolls, for tying the caves to Khirbet Qumran. What does the evidence of the scrolls themselves add to the picture?

Scroll Evidence

Much has been made of the fact that no scrolls were excavated from the ruins of Qumran.³⁶ That argument, however, is a red herring. First, it is more correct to say that no scroll fragments were excavated from the *buildings* at Qumran. If we view Qumran as an entire occupational site, as suggested above, then scrolls were found at Qumran, in Caves 4Q–5Q and 7Q–9Q.³⁷ Second, the fire that destroyed Qumran at the end of de Vaux's Period 2 consumed all the organic material in the buildings. As de Vaux states, "The end of Period II is marked by a violent destruction . . . all the rooms of the south-west and north-west were filled with debris from the collapse of the ceilings and superstructures to a height which varies between 1.10 m. and 1.50 m. Iron arrow-heads have been recovered, and almost everywhere a layer of a powdery black substance gives evidence of the burning of the

---

35. Magness, "Why Scroll Jars?," 163. Magness has argued that these cylindrical jars (and the ovoid jars, of the same general type) were used primarily for storage of the ritually pure food of the Qumran community. This would certainly account for the function of the jars sunk into the floors at the site, but what about the numerous examples from the caves? Magness suggests that the inhabitants were storing supplies of pure food and drink in the caves; this seems unlikely given the distance between the limestone cliff caves, where most of the scroll jars were found, and the buildings. In the absence of tests for food residue in the jars, her suggestion remains conjectural.

36. See, for example, Golb, "Who Hid?," 80; Hirshfeld, "Qumran," 239.

37. Pfann, "Reassessing," 154.

roofs."³⁸ Therefore one should not expect to find scraps of parchment or papyrus in the ruins themselves.

A more salient question would be whether or not there is any evidence for scribal activity in the ruins of Qumran? The answer is affirmative. There were, of course, the famous three inkwells from L30 and 31 (labeled by de Vaux "the Scriptorium"). Gunneweg and Balla list five more, although four are of uncertain provenance.³⁹ Associated with the inkwells were plastered benches and tables, which de Vaux believed were writing desks. It is more likely that the tables were a type of worktable, probably used for the preparation of scrolls for copying and for scroll repair.⁴⁰

Further evidence for scribal activity at the site comes from the inscriptional material. Lemaire has published almost all of the inscribed material found in the ruins of the khirbeh and in the caves.⁴¹ Gunneweg and Balla have analyzed the inscribed material found in the buildings as follows: fifty-one ostraca in Hebrew/Aramaic script, eleven in Greek, and three in Latin. They suggest, based on the concentration of inscribed materials in certain spots, that L124, 130, 61 and 30 were "centers of scribal activity at Qumran." Sixteen ostraca, the largest number, were discovered in L120, a "storage room-complex."⁴² Unfortunately, most of these loci contained fill of some kind (the exception is L30); therefore it is not possible to determine where those ostraca originated.⁴³

However, evidence of on-site scribal activity were found among the inscriptions. Two abecedaries were unearthed, KhQ161, found in Trench A, and KhQ2289, found in L135. KhQ 2207, a "practical student exercise" found in L129, contains practice sentences.⁴⁴ In his 1996 survey, Strange uncovered an inscribed ostracon, along the wall of the settlement, which is

---

38. De Vaux, *Archaeology*, 36.

39. Gunneweg and Balla, "Neutron Activation," 32. See also Crawford, *Scribes and Scrolls*, 195.

40. See my discussion in Crawford, *Scribes and Scrolls*, 185–88.

41. Lemaire, "Inscriptions," 341–88.

42. Gunneweg and Balla, "Possible Connection," 393–94. They also note that no inscriptions on pottery were found in caves 1Q, 2Q, 3Q, and 11Q (although inscriptions were discovered in 6Q), as opposed to Caves 4Q–10Q, further evidence that the limestone cliff caves had a different function than the marl terrace caves.

43. See also "Economic Activity" 50 in this volume.

44. Gunneweg and Balla, "Possible Connection," 394.

a deed of some sort.⁴⁵ It is likely that these ostraca were written at Qumran, that is, in and around the ruins of the building.

Further, the discovery of over 100 leather tabs in 8Q, one of the caves located underneath the terrace on which Qumran sits, is evidence for scroll manufacturing larger than a private collection. Whoever lived in or used 8Q must have been making or storing those scroll tabs for a collection of scrolls, whether for new scrolls or the repair of old scrolls. It does not take a tremendous leap of the imagination to suppose that the scrolls in question were in the settlement at Qumran. Further, skins in various stages of preparation for writing were found in 4Q and, according to Stacey, in three caves near Qumran, including "thin pieces to be used as parchment," again pointing to the production of scrolls in the khirbeh.⁴⁶

Let us now look at the types of scrolls found in each cave. Some caves contained collections that seem to have been for the private use of an individual. We have already mentioned that 7Q (a residential cave on the Qumran terrace) contained only Greek manuscripts, perhaps indicating an inhabitant with a particular interest in Greek compositions.⁴⁷ 8Q, located next to 7Q, contained two biblical manuscripts and a hymn or prayer scroll. Caves 9Q and 10Q did not contain any identifiable manuscripts. 5Q, part of the same cave complex as 4Q on the southwest spur of the marl terrace, contained seven biblical manuscripts, ten (?) groups of fragments that remain unclassified, four small previously unknown works (5Q9, 10, 13, and 14), and, most interestingly, one manuscript of the Serekh ha-Yaḥad, one manuscript of the Damascus Document, and one manuscript of the Aramaic New Jerusalem. All three of these works have been labeled as sectarian or affiliated texts,⁴⁸ which give their unique character to the Qumran collection. These small corpora are not the remnants of a larger library hidden by refugees fleeing from Jerusalem but were used by the people who lived at Qumran for study or private devotion. The caves are humanmade and grouped together, on the same terrace on which Qumran sits. The

---

45. Strange, "Excavations," 51, and the bibliography cited there. See also "Economic Activity" 50 in this volume.

46. Stacey, "Seasonal," 14.

47. It is also possible that manuscripts from the Greek language section of the overall collection was stored in this cave, in anticipation of the Roman attack in 68. The fact that the manuscript fragments were found on the steps leading into the cave lends credence to this possibility. See Crawford, *Scribes and Scrolls*, 136.

48. See Crawford, *Scribes and Scrolls*, 11–16, for definitions of "sectarian" and "affiliated."

most logical assumption is that the people who used these caves (and their scrolls) came from Qumran.

What of the caves that contained larger collections, i.e., Caves 1Q, 2Q, 3Q, 4Q, 6Q, and 11Q? Let us first consider Caves 1Q–3Q, 6Q and 11Q, the limestone cliff caves that were never meant for long-term habitation. Each of these caves contained their share of "biblical" manuscripts,[49] which could have been the property of any group of Jews in the Second Temple period. These caves also included compositions from the "Apocrypha" and "Pseudepigrapha," which would likewise have been of general interest to Jews of the period.[50] An example of this type of composition are the fragments of the Wisdom of Jesus ben Sirach found in 2Q. However, all of these caves (with the exception of 2Q) also included compositions that have been labeled sectarian, that is, as belonging to a specific wing of the Judaism of the period, with specific and often unique legal, theological, and historical interests that were not shared by wider Judaism. These compositions also share a recognizable sectarian language that sets them apart from other Jewish composition of the period.[51] For example, 1Q and 3Q contained pesharim, a form of interpretative composition unique to the Qumran collection.[52] We have already mentioned the Serekh ha-Yahad and the Damascus Document, sectarian compositions located in 5Q. Copies of the Serekh were also found in limestone cliff caves 1Q and (possibly) 11Q, and a copy of the Damascus Document was found in 6Q. In addition, one very important group of texts that were found in these caves are texts that either argue for or accept without argument the solar calendar. These works include the books of Enoch (1Q, 2Q and 6Q), Jubilees (1Q, 2Q, 3Q, and 11Q), the Temple Scroll (11Q), and Aramaic Levi (1Q, 4Q).[53] This favoring of the solar calendar indicates a division from contemporary Temple

---

49. I prefer the term "classical literature of ancient Israel," since most of the compositions now considered "biblical" were composed centuries before the settlement at Qumran was founded, and long before there was a Jewish canon of scripture. Crawford, *Scribes and Scrolls*, 11.

50. The terms "Apocrypha" and "Pseudepigrapha" are modern (and Christian) terms used to categorize works that belong to the deuterocanon or are noncanonical. A better description is general Jewish literature composed in the Hellenistic and Roman periods. Crawford, *Scribes and Scrolls*, 11.

51. Newsom, "'Sectually Explicit,'" 167–87; and Dimant, "The Library of Qumran," 170–76.

52. For a general discussion of the peshers, see Lim, *Pesharim*.

53. See Jacobus, "Calendars."

practice and argues against the proposition that these scrolls came from a Temple library or collection.

Finally, we turn to Cave 4Q. 4Q contained the largest collection of manuscripts and ties all the other cave collections to itself and to each other. Recall that 4Q is a humanmade cave, in the southwest spur of the marl terrace. According to the testimony of the Bedouin who opened the cave in 1952, the excavator de Vaux, and Milik and Cross, who first examined the scroll fragments, the scrolls were deposited on the entire floor of chamber 4a; they seem to have been deposited with no apparent order, and they were covered with a layer of debris that had sealed them in in antiquity.[54] Therefore it is clear that the 4Q manuscripts were deposited in the cave deliberately, for a specific reason or reasons.

Can we determine that reason or reasons? First, let us examine the 4Q manuscript collection. 4Q contained works from all the categories mentioned above, i.e., classical literature from ancient Israel, general (nonsectarian) Second Temple period Jewish works, sectarian compositions, and affiliated texts. Further, almost every composition found in the other ten caves is also found in 4Q. There are exceptions: two of the pesharim from 1Q (Micah, Habakkuk) were not found in 4Q; the Genesis Apocryphon is also unique to 1Q; and fragments of the Wisdom of Jesus ben Sirach were only found in 2Q.[55] But these are exceptions that prove the rule: 4Q provides a cross section of the Qumran collection. Further, all the paleographical dates of the skin and papyrus manuscripts from 4Q fall within the same broad range, mid 3rd century BCE to mid first century CE,[56] the same range as the paleographical dates of the manuscripts from the other caves.[57] Finally, individual scribal hands repeat between 4Q and the other caves. For example, the scribe of 1QS also copied 4QSam^c, 4QTestimonia,

---

54. De Vaux, *Archaeology*, 100. See also Milik, *Ten Years*, 17; and Cross, *Ancient Library*^{3}, 34n1.

55. These are all "single-copy" manuscripts. For a complete discussion, see Crawford, "Single-Copy," forthcoming.

56. Popović et al., "Dating," 11–13, have recently argued that the dates of the earliest manuscripts should be raised to the first half of the third century BCE.

57. 4Q contained the oldest manuscripts found at Qumran, as well as the youngest. See Crawford, *Scribes and Scrolls*, 141–46.

and 4QNarrative G, and made corrections on 1QIsa^a.[58] These material facts tie the scrolls from the eleven caves into a common collection or corpus.[59]

The makeup of this Qumran corpus is distinctive. The previously unknown works, especially the sectarian and affiliated texts, point to a deliberate collection with a specific point of view. The aforementioned favoring of the solar calendar is one peculiar characteristic of this corpus. Another is the specific legal interpretations found in the corpus, which sometimes embrace positions related to those ascribed to the Sadducees in the Mishnah, rejecting the Pharisaic positions, but often are peculiar to the Qumran corpus (that is, are neither Sadducaic or Pharisaic).[60] An example of this legal stance is the rejection of uncle-niece marriage, articulated in the Damascus Document (CD 5:7-8; 4Q270 2 ii 16) and mentioned in the Temple Scroll (11QT^a 66:16-17) and 4QHalakah A (4Q251 17 2-5). Many of the texts from the corpus share an eschatological outlook that gives the collection a particular emphasis (e.g., the War Scroll, Pseudo-Ezekiel, and Pseudo-Daniel). New Wisdom or Sapiential works have surfaced in the corpus, with distinctive features such as cosmological and eschatological speculations.[61] The exegetical texts, especially but not limited to the pesharim, display a distinctive interpretive stance, a shared vocabulary, and a common attitude toward contemporary events.[62] All of these attributes again tie the Qumran corpus together as a deliberate collection, and argue against the notion that it is simply a general Jewish collection of the Second Temple period.

Further, what is not found in the Qumran corpus is as important as what is. There is no evidence for literature that could be described as "Pharisaic" in nature.[63] There are no texts of an openly historical character, such as First or Second Maccabees. No works from pagan or Christian literature were discovered. Personal legal or business documents are almost

---

58. Crawford, *Scribes and Scrolls*, 161. Tov, *Scribal Practices*, 23, Table 2, takes a more conservative approach, noting that one scribe copied 1QS and 4QSam^c, as well as making corrections to 1QIsa^a.

59. Pfann, "Reassessing," attempts to separate the various cave collections, ascribing them to different Jewish groups from the era. However, his arguments are not convincing.

60. See, for further discussion, the edition of Miqṣat Ma'ase ha-Torah by Qimron and Strugnell, *DJD 10*, and the accompanying articles. See also Schiffman, *Reclaiming*, 249-55.

61. Dimant, "The Library of Qumran," 174; Goff, "Wisdom," 453-55.

62. Bernstein, "Interpretation of Scriptures"; Lim, *Pesharim*.

63. Shavit, "Qumran Library," 304.

entirely absent.⁶⁴ This last statement contrasts sharply with the corpora from Naḥal Ḥever and Wadi Murabba'at, which we know were the property of refugees fleeing from the conflicts of the first and second centuries CE. The vast majority of those documents are deeds of sale, leases, loans, marriage contracts and the like.⁶⁵ Again, this evidence points to the Qumran corpus as a distinctive collection, made by a specific group of Jews over a relatively long period of time.

Where did this collection come from? Although popular opinion has long held that scholars believed that all the Qumran scrolls were written and/or copied at Qumran itself,⁶⁶ this has never been the scholarly consensus. For example, Cross, in 1957, states, "Three very old documents have been found in Cave IV. Presumably they are master scrolls, imported into Qumrân at the founding of the community."⁶⁷ As Cross implies, it is impossible that the scrolls with a paleographic date prior to the early first century BCE were copied at Qumran. Even more importantly, there are no scrolls with a paleographic date later than the destruction at Qumran around the time of the Great Jewish Revolt against Rome.⁶⁸ Almost all of the paleographic dates of the manuscripts coincide with the archaeological dates assigned to the Second Temple phase at Qumran.⁶⁹ That observation alone should at least lead to some attempt at an explanation.

To summarize the evidence of the scrolls: The Qumran corpus is a deliberate collection, with distinctive features that set it apart from what might be expected in a general Jewish library of the Second Temple period. There is a common range of paleographic dates across the eleven caves. The contents of each cave (with the exception of the Greek corpus from 7Q) overlap with each other and especially with 4Q. There is no difference between the corpora found in the limestone cliff caves and those found in

---

64. See the list in Lange and Mittman-Richert, "Annotated List," 144. They note that the editor of these documents, Ada Yardeni, calls the provenance of several Cave 4Q documents into question. She argues convincingly that 4Q351–354, 356–58 come from Naḥal Ḥever. Yardeni, "Appendix," 283–84.

65. Lange and Mittman-Richert, "Annotated List," 152–60.

66. For an early popular treatment of the Dead Sea Scrolls that embraces this position, see Wilson, *The Scrolls from the Dead Sea*.

67. Cross, *Ancient Library*³, 43.

68. The paleographic dates assigned to the manuscripts have been confirmed by Carbon-14 dating. See Doudna, "Carbon-14 Dating," and the bibliography cited there. The Copper Scroll is an exception; see footnote 12.

69. Webster, "Chronological Index," 351–446.

the marl terrace caves. It is a Jewish religious collection, with almost no business documents.

We have established that it is most likely, based on the archaeological and textual evidence, that the manuscripts from the caves on the marl terrace had to have originated at Qumran. Can the same be said for the limestone cliff caves?

De Vaux gave an early summation of the argument that the scroll collection found in the caves came from Qumran: "When we reflect that the manuscripts are numerous and the pottery plentiful, that the manuscripts constitute a homogeneous group, and that the pottery belongs to a single period, it is difficult to resist the conclusion that the manuscripts were deposited or abandoned in the caves at the same time as the pottery."[70] Have the arguments made by de Vaux on the basis of the archaeological evidence been strengthened or weakened in the subsequent years? In my opinion they have been strengthened. Thorough studies of the pottery found in the caves and excavated at Qumran have shown that, while the corpus fits into the regional pottery types found in the Judean Desert in the vicinity of Jericho, there are distinctive features in the caves/Qumran corpora that tie those two strongly together. These include, but are not limited to, the ubiquity of the hole-mouth cylindrical storage jars in the caves and at Qumran. A reinvestigation of the caves has discovered paths and staircases leading from the settlement to the caves. All the caves dug into the marl terrace lie within the archaeological boundaries of Qumran.

Conclusions

The Qumran caves scroll deposits are demonstrably one deliberate collection. How and when were they deposited in the caves? Two theories have been proposed. The first is that the caves were *genizot* for the Qumran community. The second is that the scrolls were deposited in the caves as hiding places, in the face of the Roman attack that destroyed the settlement.

The idea that 1Q was a genizah, a storage place for old, worn out, no longer usable manuscripts, was first mentioned by Eleazar Sukenik in the first flush of the discovery of 1Q, and found some early supporters.[71] The idea was rejected by de Vaux, however, and, as more scroll caves were

---

70. De Vaux, *Archaeology*, 102. See Ullmann-Margalit's discussion of de Vaux's hypothesis and its strengths and weaknesses in *Out of the Cave*, 41–48.

71. As quoted by Taylor, "Buried Manuscripts," 1.

discovered, it fell out of favor.⁷² Joan Taylor has recently renewed the argument in its favor. She argues that the method of storing wrapped scrolls in jars in the limestone cliff caves is in fact a method of "burial," appropriate for a genizah.⁷³ The function of the caves in the marl terrace, according to Taylor, may point to "scroll-processing for preservation-burial," but this is uncertain.⁷⁴

Although Taylor makes several persuasive points on the basis of the archaeological evidence, the genizah theory does not adequately account for all the scroll evidence. First, a genizah is meant to be a storage place for old, worn out, no longer usable manuscripts, but two of the manuscripts stored in jars, 1QIsa^a and 11QT^a, were in excellent condition when deposited in their respective caves. 1QIsa^a is an older manuscript (c. 125–100 BCE), but it remained completely whole and usable. 11QT^a's paleographic date is only 25 BCE–25 CE; it seems to have been in good condition when it was discovered; its deterioration was caused by its adventures *after* its removal from 11Q.⁷⁵

Second, the overall paleographic profile of the collection argues against the limestone cliff caves being genizot in the generally accepted sense. The oldest manuscripts in the collection come from 4Q, while caves 2Q, 3Q, and 6Q have collectively later dates.⁷⁶ Stökl ben Ezra has demonstrated, using statistical analysis, that the paleographic profile of the manuscripts from 1Q and 4Q is on average older than that from 2Q, 3Q, 5Q, 6Q, and 11Q.⁷⁷ Pfann has charted the paleographic dates of the manuscripts from the larger scroll caves (1Q, 3Q, 4Q, 5Q, 6Q, and 11Q). His charts indicate that the peak paleographic date for manuscripts from 1Q, 4Q, 5Q, and 6Q is the first century BCE, and for 3Q and 11Q the first century CE.⁷⁸ This paleographic concentration is what we would expect; the settlement was founded c. 100–75 BCE and destroyed in 68 CE. The inhabitants would have brought older scrolls in at the beginning of the settlement and collected

---

72. As Taylor points out, de Vaux's concept of the function of a genizah was incorrect; he thought manuscripts stored in a genizah were texts rejected by the community, that is, heterodox. Taylor, "Buried Manuscripts," 3; de Vaux, *Archaeology*, 103.

73. Taylor, "Buried Manuscripts," 10–16.

74. Taylor, "Buried Manuscripts," 23.

75. Yadin, *Temple Scroll*, I: 9–39.

76. Webster, "Chronological Index," 375–77.

77. Stökl ben Ezra, "Old Caves," 315–18.

78. Pfann, "Reassessing," 157–58, 160.

and/or manufactured new scrolls while they lived there. Many of these new scrolls could easily have been brought in from other parts of the country, including Jerusalem. Both the paleographic findings and the physical state of 1QIsa^a and 11QT^a do not coincide with the idea that the limestone cliff caves were exclusively genizot for old, worn out, or otherwise unusable manuscripts. However, it is certainly possible that some older manuscripts were stored away in certain caves (according to Stökl ben Ezra's statistics, 1Q and 4Q), before the end of the settlement.

The second scenario, the "quick hiding" scenario, has been championed by de Vaux, Cross, Stegemann, VanderKam and others.[79] This scenario continues to have much to recommend it. The archaeological evidence from 3Q and 4Q, the only major caves where all (3Q) or a substantial portion (4Q) of the manuscript evidence was undisturbed and professionally excavated, indicate that the scrolls in 3Q were probably deposited all at once, or, in the case of 4Q, that the scrolls were in disorder when they were placed in the cave.[80]

Concerning 4Q, de Vaux states, "the many fragments recovered by us from Cave 4 went right down to the original floor of the cave."[81] To quote Cross again, "the relatively small quantity of fragments from the deepest levels of the cave [4Q] nevertheless represented a fair cross section of the whole deposit in the cave."[82] Cross does not indicate that only paleographically earlier manuscripts were found at the bottom layers of the cave, which we would expect if 4Q were a genizah.[83] Rather, according to de Vaux et al., the manuscripts were placed in the large collection caves, 1Q, 2Q, 3Q, 4Q, 6Q and 11Q, over a relatively short period of time.

Given the fact that all these caves contained manuscripts with the latest paleographic dates in the Qumran series (c. 1-70 CE),[84] it is logical to look for an event that would precipitate the manuscripts' rapid storage in the caves. That event has to be the anticipated attack on the settlement by

---

79. Originally argued by de Vaux, *Archaeology*, 106-9; Cross, *Ancient Library*^{2}, 62; VanderKam, *Dead Sea Scrolls Today*, 108. For an imaginative reconstruction of how this was done, see Stegemann, *Library*, 58-79.

80. See now Fidanzio's preliminary report on the deposition in 3Q: "Deposition," 84-101.

81. De Vaux, *Archaeology*, 100.

82. Cross, *Ancient Library*^{2}, 27n32.

83. As Pfann, "Reassessing," suggests (147, 149).

84. Webster, "Chronological Lists," 374-75.

PART 1: QUESTIONS OF ARCHAEOLOGY

the X Roman Legion Fretensis, operating in the region of Jericho in 68 CE.[85] That this attack in fact occurred is demonstrated by the destruction layer at Qumran, the Roman arrowheads in the destruction debris, and the reuse of the site as a Roman army camp in Period 3.[86]

All of these facts create a strong chain of evidence that it was the inhabitants of Qumran who owned the scroll collection and who at first stored, and then later *in extremis* hid, the majority of the scrolls, at first using the relatively inaccessible caves in the limestone cliffs for long-term storage and the marl terrace cave 4Q for more accessible storage, but then, in the emergency of the impending Roman attack, in the marl terrace caves. The scrolls must have been precious to them, since they made at least some effort to protect them from the elements by wrapping some in linen and even storing a few in a jar. They did not hide coins or other wealth; the scrolls were their only concern. Did they hope to return and recover them? Probably, but that was not to be, and their discovery was left to the curiosity of Bedouin shepherds in 1947.

Appendix

Since this article was published in 2012 I have refined my thinking concerning the deposition of the manuscripts in the caves. Critical to my understanding now is the difference between the deposition practice in the large limestone cliff caves (1Q, 2Q, 3Q, and 11Q), and that of the marl terrace caves (4Q, 5Q, 7Q–10Q).[87] The limestone cliff caves, which are located

---

85. Cross, *Ancient Library*², 60–62.

86. Stökl ben Ezra proposes two events that precipitated hiding; 1Q and 4Q were used at the time of the first fire that destroyed the buildings in 9/8 BCE, while caves 2Q, 3Q, 5Q, 6Q, and 11Q were used in 68 CE ("Old Caves and Young Caves," 327–28). However, Mizzi and Magness have demonstrated that the site was never destroyed and abandoned, but was continuously inhabited by the same group from c. 100–75 BCE until its destruction in 68 CE ("Was Qumran Abandoned?," 302–3, 314–17, 319–20). Nevertheless, the suggestion that some manuscripts were hidden or stored away earlier than 68 is certainly possible and can be argued as part of the overall deposit scenario. Doudna makes the sweeping suggestion that all the scrolls were deposited in the caves in the first century BCE, dismissing the first century CE paleographic dates. "Legacy," 146–56.

87. 6Q, which is located in the cliff face above the Wadi Qumran, below the aqueduct leading to the site, is more like the marl terrace caves than the other limestone cliff caves. It is within the built parameters of Qumran and its manuscripts would appear to have been deposited on the floor of the cave rather than stored in jars. For the location of 6Q, see Fidanzio, "Searching," who says: "6Q . . . is closer to the settlement than the other

between two and three kilometers from the settlement, are connected to it only by rough paths. According to recent work by Fidanzio, Taylor, and Mizzi,[88] it now seems very likely that a majority of the manuscripts found in the limestone cliff caves (with the exception of 6Q), were originally wrapped in linen, stored in sealed scroll jars, and placed in the cave. They were not meant to be retrieved; thus, the purpose of 1Q, 2Q, 3Q, and 11Q would appear to have been permanent or long-term storage.

On the other hand, 4Q, 5Q, and 7Q–10Q are humanmade caves, part of the built environment of the settlement (it is probable that 4Q and 5Q were originally part of one cave complex). The manuscripts in 4Q and 5Q were found packed on the floor of the caves; they were not wrapped in linen or stored in jars.[89] The manuscripts discovered in 7Q were recovered from the lower part of the stairs leading into the cave.[90] This data suggests that these caves were never used for a permanent, long-term type of storage, but were meant to be retrieved. The placement of the fragments in 7Q suggests haste in deposition.

Thus, I believe that the Qumran caves actually present us with two different storage scenarios: permanent, long-term storage in the limestone cliff caves, and temporary, in some cases emergency, storage in the marl terrace caves.

---

natural caves; laying below the aqueduct that served the settlement, it was not isolated as the other natural 'scroll' caves; it is possible to access Cave 6Q reaching the limestone cliff through the marl terrace. Its topography, and its geological setting, place Cave 6Q halfway between natural and artificial caves" (11).

88. Fidanzio, "Searching," and Humbert and Fidanzio, "Qumrân Cave 11Q"; Taylor, Mizzi, and Fidanzio, "Revisiting"; Taylor, "Buried Tombs."

89. It is possible that there were shelves built in the walls of the principal chamber of 4Q, which collapsed in antiquity, depositing at least some of the scrolls on the floor of the cave. Crawford, *Scribes and Scrolls*, 133.

90. De Vaux, "Archéologie¹," 27.

2

Qumran Cave 4Q
Its Archaeology and its Manuscript Collection

QUMRAN CAVE 4Q HAS been described as the mother lode of the Judean Desert caves, and as the hub of the Qumran manuscript collection. Situated a stone's throw from the buildings of Qumran, on the southern spur of the western marl plateau, its mere location argues for a connection with the Qumran settlement. Added to that are the many connections between the 4Q manuscript collection and the manuscript collections in the other ten Qumran caves.[1] This article will investigate the archaeology of Cave 4Q, followed by a glimpse at the nature of its collection. By bringing together these two types of evidence, a plausible reconstruction of the function of 4Q in the late Second Temple period can be created.

The Archaeology of Cave 4Q

Cave 4Q is actually two caves adjacent to one another, 4a and 4b, hollowed out from the marl plateau situated immediately to the west of the plateau on which the building remains of Qumran are located. It was first opened by Bedouin tribesmen in 1952.[2] Once they began to bring their manuscript

---

1. See Crawford, "Qumran Collection," 120–25.
2. Because the Bedouin did not distinguish fragments from 4a and 4b, but instead mixed them together, the two caves were collectively designated "Cave 4Q." The Bedouin who removed fragments from these caves claimed that most of them originated in 4a,

finds to the Palestine Archaeological Museum for sale, Roland de Vaux and G. Lankester Harding discovered the location of the cave and removed the clandestine diggers. De Vaux then undertook the excavation of the cave in September of 1952. A preliminary report of the findings, written by de Vaux, was published posthumously in DJD 6.[3] According to de Vaux's report, the archaeologists explored for themselves the lower layers of the cave and one small concealed chamber (probably de Vaux's "un réduit obscur" or "obscure nook"; see below), as well as discovering the original entrance (the Bedouin had dug their own entrance). Although by the time the archaeologists entered the cave, the Bedouin had already removed at least a meter of debris containing manuscript fragments, de Vaux and his workers collected nearly 1000 fragments from perhaps 100 manuscripts.

4a's principal chamber (Chamber 1) had an east-west orientation; it was 8 m. in length and a maximum of 3.25 m. in width, with a maximum height of 3 m. It is open to the east (toward the settlement) by a "window" that overlooks the ravine that separates caves 4Q–5Q and 10Q from the south end of the marl plateau on which the ruins of Qumran sit. In front of this "window" an oblong trench one meter long was dug, .65 m. deep. Chamber 1 also had small niches hollowed out of its walls above floor height.[4] According to de Vaux, "almost all" of the recovered documents and pottery came from this chamber.[5]

In the center of the south wall of Chamber 1, a second chamber (Chamber 2) was dug toward the south. It sits at a higher level than Chamber 1. Its ceiling and most of its walls have eroded away. At the time of its discovery it did not contain any documents or pottery.

A third chamber was dug at a southwest angle from the main chamber, at a lower level. It was not more than 2 m. in height, 2 m. long and 2.5 m. in width.

Between Chambers 2 and 3 an "obscure nook"[6] was dug out from the south wall, which was accessed by an irregular descent cut into the floor of

---

with almost none from 4b; these claims were borne out by the fragments found by the archaeologists, most of which also came from 4a. Thus, de Vaux deemed 4a the more important of the two. "Archéologie^2," 9.

3. All of the following information unless noted is taken from de Vaux, "Archéologie^2," 3–22. See also Milik, *Ten Years*, and Cross, *Ancient Library*^{2}. Milik was present at the excavation of 4Q and Cross was the first to examine its excavated fragments.

4. See the plans drawn by de Vaux in DJD 6, Figs. 1, 2, and 3; 10–12.

5. De Vaux, "Archéologie^2," 9.

6. De Vaux, "Archéologie^2," 9.

Chamber 1. It was sunk 1.3 m. below the floor, and was 1.45 m. in height. According to de Vaux, it contained much debris that had slid down from Chamber 1, in addition to a small jug.

The original entrance to 4a was constructed to the north; it consisted of a circular opening with a sunken passage that slopes gently down several meters, finishing in several steps that issue out in the north wall of Chamber 1. In the passage de Vaux discovered a lamp, which he dated to the first century CE.[7]

Finally, a small trench between 4a and 4b had been formed by erosion; some fragments, pottery and phylactery cases had drifted into it, evidently from Chamber 1.[8]

To summarize: Cave 4a was intentionally dug into the marl terrace which lies to the west of the buildings of Qumran; it was visible and easily accessible from the settlement. Entrance was made from above, coming south on the ridge of the marl plateau, and consisted of an opening, ramp and stairs. The cave consisted of one principal chamber (Chamber 1), with two smaller chambers dug off it (Chambers 2 and 3). All three chambers were high enough for an adult male to stand in. Chamber 1 contained a niche dug into the floor below its "window," as well as a small space (the "obscure nook") accessed from its floor.

4b is situated immediately to the west of 4a. A trench connects the two caves (see above). 4b consists of one chamber, oriented east-west, which is 5.5 m. long, about 2 m. wide, and 2.15 m. in height. Originally it had a second chamber on its east, about 1.7 m. lower, which has been carried away by erosion. On the west, 4b had a large open bay in the cliff face, overlooking Wadi Qumran. The cave's entrance was an opening in its north wall, with a steep passage now almost entirely eroded, which stopped on a platform from which one jumped down into the cave.

Material Remains Recovered from Cave 4Q

Pottery and other debris (in addition to manuscript fragments) were recovered from both caves (although de Vaux described 4b as "very nearly

---

7. De Vaux, "Archéologie²," 17–18.

8. Although de Vaux believed that this trench was formed by erosion, Humbert has suggested that it was made as a deliberate connection between 4a and 4b. Humbert, "Cacher," 52–55.

sterile").⁹ Both de Vaux and Mizzi, who has examined the small finds from 4Q, comment on the overall dearth of small finds coming out of the two caves.¹⁰ According to de Vaux, almost all of the pottery, which was very broken, came from 4a. His inventory consists of eleven cylindrical or ovoid jars (aka "scroll jars"), one bag-shaped jar, three bowl-shaped lids, one "casserole," five bowls, three plates, two jugs, one juglet (this was located in the "obscure nook"), and one Herodian lamp.¹¹ All of the recovered pottery dates from the first century BCE to the first century CE (with the exception of the lamp), thus matching the dates of the pottery recovered from the buildings of Qumran.

Other small finds included seventeen phylactery cases, thirteen of which were published by Milik in DJD 6.¹² In addition, de Vaux mentions recovering debris of cloth, wood and leather (uninscribed?¹³), but does not specify further what these were. In her 2003 inventory, Bélis lists a fragment of linen with a border, and a leather thong.¹⁴

The floor of 4b was covered in palm branches, spread to a thickness of .25 meters. Underneath the palm branches was a powdery layer mixed with ash, then a layer of brown dust.¹⁵ Finally, Fields, from an interview with the Bedouin diggers, states that they found pieces of wood in the cave, which they threw into the wadi as worthless.¹⁶

The Function of Cave 4Q in the late Second Temple Period

In light of the archaeological evidence presented above, what can be said about the function of 4Q from the first century BCE through the first century CE? The original excavation of the caves would have been an enormous

---

9. De Vaux, "Archéologie²," 13.

10. De Vaux, "Archéologie²," 52; Mizzi, "Miscellaneous," 137.

11. De Vaux, "Archéologie²," 15–20; see also Fidanzio and Humbert, "Finds," 275. Mlynarczyk has redated this lamp to between the late first and early third century. "Terracotta Oil Lamps," 116–17.

12. According to Milik three of these were found by the excavators, while the rest were purchased from the Bedouin. Milik, "Tefillin," 34. Adler has identified a possible additional four cases; see Adler, "Distribution," 163n4.

13. See Fields, *History*, 153.

14. De Vaux, "Archéologie²," 15. Bélis, "Des textiles," Tableau 1, 212–18.

15. De Vaux, "Archéologie²," 13.

16. Fields, *History*, 150.

undertaking, requiring much manpower and time.[17] It is impossible to determine when the caves were actually excavated; the presence of the datable pottery and the manuscripts point to the late Second Temple period, when the settlement at Qumran was constructed. In a plausible scenario, David Stacey has suggested that the marl caves were dug to supply clay to make the mud bricks that were used to construct the buildings.[18] However, it is worth remembering that a small settlement existed at Qumran in the Iron II period.[19] Cross suggested in an interview that the marl caves, including 4Q, were originally constructed as Iron Age tombs.[20] If the caves were originally used as burial caves, however, they would have been thoroughly cleaned out, presumably when the site was reinhabited in the late Second Temple period. It is possible that 4b was used as sleeping quarters; the palm fronds covering the floor would support this hypothesis. On the other hand, the very small amount of pottery fragments recovered from both 4a and 4b, the majority of which are storage jars rather than small personal use items, indicates that the caves were only briefly, if at all, used as sleeping quarters.

The largest artifact found in 4Q is the manuscript collection itself, and thus it must be the first consideration when seeking to determine the cave's function. De Vaux was unequivocal in his identification of the caves as sleeping quarters, which were only put into use for scroll storage in the emergency situation of the impending Roman attack.[21] In fact, he suggests that the scroll fragments recovered from 4b were private use manuscripts, left behind when the settlement was abandoned, like those manuscripts in 7Q, 8Q and 9Q.[22] However, since we do not know precisely which manuscripts came from 4b, it is difficult to test his theory.

The majority of the fragments seem to have come from 4a, and according to the testimony of de Vaux, Milik and Cross, were found lying packed on the floor of the cave, underneath at least a meter of debris. De Vaux states that most of the fragments were recovered from Chamber 1, where they had been deposited "pell-mell" ("en vrac"). He also notes that fragments of the same manuscripts were dispersed in every layer of the

17. Humbert, "Cacher," 6.
18. Stacey and Doudna, *Qumran Revisited*, 37.
19. De Vaux, *Archaeology*, 1.
20. Shanks, *Frank Moore Cross*, 114.
21. De Vaux, "Archéologie²," 21.
22. De Vaux recovered "several written fragments" from the bed of palms in 4b. De Vaux, "Archéologie²," 13.

deposit.²³ Fragments were also recovered from the trench between 4a and 4b, and in the "obscure nook" cut into the floor of Chamber 1.

Milik, describing the Bedouin find in an early publication, says, "They had already turned over several cubic metres of earth when, suddenly, their hands came upon a compact layer of thousands of manuscript fragments."²⁴ Cross, the first scholar to systematically examine the excavated fragments from Cave 4Q, noted, "I was struck with the fact that the relatively small quantity of fragments from the deepest levels of the cave nevertheless represented a fair cross section of the whole deposit in the cave, which suggests . . . that the manuscripts may have been in great disorder when originally abandoned in the cave."²⁵ This combined testimony, that the scrolls were laid in layers on the floor of the cave, with no discernible order, appears to support the "quick hiding scenario" championed by de Vaux.²⁶

However, other archaeological evidence may point to the use of the caves as longer-term storage for scroll manuscripts. It has long been suggested that the niches in the walls of Chamber 1 may have been used as support holes for shelving.²⁷ No wood remnants that may have been used for shelves were recovered from the chamber, but the Bedouin did claim to have discarded pieces of wood that they found in the cave.²⁸ If there were in fact shelves on which manuscripts were stored, and these shelves disintegrated in antiquity and fell to the floor of the cave (possibly because of an earthquake), it might explain the disarray of the manuscripts on the cave floor. If 4a was used as a storage cave for manuscripts over the course of the life of the Qumran settlement, the dearth of small finds associated with habitation and the large number of manuscripts found there would be

---

23. De Vaux, "Archéologie²," 4, 21.

24. Milik, *Ten Years*, 17.

25. Cross, *Ancient Library²*, 27n32. See also Cross, "Reminiscences," 935, where he says, "I had a cross-section of Cave 4 manuscripts, eloquent evidence of the chaotic mix of fragments surviving in the cave." Regarding 4QSamª, a late first century BCE manuscript, Cross states, "In the lowest subterranean level of the cave, in a small pit, twenty-seven fragments of 4QSamª were found." Cross et al., *1–2 Samuel*, 2. This "pit" could refer either to the trench in front of the "window" in 4a, or the "obscure nook" in the same cave. In any case, the fragments came from the lowest level of the cave.

26. De Vaux, *Archaeology*, 105.

27. See Schiffman, *Reclaiming*, 56. The niches were evidently not used for lamps, since there is no soot blackening the walls around them. I thank Jodi Magness for this observation.

28. Fields, *History*, 153.

explained.[29] However, it would not explain why fragments were discovered packed into every part of Chamber 1 and its nook; for that, the "quick-hiding" scenario offers a better explanation.

In sum, the archaeology of Caves 4a and 4b presents the following picture. Cave 4a, in spite of being manmade and having good light and air, does not seem to have been used for long-term habitation in the late Second Temple period, during the time the Qumran settlement was inhabited. Rather, a plausible scenario is that it was used for the short-term or temporary storage of scrolls;[30] then towards the end of the first century CE, most likely in anticipation of the Roman attack on the settlement in 68, a larger collection of scrolls was abandoned in the cave.

4b may have been used as sleeping quarters, given its palm leaf flooring, but if it was very little material evidence of that remains. On the other hand, relatively few scroll fragments were found there either, so it seems clear that it was not used for scroll storage. In that way 4b more closely resembles Caves 7Q, 8Q, and 9Q on the other side of the ravine, which were certainly used as workshops and sleeping quarters.

The next step is to investigate the contents of the scrolls collection abandoned in 4a, to see if it can help to determine when, how and why it ended up there.

The Cave 4Q Scroll Collection

An overview of the 4Q manuscript collection demonstrates how diverse and broad it was. It contained multiple copies of the classical literature of ancient Israel, which later became the Jewish canon of scripture (usually referred to as "biblical" or "scriptural" in the literature). It contained a cross-section of later Second Temple literature (with some notable exceptions), including previously unknown works.[31] 4Q also contained what has been identified

---

29. Taylor suggests an alternative scenario: Cave 4Q was used as a temporary storage place for manuscripts being prepared for burial in a genizah. She suggests the shelves were removed in Period 3 (the post-sectarian phase of the settlement), thus explaining the disarray of the manuscripts. Taylor, "Buried Manuscripts," 291–92. See also Pfann, "Reassessing," 152.

30. As opposed to the long-term or permanent storage scenario we find in the limestone cliff caves 1Q, 2Q, 3Q, and 11Q. See Crawford, *Scribes and Scrolls*, 318.

31. This includes books which date from the third century BCE onwards, such as the Enoch literature, Tobit and Jubilees. The exceptions are works supportive of the Hasmonean regime and clearly Pharisaic compositions. See Crawford, "The Qumran

as sectarian (or core *yaḥad*) literature,[32] such as the Damascus Document and the Community Rule. Three languages, Hebrew, Aramaic and Greek, are represented, as well as four scripts, the square script, paleo-Hebrew, the cryptic script, and Greek. Finally, it contains several idiosyncratic elements that are important for understanding the character of its manuscript collection.

The contents of the 4Q scroll collection have been the subject of two recent major studies, by Devorah Dimant and Charlotte Hempel respectively.[33] I will briefly summarize their conclusions before adding my own observations.

Dimant, while offering an overview of the entire collection, notes the central position of 4Q, which contained 74% of the recovered manuscripts.[34] She divides the collection into five groupings, all of which were present in 4Q: a) biblical manuscripts; b) sectarian literature, which she defines as works containing particular terminology, style and ideas linked with the life and ideology of the Qumran community; c) non-sectarian texts, which by definition do not contain (b); d) intermediary texts, which do not contain sectarian terminology but have affinity with sectarian ideas; and e) Aramaic literature.[35] Dimant emphasizes a curatorial process of "tendentious selection and exclusion."[36] She suggests that 4Q, because it contains specimens from all five groups and its position vis-à-vis the Qumran buildings, served as a library for the community.[37]

Hempel, by her very title, emphasizes the diverse nature of the 4Q collection. While acknowledging the connections of 4Q with the manuscripts found in the other Qumran caves, she recognizes its distinctive elements. The fifty-five mostly papyrus texts written in cryptic script form one idiosyncratic element in the collection. She notes that access to this material would have been "highly selective and restrictive."[38] Another distinctive el-

---

Collection," 120–22.

32. The formulation is Ben-Dov's, "Demonic Deuteronomy," 268.

33. Dimant, "Qumran Manuscripts," and Hempel, "'Haskalah.'"

34. Dimant, "Qumran Manuscripts," 36.

35. I use a slightly different classification system for the Qumran manuscripts: 1) the classical literature of ancient Israel; 2) Hellenistic-Roman non-sectarian works; 3) affiliated texts; and 4) sectarian texts. See Crawford, *Scribes and Scrolls*, 11–16, for definitions and discussion.

36. Dimant, "Qumran Manuscripts," 31, 38.

37. Dimant, "Qumran Manuscripts," 36, 40.

38. Hempel, "'Haskalah,'" 316.

ement in the 4Q collection addressed by Hempel is the numerous calendar texts discovered there, texts that would have required a high degree of technical expertise in their readers.[39] Hempel also argues for a particular connection between the contents of 4Q and the office of the Maskil, pointing especially to the cryptic script texts and the calendrical literature.[40]

Other characteristics of the 4Q collection that Hempel brings out are the multiple attestations of many compositions, often in different forms, and the "workaday quality" of a number of texts.[41] In her conclusion, Hempel argues that 4Q "comprises the most eclectic and scholarly corner of the collection," and was "the learned hub of the Qumran elite."[42] Dimant's study demonstrates the breadth of the 4Q collection, while Hempel's highlights some of its unique elements.

Another important observation (not made by either Dimant or Hempel) is that, according to both paleographic and C-14 dates, 4Q preserves the full range of manuscript dates found at Qumran. It contains the oldest manuscripts in the entire Qumran corpus, from the mid-third century BCE, while also containing manuscripts from the third quarter of the first century CE, and all the periods in between.[43]

Like Hempel, I believe that the unique elements of the 4Q collection are important clues for determining what it was, and why and when it was deposited in the cave. There are four elements I would like to highlight: 1) the oldest manuscripts in the collection; 2) the number of single copy works; 3) the presence of esoteric texts requiring specialized knowledge;

---

39. Hempel, "'Haskalah,'" 319–29.
40. Hempel, "'Haskalah,'" 317–19.
41. Hempel, "'Haskalah,'" 330–31, 332–33.
42. Hempel, "'Haskalah,'" 336, 337.

43. According to Webster's index, there are five manuscripts, all from 4Q, whose date ranges fall in the mid- to late third century BCE: 4QExod-Lev^f, 4QSam^b, 4QpaleoDeut^s, 4QJer^a and 4QEnastr^a ar. Webster, "Chronological Index," 378. For the first century manuscripts, see Webster, "Chronological Index," 351–446. Stökl ben Ezra has demonstrated that the 4Q manuscript collection as a whole is statistically older than those of other Qumran manuscript caves. He suggests on that basis that there were two sub-collections in 4Q, the first deposited prior to the fire in 9–8 BCE, and the second at the time of the Roman attack in 68. Stökl ben Ezra, "Old Caves," 316. But that "two distinct deposits" scenario is unnecessary; rather, scrolls could have been deposited in 4Q continuously over the length of its usage. Addendum: In a recent article, Popović and his team have stated that, on the basis of their new C-14 dating and AI paleography tool, the paleographic date ranges of the Qumran manuscripts are older (by about half a century) than previously thought. Popović et al., "Dating," 7.

and 4) "working" texts, such as student exercises and brief lists. Some of the items to be discussed will fall into more than one category.[44]

The Oldest Manuscripts in the Collection

As noted above, Cave 4Q contained an unusually high proportion of paleographically older manuscripts, certainly older than the site of Qumran itself. The general consensus among archaeologists now is that the Second Temple settlement at Qumran began c. 100–75 BCE.[45] Accepting that date, at least eighty-five manuscripts, seventy-nine in the square script, five paleo-Hebrew manuscripts, and one Greek manuscript, can be dated prior to the beginning of the settlement.[46] That means that about one-fifth of the 4Q collection is older than the settlement and were brought from elsewhere to the region of Qumran.[47] The majority of these manuscripts (fifty-two) are from the classical literature of ancient Israel. However, fully thirty-nine fall into my categories 2–4. Of these, nine are sectarian. This indicates that the sectarian group that composed and/or copied these sectarian texts was *already in existence* prior to the founding of Qumran; thus, the scroll collection cannot be tied solely to the settlement. That is, because these scrolls were brought from outside and are older than the settlement, we must assume that the group who owned them is older than the settlement, and that Qumran is only one of the places where they were located. At the same time, according to the testimony of de Vaux, Milik and Cross, the 4Q scrolls were not found in layers according to age (with the most recent manuscripts on top and the older ones underneath), but mixed together. Thus we cannot determine if the older scrolls were placed in the cave earlier, or separately. It is possible that this was the case, but unfortunately it is not provable now.

---

44. It is important to remember, as we catalogue works by various means, that we do not have the entire collection as it existed in antiquity. There is good evidence that 4Q was disturbed between the time of the final deposition of manuscripts and its discovery in 1952. See Taylor, "Buried Manuscripts," 299.

45. See Magness, *Archaeology*², 64–78.

46. According to Webster, "Chronological Lists," 419–34. I have not included the Cryptic A manuscripts, whose paleographical dating is much less certain, in this count.

47. According to Popović's revised dating, that percentage would be higher.

PART 1: QUESTIONS OF ARCHAEOLOGY

Single-Copy Works[48]

4Q had a large number of single-copy works, from all parts of its collection. From the classical literature are single copies of Kings (4Q54), Lamentations (4Q111), Ezra-Nehemiah (4Q117), and Chronicles (4Q118).[49]

From general Jewish literature of the period (both non-sectarian and affiliated) we find single copies of many different genres of texts. The following list is by no means complete, but includes Aramaic translations of Leviticus and Job (4Q157, 158), various types of parabiblical literature, such as the Visions of Samuel (4Q160) or the Admonition on the Flood (4Q370), and liturgical texts such as Personal Prayer (4Q443) or Purification Liturgy (4Q284). There are also texts that have been identified as wisdom texts, including the Wiles of the Wicked Woman (4Q184). Many single-copy works fall into the category "sectarian." These include the peshers on Micah, Nahum and Zephaniah (4Q168–170). There are also several single-copy anthologies like the Testimonia (4Q175). A number of single-copy works may be termed esoteric, that is, requiring specialized knowledge or interest, such as Zodiology and Brontology ar (4Q318) and Physiognomy/Horoscope (4Q561). Finally, there are collections of laws and rules, such as Miscellaneous Rules (4Q265).

The presence of all these single-copy works points to the working quality of the Cave 4Q collection.[50] By "working quality" I am referring to two different things. The first is the desire of a scholarly community to have as complete a collection as possible; this explains the presence in 4Q of literary works that otherwise did not figure prominently in the Qumran collection as a whole.[51] The second is the draft-like quality of some of these works, such

---

48. Although I am emphasizing here works that occur in single copies, the presence of works that occur in multiple copies is equally important, indicating as it does the desire of the owners of the scrolls to preserve those copies of what must have been important texts in their worldview. As examples from all parts of the collection, 4Q contained at least twenty-three copies of Deuteronomy, twelve copies of various books of Enoch, nine copies of Jubilees, ten copies of the Serekh ha-Yaḥad (the Community Rule), and eight copies of the Damascus Document. See also Hempel, "'Haskalah,'" 329–31.

49. According to Tov, *Revised Lists*, 28–32.

50. Two of the works listed above are classified by Hempel as having a "workaday quality": 4Q265 and 4Q175. Hempel, "'Haskalah,'" 332–33.

51. See also Popović, "Scroll Storehouse," 554, who notes the "scholarly, school-like collection of predominantly literary texts."

as 4Q175, which is a simple collection of passages around a theme.[52] These qualities point to the learned scribal character of the 4Q collection.

Esoteric Texts

We know from the study of Mesopotamian textual troves found by excavators *in situ* that scribes collected works pertaining to their specializations, including astronomical/calendrical lore and augury/divination.[53] At a house in Uruk occupied by two families of scribes in the fifth-fourth centuries BCE, tablets were discovered containing incantations and medical texts. The library in the Shamash Temple in Sippar contained omens, incantations, and mathematical and astronomical texts.[54] The presence of the same types of texts in the 4Q collection is striking. They include thirty examples of calendrical texts, including the mishmarot and the copies of Astronomical Enoch, as well as a horoscope (4Q186), an exorcism (4Q560), an incantation (4Q444) and the previously mentioned 4Q318 and 4Q561. The occurrence of the cryptic script texts also points to specialized, esoteric knowledge. The presence of these documents in 4Q indicates to my mind the scribal character of this collection; these are the types of texts that only highly trained scholar scribes would have possessed.[55]

"Working" Texts

We have already suggested that some of the single copy manuscripts found in 4Q, such as 4Q175, had a draft-like quality, indicating that they were working notes of some kind. We can add to the list of draft-like documents, beginning with the three scribal exercises found in 4Q: 4Q234, 341, and 360. These three documents were penned by scribes practicing their trade;

---

52. This was also noted by Steudel, *Midrasch*, 178–81, and Popović, "Scroll Storehouse," 577, who suggests that texts such as these may represent "personal scholarly notes." Many of the so-called "biblical" texts may in fact be simple anthologies of passages; for examples see 4QDeutj, 4QDeutn and 4QRP D, E (4Q366 and 367). See now my articles on excerpted texts in Crawford, *Text of the Pentateuch*, 269–81.

53. Crawford, *Scribes and Scrolls*, 34–35.

54. See Crawford, "Qumran Collection," 110, 114–15, for discussion and bibliography.

55. Hempel, "'Haskalah,'" 319, argues for the connection of this aspect of the collection, especially the cryptic script and calendar texts, with the Maskil. This is possible, but requires a rather large leap from the references we have to this leadership figure to stating that part of the 4Q collection consists of a "Maskil collection."

4Q234 contains short words written in three different directions, 4Q341 preserves a series of letters and some names, and 4Q360 is again written in different directions and repeats the name "Menachem" three times.

Other draft-like documents include the List of Netinim (4Q340), List of False Prophets (4Q339), and Rebukes Reported by the Overseer (4Q477). I have argued elsewhere that the presence of these scribbled exercises and notes in 4Q indicates the local nature of the collection; that is, it is highly unlikely that such draft-like documents would have been transported to Qumran from Jerusalem or elsewhere. Their place of origin must have been Qumran.[56] Here I would emphasize that their presence indicates that the site of Qumran (which includes 4Q) seems to have had an active scribal contingent living there during the first century BCE through its destruction in 68 CE.

By examining the collection through the lens of the four categories above, the breadth of the 4Q corpus becomes clear. Given the age of a portion of the manuscripts, one can argue that this collection was the product of a long-term collection process, which stretched from at least the beginning of the first century BCE, when the oldest manuscripts began to be assembled (according to the archaeology of both 4Q and the settlement at Qumran), through the late first century CE. Because we do not know the place of origin of the pre-100 BCE manuscripts, we cannot say with certainty where this collection process began, but it certainly continued at Qumran.

The large number of single-copy works, some of which are also esoteric texts or what I have termed "draft-like" texts, points to the working quality of the 4Q collection. That is, this collection was not a frozen relic of a collection brought from elsewhere to be hidden in the caves, as several scholars have suggested,[57] but was a living collection, being used and added to up until its final deposit in the caves.

Conclusions

Putting the archaeology of 4a and 4b together with an examination of the manuscripts discovered in them allows for certain conclusions to be drawn. The fact that 4b was most likely used as a dwelling cave indicates that that was possibly the original purpose of 4a as well. However, 4a was not used

---

56. Crawford, "Qumran Collection," 129.

57. For various scenarios, see, e.g., Golb, "Khirbet Qumran"; Magen and Peleg, "Ten Years"; and Stacey and Doudna, *Qumran Revisited*.

as a dwelling cave for long, if at all. The fact that scroll manuscripts were packed into the cave, beginning on its floor and in its niches, indicates that its primary use was for storage. If there were shelves in the cave in antiquity, which would indicate an orderly placement of scrolls that could later be easily located and retrieved, a short-term storage scenario is suggested. On the other hand, the testimony of de Vaux, Milik and Cross (and the Bedouin) pictures a more haphazard deposit, with no discernible order.

The pre-100 BCE dates of at least 25% of the 4Q manuscripts show a collection that began to form at least a century before the earliest pottery from the cave, which is late Hasmonean. Thus, the cave was not the original home of that part of the collection, and we may extrapolate that the same is true for perhaps most of the other manuscripts in the corpus. On the other hand, the working quality of many of the manuscripts, especially the student exercises, argues for a nearby origin. The most likely place is the settlement at Qumran; 4Q is part of its archaeological landscape, and the marl caves on its plateaus were used as dwelling caves.[58]

Thus, the following highly plausible scenario may be sketched: Caves 4a and 4b were dug or re-excavated at the beginning of the first century BCE as dwelling caves, at the same time as the first Qumran buildings were constructed. At some point in time, perhaps as early as the mid-first century BCE, 4a began to be used as storage for older or surplus manuscripts from the settlement, where, among other activities, scribal work was taking place. At the time of the Roman destruction of Qumran in 68, the bulk of the manuscript collection from the buildings was taken up and deposited in 4a and other marl terrace caves (conveniently close to the buildings), in some degree of haste and disorganization. This scenario accounts for both the age of the collection and its large concentration of single-copy, working quality texts (including texts demanding specialized, esoteric knowledge), as well as the unsystematic layers of scrolls found in the deposit levels of Cave 4a.

---

58. Crawford, "Caves, Scrolls and Buildings," pages 3–23 in this volume.

3

The Inscriptional Evidence from Qumran and Its Relationship to the Cave 4Q Documents

OSTRACA, I.E., BROKEN SHERDS of pottery, are the ubiquitous archaeological remains from ancient Israel and Judah. They served as "scratch paper" for the ancients, leaving an important record of everyday activities, particularly regarding trade and education, as well as onomastic lists for various ethnic groups.

The inscriptions from Khirbet Qumran have now been fully published by Lemaire,[1] affording a unique opportunity to study an inscriptional corpus in conjunction with a corpus of literary scrolls that were untouched after antiquity. I am convinced, by a plethora of archaeological evidence, that the scrolls found in the eleven caves in the vicinity of Khirbet Qumran are part of the archaeological landscape of Qumran,[2] and it is thus legitimate, and in fact necessary, to study the scrolls and other archaeological remains from the caves in conjunction with the archaeological remains from the buildings of Qumran.

---

1. Lemaire, "Inscriptions," 341–88. The information which follows is taken from Lemaire's publication, unless otherwise noted.

2. For discussion, see Magness, *Archaeology*², 44–46, and Crawford, *Scribes and Scrolls*, 123–24, 130.

The Inscriptional Evidence from Qumran

Because of the massive fire that swept over Qumran in the destruction of 68, very little organic material survives from the khirbeh.[3] Thus, no material remains of manuscripts were found. We must therefore rely on the ostraca found at the site to give us any information we can glean about writing activities in the buildings. Given the presence of inkwells, it is certain that some writing activity took place there, but of what type and for what purpose? I will attempt to answer that question in the first part of this paper; in the second I will investigate whether any connections can be drawn with the scroll collection from Cave 4Q, the main manuscript cave.

Languages of the Inscriptions

The inscriptions found at Khirbet Qumran were either on ceramic remains, both on intact vessels and on pieces of vessels, or on stone seals or weights. The ceramic inscriptions were either incised into the clay before firing, or scratched, written, or painted on after firing. If the inscription was written or painted on after firing, it was done either with black carbon ink or red ochre.[4]

The inscriptions found in the khirbeh are written in Hebrew/Aramaic (often it is difficult to determine if the language is Hebrew or Aramaic), Greek, and Latin in the form of Roman numerals. Forty-nine Hebrew/Aramaic inscriptions were discovered (thirteen are marked by Lemaire as questionable), seven in Greek (one marked as questionable), one in Latin, two with Hebrew/Aramaic letters and Roman numerals, and four in which the language is unidentified. In addition, two inscriptions in paleo-Hebrew from the Iron 2 period, including a *lmlk* stamp seal, were discovered. Finally, there were six graffiti that contained only figures such as lines.

The caves yielded the following inscriptions: one in Heb/ar from 4Q, one Heb/ar and one Greek inscription from 6Q, one Heb/ar, one Greek, and one uncertain inscription from 7Q, one inscription in Heb/ar from 8Q, and one Heb/ar from 10Q. No inscriptions were discovered in 1Q–3Q, 5Q, 9Q, and 11Q.

The fact that inscriptions were found in three languages, Hebrew, Aramaic and Greek, indicates some degree of trilingualism in the Qumran

---

3. De Vaux, *Archaeology*, 36, and Magness, *Archaeology*², 63. Some carbonized linen was found in L96.

4. Gunneweg and Balla note that red ochre was found in L2 in the main building, indicating that it is possible that the red painted inscriptions were made at Qumran. Gunneweg and Balla, "Possible Connection," 391.

settlement. However, it will be important in this regard to study the find sites, the stratigraphic dates, their chemical group (if available) and the genres of the inscriptions for clues about distribution and use of languages. Therefore I will now turn to the find sites.

Provenance and Date of the Inscriptions

When studying the locus numbers associated with the inscriptions, it is evident that inscriptions were found scattered in every area of the site, including the main building, the southeast annex that contained the pottery kiln (including the two sherds found by James Strange in 1996 along the base of the eastern wall),[5] and in the western industrial complex. At least one inscription was found in the following loci: Trench A, West Trench, 4, 8, 10A, 15, 23, 27, 28, 29, 30, 34, 35, 38, 39, 54, 59, 61, 63, 73, 78, 84, "east of" 84, 89, 110, 111, 116, 121, 124, 125, 129, 130, 135, and 143.[6] There were, however, loci where more than one inscription was found, which is of interest because it may indicate a concentration of writing activity in those areas. These loci fall into three groups.

In the main building, more than one inscription was found in L30, 34, 35, and 39. L30, which yielded three inscriptions, is the room identified by de Vaux as "the scriptorium"; three inscriptions were found there. However, one of these, a Greek stone seal (KhQ439), comes from de Vaux's Period III[7] (marked as questionable; see below), after the community settlement was destroyed. Two inscriptions were found in L34, a "small room" in the southeast corner of the main building in de Vaux's Period II. L35, also with two inscriptions, is a room next to L34 in the southeast quadrant. L39, where two inscriptions were found, is a "square chamber" in the northeast quadrant of the main building. Thus, no real pattern emerges for the inscriptions found in the main building.

---

5. Strange, "Excavations," 41-54.

6. The loci numbers and their descriptions are taken from Humbert and Chambon, *Fouilles de Khirbet Qumrân*, which transcribes de Vaux's field notes.

7. De Vaux divided the Greco-Roman period at Qumran into four distinct "periods:" Period IA, 135-100 BCE; Period IB, 100-31 BCE; Period II, 4 BCE-68 CE; and Period III, 68-c. 135 CE. Magness and Mizzi have shown, however, that the site was continuously inhabited during the Second Temple period from the first quarter of the first century BCE until its destruction in 68 CE and cannot be subdivided into smaller periods. See Magness and Mizzi, "Was Qumran Abandoned."

The loci of the southeastern annex where more than one inscription was found are L61 (three inscriptions), L84 (two, including the inscription found to the east) and L143 (two). L61 and 84 are workrooms associated with the pottery kilns, while L143 is a "small shelter" at the furthest southern end of the southeast annex. The association with the pottery kilns is natural, since there presumably would have been more available sherds there than elsewhere in the settlement; thus, no special significance should be attached to these find sites.

The western industrial complex had five loci where more than one inscription was found: L110 (the large round cistern; four inscriptions), L111 (three inscriptions), L124 (which de Vaux described as "a solid mass of masonry to support the building of the storeroom to the west of the western outbuilding"; seven or eight inscriptions),[8] L129 (two) and L130 (two). A total of nineteen or twenty inscriptions were found in this area.[9] This may seem at first glance to be an important indicator of writing activity in the western industrial complex, but it must be noted that in the two loci where the most inscriptions were found, L110 (four) and L124 (eight), the pottery sherds were either fill that had drifted into the round cistern (L110), or were deliberately used to reinforce a wall (L124). Thus, these sherds most likely came from elsewhere around the site and give no information about writing activity in this area.[10] Taken together, then, the find sites of the inscriptions give no indication of a concentration of writing anywhere in the ruins.

The dates of the inscriptions are quite difficult to determine, except within broad parameters. None of them contain any kind of date formula. De Vaux registered two of the inscriptions as belonging to the Iron II period, three from his Period I,[11] thirty to Period II, three to Period III, and one to Periods II or III. Six are noted as surface finds, while ten are from unstratified contexts. The majority of the inscriptions, therefore, come

---

8. Following the translation of Pfann, *Excavations*, 6. De Vaux's note reads: "Massif de fondation pour soutenir les magasins à l'ouest des dépendances, construits au bord abrupt du wadi." Humbert and Chambon, *Fouilles de Khirbet Qumrân*, 14.

9. See also Gunneweg and Balla, "Possible Connection," 393, who have slightly different counts.

10. *Contra* Gunneweg and Balla, "Possible Connection," 393, who argue that it is unlikely that this is in fact a dump. However, de Vaux does not describe L124 as a dump, but as a reinforcement for a wall.

11. See also Cross and Eshel, "Ostraca from Khirbet Qumran," 509, where Cross dates KhQ 3 (= KhQ161) to Period I.

from de Vaux's Period II, which is unsurprising, since Period II was the last major habitation of the site.[12] Eight of the thirty, however, are from the fill in L124, which is a reuse. Thus, their actual date is indeterminate. If we subtract these eight from Period II and add them to the surface/unstratified group, twenty-four are now of indeterminate date, while twenty-two can be securely located in Period II. The Period II inscriptions, however, still outweigh those of the other periods by a significant margin.

Scientific Analysis

A selection of the sherds were subjected to Instrumental Neutron Activation Analysis, in order to determine the locality of the clays from which the vessels were made.[13] There are four chemical groups as identified by Gunneweg and Balla:

Chemical Group 1: local to Qumran. Five of the ostraca tested belonged to this group: KhQ386, 621, 2176, 2556 and 7Q6. Four of these were in Heb/ar; one had ten lines in ink. None were in Greek or Latin.

Chemical Group 2: clay from the Hebron/Motsa formation.[14] Nine ostraca were made from this clay: KhQ425, 425c, 1313, 1401, 2109, 2125, 2507, 2553, and 2554. Eight of these inscriptions were Heb/ar, while one bore a Latin number.

Chemical Group 3: Jericho. Fourteen ostraca were made of clay that Gunneweg and Balla identify as coming from Jericho (but see below): KhQ387, 426, 461, 635, 680, 681/691, 711, 979, 1110, 1650, 2587, 2609, and 3759. Seven of these were Heb/ar, four were Greek, one was uncertain, and two had lines or incisions.

---

12. De Vaux notes that only the north wing of the main building was reoccupied during Period III (De Vaux, *Archaeology*, 63–64). See also Taylor, "Kh. Qumran," 133–46.

13. Gunneweg and Balla, "Neutron Activation Analysis," 3–54. Magness gives a concise definition of INAA: "a nuclear method to determine the chemical composition of clay or pottery, with groupings based mainly on the trace elements present." Magness, "Connection," 187.

14. The Motsa Formation is the most well-known and widely utilized clay formation in Judea (it is still in use at the present day). See Michniewicz and Krzysko, "Provenance," 59–100, and Magness, "Connection," 190.

The Inscriptional Evidence from Qumran

Chemical Group 4: Edom (Nabatea). Two sherds, KhQ2416 and 2417, both from L130 and with the same type of inscription, Heb/ar letters plus Roman numerals, were made of this geographically distant clay.

Gunneweg and Balla make the assumption that those sherds from chemical groups 2–4 were imported into Qumran after firing.[15] If this assumption is correct, it would mean that any sherds with incised inscriptions, made on the clay before firing, would not contain information (e.g., names) directly pertaining to the Qumran site, although those with inked or painted inscriptions could have been written at Qumran. However, as Michniewicz and Krzysko observe in their petrographic analysis in the same volume, it is "difficult to determine deposit provenance on the microregional scale."[16] According to them, "the clayey materials from the region of Judea are highly homogenous from the geochemical point of view," so that "no precise determination of the provenance of local pottery is possible."[17] In other words, the distinction between pottery made from "Jericho" clay and pottery made from "Qumran" clay, which Gunneweg and Balla attempt to draw, is probably too fine to be realistic, given the close geographical proximity of Qumran and Jericho.[18] Further, Michniewicz and Krzysko observe that clays close to Qumran were not used to manufacture *pottery* at Qumran,[19] so the "Qumran designation is misleading."[20] Thus, it seems safest to assume that the clays used in Groups 1, 2 and 3 came from the general area of Judea, with a preference for the good clay of the Motsa Formation. Therefore, INAA analysis does not contribute very much to our knowledge of the provenance of the inscriptions. The exception is the two sherds from Chemical Group 4, the Edom/Nabatea group, which we may assume were imported.

---

15. Gunneweg and Balla, "Possible Connection," 391–92.
16. Michniewicz and Krzysko, "Provenance," 60.
17. Michniewicz and Krzysko, "Provenance," 76.
18. See also Magness's conclusions in "Connection," 194.
19. Rather, it was used for kiln linings, oven covers, clay balls, etc. Magness, "Connection," 189.
20. Michniewicz and Krzysko tested clays taken from deposits from the coast of the Dead Sea, from the Wadi Qumran estuary, from deposits underneath cave 4Q, and from above the aqueduct. None of this clay was found in the ceramics subjected to petrographic analysis. Michniewicz and Krzysko, "Provenance," 62, 74, 76.

Part 1: Questions of Archaeology

Genres of the Inscriptions

Finally, we must look at the genres of these inscriptions. These are difficult to ascertain, since the inscriptions are often very broken, and only a letter or two remains. However, some inscriptions can be identified by type, or at least by a descriptive category.

I will begin with those inscriptions which seem to have something to do with measurements, trade, or economic transactions. Four inscriptions, KhQ2416, 2417, 2538 and 6Q1, may indicate a weight, measurement, or quantity. They are all found on pitchers or storage jars. Two (2416 and 2417) combine Heb/ar letters with Roman numerals.[21] Four inscriptions, KhQ461, 2554, 2261c and 4Q1, seem to have to do with trade or import/export. Two of these, 2554 and 2261c, are identical and found in the same locus (L124; note, however, that this is fill reinforcing a wall). Five inscriptions (KhQ386, 680, 1095, 2115 and 3759) are simple lines or incisions, which may indicate counting or calculation. Finally, there is one deed of gift or sale, the KhQOstracon 1 found in the 1996 Strange excavation.[22]

Another group of inscriptions contains marks of identity. Three seals were discovered, two in Greek (KhQ439 and 2145), and one with a rosette and what appears to be two paleo-Hebrew letters (KhQ2208).[23] Their function is transparent. Less obvious in function are the inscriptions that just contained a single name. There are nine of these, all in Heb/ar, and all bearing a Jewish name, some common in the late Second Temple period: KhQ621 (Yoḥanan Ḥatla), 935 (שלי; ŠLY), 1313 (Ḥoniah), 1416 (Meshullam), 1650 (Eleazar), 2108 (Pinḥas), 2125 (שמעאל; Samuel?),[24] 2136 (שוה; ŠWH), and 2507 (Eliezrah). None of the names repeat, although there is one Eleazar and one Eliezrah. Of the eight, five (621, 935, 1650, 2136 and 2507) were found either on intact vessels or remains of once intact vessels, which may indicate ownership of some kind. In this last group one might

---

21. These are the two ostraca made from clay from the Edom/Nabatea region.

22. Published by Cross and Eshel, "Ostraca," 18–27, and "Ostraca From Khirbet Qumran," 497–507. Two subsequent articles, by Yardeni and Puech respectively, dispute some of the readings of Cross and Eshel, who read the word ליחד in line 8, thereby connecting the deed to the יחד referred to many times in the Serekh ha-Yaḥad. Yardeni and Puech both instead read [לכול אילן אח ("all the oth[er] trees"). All agree, however, that it is a deed transferring property. Yardeni, "Draft," 236; Puech, "L'ostracon," 3.

23. KhQ439 and 2208 are dated to Period 3. KhQ2145 is unstratified.

24. The reading is uncertain. Lemaire, "Inscriptions," 359.

The Inscriptional Evidence from Qumran

wish to include the רומא ("rûma'" or "rôma'") inscriptions, KhQ681/691 and 7Q6, if "rûma'" is a proper name and not a geographic indicator.[25]

A second group of ostraca containing common Jewish names of the period appears to be concerned with trade or import/export. Four contain the Aramaic word לאפך, "to return," which seems to indicate trade. One vessel, KhQ2553, has two names, Shimon bar Yonatan and Mattatay bar Yosef. KhQ2554 and KhQ2661c have the same inscription: שנים ולי לאפך "two, and to PN?/to me?, to return." Lemaire suggests that the PN could be "Julia."[26] However, one can also understand it simply as "and to me." 4Q1 has the name Yair. The two ostraca from Chemical Group 4 (KhQ2416 and 2417), the Edom/Nabatean group, each has a name, גרף, GRP[27] and Zimri, followed by Roman numerals. These vessels were almost certainly imported. Finally, KhQOstracon 1, the deed of gift or sale, contains in lines 2, 9 and 14 the name "Ḥoni, son of[," in line 3 "Eleazar son of Naḥmani," and in lines 10 and 14 "Ḥisday, slave of Ḥoni."[28] Two of these names, Ḥoni/Ḥoniah and Eleazar, are found in other inscriptions (KhQ1313 and KhQ1650 respectively), but it is impossible to tell if they are the same people.

Finally, there is a Greek seal, KhQ439, possibly from Period 3, bearing the name "Joseph." Whether or not any of these names belonged to inhabitants of the khirbeh is impossible to determine, although that remains a possibility.

Four inscriptions are single letter inscriptions, all on intact vessels. Three are Heb/ar, while one is probably Greek. KhQ1110 has the Hebrew letter ש, while KhQ1403 and 8Q10 have the letter ט. This ט may stand for טהר, "pure," or טמא, "impure." 6Q2 has a M.

---

25. De Vaux noted that the name is attested in Nabatean and Palmyrene, and may be related to רמי at Elephantine. He suggests that the Greek name Ῥούμας, frequent at Dura Europos, is a transcription of the Aramaic form. De Vaux, "Archéologie," 30. Alternatively, Pfann proposed that it should be read as an abbreviation of תרומא, a variant spelling of תרומה. Recently, Mizzi has made a detailed study of 7Q6, which appears on a jar in cave 7Q ("'Rome at Qumran"). He tentatively suggests that the inscription is in fact a GN, and might indicate that the contents of the jar were were either for export to Rome or were to be set aside to pay taxes to Rome (369–70, 373).

26. Lemaire, "Inscriptions," 368.

27. The reading and interpretation of this inscription is uncertain. Lemaire, "Inscriptions," 363–64.

28. According to the reading of Cross and Eshel, "Ostraca From Khirbet Qumran," 497–507. Neither Yardeni nor Puech read "Ḥisday, slave of Honi."

Finally, there are three ostraca that have been identified as student exercises. Two, KhQ161[29] and KhQ2289, are Hebrew abecedaries. KhQ2207, a stone plaque with five lines of writing, has an unknown content; the letters, which are roughly formed and irregular, are random, rarely forming any recognizable word. Lemaire suggested that this was "probably an incomplete apprentice scribe's exercise."[30]

To summarize thus far, the inscriptional evidence from the khirbeh and the caves allows us to make the following statements. 1) Some kind of scribal practice was going on, given the presence of scribal exercises. 2) Trade into Qumran from outside the settlement is also indicated. 3) Hebrew and Aramaic were the common languages of the settlement, along with an ability to at least decipher Greek letters and Roman numerals.

Cave 4Q Manuscripts

Next, let us turn to some manuscript evidence from cave 4Q, which may provide us with some connections to the inscriptional evidence. We begin with perhaps the most pertinent connection, the presence of scribal exercise fragments in 4Q. 4Q234, 341, and 360 have all been identified as scribal exercises. 4Q234, Exercitium Calami A, written in a first century BCE script and penned in various directions, may contain a quotation of Gen 27:19-21, but this identification is uncertain, since only two words are extant.[31] 4Q360, Exercitium Calami B, in an early Herodian bookhand, is also penned in various directions. It contains the name Menaḥem, repeated three times.[32] Although this is in the realm of speculation, it seems possible that here we have the name of the scribe himself. 4Q341, Exercitium Calami C,[33] is clearly a writing exercise. Lines 1-3 contain a series of letters, sometimes alphabetical. Lines 4-7 and 9 contain some personal names: Magnus, Malchiah, Mephiboshet, Gaddi, Dalluy, Hyrcanus, Vanni and Zakariel. In addition, there is a name written in the right-hand margin,

---

29. KhQ161 was also published by Eshel as KhQOstracon 3 (Cross and Eshel, "Ostraca From Khirbet Qumran," 509-14). According to Eshel, the script is "transition to Herodion," that is, mid-first century BCE (509).

30. Lemaire, "Inscriptions," 360. See also Taylor, "4Q341," 141.

31. Yardeni, "4QExercitium Calami A," 185-86.

32. Yardeni, "4QExercitium Calami B," 297.

33. *Olim* 4QTherapeia, 4QList of Proper Names. Naveh, "4QExercitium Calami C," 291-93. See also Taylor, "4Q341."

Omriel(?). The name Mephiboshet has an obvious biblical reference (2 Sam 9), and Hyrcanus may refer to the Hasmonean John Hyrcanus. However, the most likely explanation for the list of names is that they are the names of individuals known to the scribe, who practiced his craft by writing the names of his friends.

Why were these small, seeming worthless exercises placed in Cave 4Q? 4Q234 may contain a scriptural text, but otherwise these small scraps are not even literary. I would suggest that they are part of the material from the khirbeh that was thrust helter-skelter into 4Q in anticipation of the Roman attack.[34] In any case, the presence of scribal exercises in both the inscriptional corpus and the 4Q corpus ties the two together.

The second group of 4Q manuscripts that has connections to the inscriptional evidence is the documentary texts, i.e., deeds, accounts, etc. (4Q342–359). These manuscripts are more controversial than the scribal exercises, since, while the Bedouin claimed they came from cave 4Q, Yardeni has shown that at least one (4Q347) and possibly more actually came from Wadi Seiyal.[35] On the other hand, Lange and Mittmann-Richert have argued that some of them did in fact come from 4Q.[36] To err on the side of caution, I will discuss only those documents with paleographic and/or C14 dates that fall within the dates of the Second Temple period remains at Qumran.

4Q342, an early first century CE Aramaic letter, contains the names Judah (l. 3), Eleazar (l. 3), and Elishua (l. 4). 4Q343, a Nabatean letter from the middle of the first century BCE, contains the name Shimon in line 13, and possibly an unknown proper name in line 14. 4Q345, an Aramaic or Hebrew deed of the middle-late first century BCE, contains the name

---

34. Stökl ben Ezra has suggested that 4Q material from the first century BCE and earlier may have been hidden there prior to 9–8 BCE. Stökl ben Ezra, "Old Caves," 327–28. However, the only record I have found concerning the state of the excavated materials from 4Q is that of Cross from 1958, who remarks, "I was struck with the fact that the relatively small quantity of fragments from the deepest levels of the cave nevertheless represented a fair cross section of the whole deposit in the cave, which suggests... that the manuscripts may have been in great disorder when originally abandoned in the cave. The paucity of sherds in the cave certainly indicates that the scrolls of Cave IV were not left stored away in jars." Cross, *Ancient Library*[1], 27n32. This suggests that perhaps the majority of the 4Q scrolls were placed in the cave quickly, prior to the Roman attack.

35. Yardeni, "Appendix", 284. Yardeni argues that none of the documentary texts originated in the Qumran caves.

36. See Lange and Mittmann-Richert, "Annotated List," 144. The documents they list as coming from 4Q are 4Q352, 352a, 353, 354, 355, 356, 357, 358, 351, 350, 346, and 345.

Part 1: Questions of Archaeology

Yeshua on the recto upper line 6, the name Hoshayah son of[on verso line 20, and Ishmael son of Shimon on verso line 21 (note the appearance of the name Shimon in 4Q343). 4Q346, an Aramaic deed of sale from the late first century BCE, contains the name Shimon (again!) on line 3, and Manasseh on line 6. 4Q348, a Hebrew deed of the middle to late Herodian period, contains the following names: Menaḥem ... son of Eleazar (upper, line 1); Shimon (upper, line 5); Yehoḥanan son of Yehosef (upper, line 9); Yehosef, Mattatyah son of Shimon and Eleazar (lower, line 14); Ḥanan and Eleazar son of Shimon, son of Ḥoni (lower, line 15); Manasseh (lower, line 17); and Shimon from the Timber Market, a district in Jerusalem (lower, line 18). The repetition of the names in this group, Eleazar (342, 348), Shimon (343, 345, 346, 348), and Manasseh (346, 348), suggests a personal archive of some kind, perhaps belonging to Shimon, whose name appears five or six times. Further, there are evident family relationships among the names: Shimon is listed as the father of Ishmael, Mattatyah and Eleazar, which also suggests a personal archive. Some of these names also occur on inscriptions from the khirbeh: Ḥoni/Ḥoniah (KhQOstracon 1, KhQ1313), Eleazar (KhQ1650, KhQOstracon 1), Yehoḥanan/Yoḥanan (KhQ621) Yehosef/Yosef (4Q1), and Shimon (4Q1). Further, in 4Q348 Shimon is identified as the son of Ḥoni, a name that appears in KhQOstracon 1.

It is important to emphasize that none of these names necessarily refers to the same individual, especially since these are common Jewish names of the period. However, the last example, that of Shimon son of Ḥoni (4Q348), gives the best possibility for a connection with an inscription, placing Shimon, the owner(?) of the personal archive found in cave 4Q into a familial relationship with Ḥoni, the giver of the gift in KhQOstracon 1. The ostracon and the deed date paleographically to the same period, which strengthens the connection.

Although there are several accounts listed among the 4Q fragments, only two seem certain to have originated at Qumran. The first is 4Q350, Account gr, which is an opsisthograph of 4Q460, Narrative Work and Prayer.[37] Yardeni suggests that since the account is in Greek it was written by non-Jews (Roman soldiers?) during the partial occupation in Period 3. This, however, seems unlikely. Why would a Roman soldier remove a manuscript from 4Q, use it to mark an account in Greek, and then put it back into the cave? It is more plausible that the manuscript's reuse actually

---

37. Yardeni, "Appendix: Documentary Texts Alleged to Be from Qumran Cave 4," 294. Larson, "4QNarrative," 369.

took place during the time of the Qumran settlement, and it eventually ended up in 4Q.

The second, 4Q355, Account C ar or heb, is written on the verso of 4Q324, Mishmarot C. Its content is illegible. The most that can be said, then, is that some accounts have surfaced in 4Q which resemble the accounts or figures in the inscriptional corpus.

Finally, I would like to compare the names found in 4Q477, Rebukes Reported by the Overseer (late Herodian script), with the names listed above.[38] The names on 4Q477 are as follows: Yoḥanan ben Ar[(2 ii 3), Ḥananiah Notos (2 ii 5), and Ḥananiah ben Shim[on] (2 ii 9). The names on this list are without argument members of the Yaḥad (2 ii 6): אנשי ה[יח]ד ("men of the[Yaḥad; 2 i 1)." Again, we find some overlap with the names already listed: Yoḥanan on KhQ621, and Shimon on 4Q2553 and especially 4Q343, 345, 346 and 348. However, the Shimon in 4Q477 is the father of Ḥananiah, not mentioned in the 4Q archive. These two names are so common that it does not seem wise to make any overt connections.[39]

Conclusions

The inscriptional evidence from Khirbet Qumran and the manuscripts from cave 4Q do exhibit some connections that add to the many pieces of evidence that tie the ruins of Qumran to the caves. The first, and most important, is the presence of scribal exercises in both places. These exercises, which are unlikely in the extreme to have been brought into Qumran from the outside, demonstrate that scribal activity and training was taking place at Qumran itself.

The second is the presence of documentary texts and accounts in the khirbeh and in the caves, evidence of commercial activity of some kind, including the sale/exchange of property, at Qumran. The third is the onomasticon listed above, consisting of a common repertoire of Jewish names from the Second Temple period. There is some recurrence of names that tie certain documents together, especially the possible personal archive of Shimon from 4Q with KhQOstracon 1, both mentioning a certain Ḥoni. On the basis of this evidence, we can therefore make the claim that there are modest written connections between the khirbeh and the caves.

38. Eshel, "4QRebukes," 474–84.
39. See also Eshel, "4QRebukes," 480.

4

Economic Activity, Trade, and Manufacture at Qumran, with a Special Look at the Inscriptions and Documentary Texts

Khirbet Qumran has received a disproportionate amount of attention in scholarly discourse for a small, archaeologically poor site geographically removed from large urban centers in late Second Temple period Judea. This is, of course, because of the discovery of the approximately 1000 fragmentary manuscripts in the nearby caves. The relationship of these scrolls to Khirbet Qumran has been the subject of much debate over the decades. I have stated elsewhere my own position, that the scrolls discovered in the eleven caves are part-and-parcel of the site and must be considered in any interpretation of it. The inhabitants of Qumran in the first century BCE and the first three-quarters of the first century CE were responsible for placing the scrolls in the caves; further, a portion of the people who lived at Qumran were scribes, whose role was the copying, repair, collecting, and storage of the scrolls that were in their care.[1]

But, of course, more than just scribal activities and manuscript collection went on at Qumran. People lived there, which means that they carried on the mundane activities of daily life. As more of the archaeological data

---

1. Crawford, *Scribes and Scrolls*, 309–20.

Economic Activity, Trade, and Manufacture at Qumran

from Qumran has become available, it becomes possible to reconstruct a more complete picture of daily life at the site.

One important question that has engaged both archaeologists and textual scholars is the question of how much contact the Qumran inhabitants had with the outside world. One of the rhetorical tropes used to describe Qumran is as a "monastery" (a completely inappropriate term for a Jewish settlement), where the inhabitants labored in a "scriptorium" and ate in a "refectory." Some of this language was in fact used by Roland de Vaux, the chief excavator at Qumran; he used the word "scriptorium" to refer to L30, and the word "refectory" for L77.[2] But he did not, to my knowledge, use the term "monastery" to refer to Qumran. However, scholars such as Geza Vermeš and J. T. Milik did use the words "monastery" and "monastic" in their handbooks, and those terms entered popular discourse through the work of Edmund Wilson.[3] Coupled with the term "ascetic lifestyle,"[4] these terms left the unfortunate impression that the inhabitants of Qumran led an impoverished, isolated life in the desert, devoting themselves exclusively to an austere, even celibate, religious practice and piety. This popular picture, however, was the result of an underappreciation of the true archaeological picture, an overreliance on the classical sources (i.e., Josephus, Philo, and Pliny), and an overinterpretation of some of the first-discovered scrolls, such as 1QS.

As more complete archaeological data became available, some parts of that data seemed to be at odds with this popular picture. This led to a number of "alternative theories," none of which has stood the test of time.[5] But the new data has also forced scholars to reevaluate that old popular paradigm, which has resulted in a more nuanced picture of the quotidian at Qumran.

One of the questions we can now pursue in the light of new data is how daily life was supported at the site. The climate of the Dead Sea region,

---

2. De Vaux, *Archaeology*, 11, 30.
3. Vermeš, *Dead Sea Scrolls*, 87 et al.; Milik, *Ten Years*, 20 et al.; Wilson, *Scrolls*.
4. Favored by Cross, e.g., *Ancient Library*[3], 68.
5. For an overview of these theories, see Crawford, *Scribes and Scrolls*, 168–70. Those that particularly concern the economic life of Qumran are Crown and Cansdale, "Qumran," who argue that Qumran was "a commercial entrepôt and a resting stop for travelers" (25), and Magen and Peleg, "Back to Qumran," who claim that Qumran was a pottery production center. See also Magen and Peleg, *Final*, 113–19. For refutations of the views of Crown and Cansdale and Magen and Peleg in particular, see Broshi, "Crossroads?" and Magness, "Review Article."

where Qumran is located, does not, and did not in antiquity, support the growing of such common commodities as wheat, barley, grapes, or olives, so how and where did the inhabitants obtain these necessary foodstuffs? How and where did they obtain the miscellaneous articles of everyday life found at the site, such as glassware or metal products? In other words, what was their economic life? Did they engage in some kind of trade and/or manufacture to support themselves?

The answer, in one sense, is obvious: they must have engaged in commerce outside their immediate vicinity, because all of the above-mentioned items must have been imported, that is, brought into the settlement from the outside. But if this is the case, what were the inhabitants trading for them? What goods did they offer on the market in exchange for their own necessities? These are the questions I will explore in this article, by examining the landscape remains, the archaeological finds, and the inscriptional and documentary evidence from the Qumran area. This investigation will make it clear that the Qumran inhabitants did not engage in any large-scale industrial production such as pottery manufacture. Qumran lacked the necessary raw materials and infrastructure; it did not have a consistent large freshwater supply; it did not sit on a major road or port;[6] and it lacked any desirable natural resource, such as an excellent clay bed, in its vicinity. It was, as stated above, a small, relatively poor, and somewhat isolated settlement, but the inhabitants did participate in some small-scale industrial production and engage in trade with the surrounding region.

The Landscape of Qumran and Its Connections in the Region

Qumran sits on a marl plateau on the northwest shore of the Dead Sea, a little removed from the sea itself (the water level was much higher in antiquity). To its north lies Jericho, a fertile oasis renowned for its balsam and date plantations, and home to the winter palaces of the last Hasmoneans and Herod the Great. Jericho had access to the shipping on the Dead Sea at the minor harbor of Rujm al-Bahr.[7]

---

6. *Pace* Crown and Cansdale, "Qumran," 32. See also Taylor and Gibson, "Qumran Connected"; and the discussion below.

7. For a discussion of Jericho and its balsam and date plantations controlled by Herod the Great, see Taylor, *Essenes*, 239–42.

Economic Activity, Trade, and Manufacture at Qumran

To the south of Qumran is the oasis of ʿEin Gedi, home to the second major balsam plantation in the Dead Sea region, as well as date plantations. ʿEin Gedi also had access to the Dead Sea at its own harbor.[8] Thus, products from Jericho could easily move on the Dead Sea to ʿEin Gedi, and vice versa. There were, however, no remains of docks or wharves on the Dead Sea connected to Qumran, which meant that sea traffic bypassed the settlement.[9]

On Qumran's west lies the Buqeiʿa Valley, guarded by the fortress of Hyrcania. In the Iron Age, barley was grown in the Buqeiʿa, but whether the practice continued in the Greco-Roman period is not clear.[10]

How was Qumran itself connected to the surrounding region? According to Taylor and Gibson, who did a thorough survey of the roads and paths in the Qumran region, Qumran was connected locally to the surrounding region by a network of what they term "rough paths" and "beaten trails." A "rough path" is a "small, private thoroughfare ... wide enough for a donkey and its load," while "beaten trails" are "makeshift tracks or trails caused by the movement of animals and humans over the same route over a long period of time."[11] One of these rough paths ran north from Qumran to at least Jericho, while another led south along the seacoast to ʿEin Gedi, although it was prone to flooding. At Jericho, the Qumran residents could connect to a road to Jerusalem.[12] To the west of the settlement, a pass adjacent to the lower part of the aqueduct led to the northwest up into the Buqeiʿa, but it was too narrow in places even for a mule.[13] Taylor and Gibson conclude that Qumran was moderately connected locally to ʿEin Gedi and Jericho, but was somewhat isolated from the main commercial centers.[14] It therefore could not have engaged in extensive commercial activity, but only local barter and trade.

---

8. Taylor, *Essenes*, 243; Barag, "ʿEin Gedi." See also Hadas, "Harbour"; Hadas, "Sailing Routes"; and Hadas, "Anchorages."

9. Taylor and Gibson, "Qumran Connected," 194.

10. Crown and Cansdale, "Qumran," 30, claim that the region was not farmed in this period. But see Har-El, "Agriculture," who suggests that the inhabitants of Qumran grew flood crops in the Buqeiʿa.

11. Taylor and Gibson, "Qumran Connected," 169–70. The western industrial section of the Qumran settlement contains stables, where pack animals could have been kept.

12. Taylor and Gibson, "Qumran Connected," 174, 176, 193.

13. Taylor and Gibson, "Qumran Connected," 182.

14. Taylor and Gibson, "Qumran Connected," 195. See also Broshi, "Crossroads?"

PART 1: QUESTIONS OF ARCHAEOLOGY

Qumran also lacks a necessary natural resource for large-scale agriculture or industry: water. The settlement itself has no natural water source; its water needs were met by the extensive water system that collected the flood waters flowing into Wadi Qumran in the hills to the west. Any gardening at Qumran would have been extremely labor intensive, involving the use of buckets of water brought from the cisterns. Thus, even with the small population at Qumran,[15] they could not have supplied their own food needs, even if the climate had allowed it.

However, three kilometers south of Qumran is the oasis of 'Ein Feshkha, which had about twenty brackish water springs (some of them have dried up since the site was inhabited); the area around the springs is marshy.[16] In the late Second Temple period, date palms, which need a great deal of moisture and heat, were cultivated at 'Ein Feshkha. In addition, fish could be caught in its pools, sheep and goats could be quartered and grazed there,[17] and some vegetables and pulses grown as well.[18] Thus, the most logical place for the inhabitants of Qumran to obtain some of their basic food supplies was 'Ein Feshkha, the closest area which could be agriculturally exploited.

De Vaux, who first excavated 'Ein Feshkha in 1958, argued that it was a satellite settlement of Qumran.[19] 'Ein Feshkha was excavated again in 2001

---

15. Estimates vary, but it seems reasonable to assume that approximately fifty people lived at Qumran at any given time. See Crawford, *Scribes and Scrolls*, 181–82.

16. Magness, "'Ein Feshkha."

17. The "enclosure" excavated at 'Ein Feshkha by de Vaux has now been identified as an animal pen. See Hirschfeld, "Excavations," 41; Magness, "'Ein Feshkha," 238; Taylor, *Essenes*, 266, who identifies the roofed area as a stable. Hirschfeld also argues that the eastern part of L105 was used to house animals (53). In addition, sheep shears (KhQ2401) were found at Qumran, although there are no certainly identified animal pens there. It is reasonable to assume that the sheep and goats belonging to the inhabitants were kept at 'Ein Feshkha, where there was a natural water supply. See Taylor, *Essenes*, 267; Pfann, "Table," 178. It should be noted that de Vaux suggested that the roofed area of the enclosure was a drying shed for dates. De Vaux, *Archaeology*, 73, and see below.

18. See Har-El, "Agriculture," 15–16.

19. De Vaux, *Archaeology*, 58–87. In 1971 Bar-Adon reported on a salvage excavation at another oasis approximately fifteen kilometers (nine miles) south of Qumran, 'En el-Ghuweir (see Bar-Adon, "Another Settlement"). Bar-Adon argued that this oasis was also a satellite settlement of Qumran. The evidence for this conclusion is very weak; unique features of Qumran are missing there, especially the hole-mouthed cylindrical jars. See Magness, *Archaeology*², 263–64. 'En el-Ghuweir was more likely another Jewish settlement found along the shores of the Dead Sea in the Herodian period.

by Hirschfeld, who agreed with de Vaux that it was connected to Qumran.[20] Its one building, a farmhouse,[21] was constructed in the second half of the first century BCE, the floruit of Qumran. Its two other architectural installations seem to have had agricultural/manufacturing purposes; these are a walled enclosure with a roofed shed to the south of the main building and a water installation to its north. Paths connect Qumran with 'Ein Feshkha. For de Vaux, the most important piece of evidence connecting the two sites was the "long wall," which runs south of Qumran down to Ras Feshkha and separates both sites from the Dead Sea while connecting them together. It is described by de Vaux as a "containing wall" for the plantations.[22] There is general agreement that Qumran and 'Ein Feshkha are part of the same archaeological landscape and should therefore be considered together when constructing a picture of life there.[23]

We can therefore argue that agricultural activities at 'Ein Feshkha helped support the settlement at Qumran. Milk products, meat, and wool came from the sheep and goats penned there. Fish were caught there and vegetables grown there, all of which could be consumed at Qumran. But it is the date palm plantation in the marshes of 'Ein Feshkha that produces what appears to have been the most important commodity at Qumran: the date.

Archaeological Structures and Finds Associated with Industrial Production at Qumran

Date Processing

Both Qumran and 'Ein Feshkha have installations that can be associated with a date processing industry. At 'Ein Feshkha, to the southwest of the main building, sits the remains of what de Vaux called "an enclosure." The

---

20. Hirschfeld, "Excavations," 70. Hirschfeld does not believe, however, that Qumran was an Essene settlement.

21. The term is Magness's. See Magness, *Masada*, 52.

22. De Vaux, *Archaeology*, 59-60. The foundations of this wall date to the Iron Age, but it was rebuilt in the late Second Temple period. De Vaux also found remains of small buildings dating to the Second Temple period between Qumran and 'Ein Feshkha, further evidence that the two sites were connected. Hirschfeld, "Excavations," 38, notes that two small springs, 'Ein Ghazal and 'Ein et-Tannur, which also could be used for irrigated agriculture, lie to the north of 'Ein Feshkha. He identifies one of the remains noted by de Vaux as a columbarium.

23. See also Netzer, "Perfume Industry?"

northern wall of this enclosure had a roofed area, which seems to have been some type of open-air shed. De Vaux suggested that this shed may have been a drying house for fresh-picked dates.[24] However, this enclosure has also been identified as an animal pen (see above, n. 17). It is possible that it had both functions. If it was only used as an animal pen, then dates picked at ʿEin Feshkha would have been dried in the sun, as was the usual practice.

To the north of the main building is a water installation, fed by one of the many springs at the oasis. This installation consists of a series of shallow basins fed by small channels.[25] The purpose of this water installation remains uncertain. De Vaux proposed that it was a tannery, i.e., a place for curing animal hides.[26] However, no traces of tannin or any remnants of animal hair were discovered in the basins, so his suggestion appears improbable. Zeuner proposed that the basins were used for raising fish (aquaculture), but positive evidence is lacking.[27] Hirschfeld suggested that the installation was used for manufacturing opobalsam perfume, but as Netzer has shown, the installation at ʿEin Feshkha is quite different from the opobalsam facility at Jericho.[28] Another proposal, first made by Netzer, is that the water installation was used for the production of date wine.[29] Since there was date palm cultivation at ʿEin Feshkha, Netzer's proposal makes the most sense of the evidence. Thus, we have another possible piece of evidence for a date-processing industry at Qumran/ʿEin Feshkha.

At Qumran itself more evidence for date processing has come to light. L75, in the southeast extension area near the pottery kilns, has been identified as a date press for the making of wine and honey.[30] In the excavations conducted by Magen and Peleg in 1993–2001, a "very large quantity" of burnt dates was found in a refuse dump just to the south of L75, while more date remains were found in a northern dump.[31] These remains indicate date-processing was occurring on a modest scale at Qumran.

24. De Vaux, *Archaeology*, 73.

25. De Vaux, *Archaeology*, 75–76; Hirschfeld, "Excavations," 55–65.

26. De Vaux, *Archaeology*, 79.

27. Zeuner, "Notes," 33–34.

28. Hirschfeld, "Excavations," 64–65; Netzer, "Perfume Industry?," 99. Another proposal for the function of this water installation was for the production of indigo dye, but indigo does not seem to have been grown at ʿEin Feshkha. Bélis, "Indigo Dye."

29. Netzer, "Perfume Industry?," 98; Broshi and Eshel, "Agriculture at Qumran?," 251.

30. De Vaux, *Archaeology*, 16, first identified L75 as a clay washing area. Pfann, "Wine Press," 213–14, first suggested that it was a wine press.

31. Magen and Peleg, "Back to Qumran," 59–60; *Final Report*, 59, 68, figs. 65, 67.

Finally, a peculiar find in the cemetery gives further support to the suggestion of a date-processing industry at Qumran. In two of the graves excavated by Magen and Peleg at the southern end of the main cemetery, a group of fifteen sealed jars containing date honey was buried.[32] Magen and Peleg, supported by Magness, have suggested that these jars were buried because the liquid contents had contracted corpse impurity and would have been unusable.[33] However, the biblical injunctions concerning ceramic vessels that had contracted corpse impurity mandate that the vessels should be broken, not buried (Lev 11:33–35; 15:12).[34] Therefore, it is unlikely that this first suggestion is correct. Magen and Peleg proffer a second suggestion, that the burial might be more practical in nature, to protect the residents from scavengers or pests, such as bees.[35] However, a burial in a shaft grave seems much too elaborate a solution for a problem that could simply be resolved by discarding the contents into a dump or the wadi.[36] Mizzi offers a third suggestion: "the jars were set apart because they were deemed sacred and thus proscribed from use."[37] In other words, he is suggesting that the jars, with their date honey, contained tithes or first-fruit offerings that had not been delivered to the temple in Jerusalem or, alternatively, a trustworthy priest. Unfortunately, a completely convincing argument has not yet surfaced; we do not actually know why the jars were buried in the cemetery. However, they do attest to the production of date wine at Qumran.

It seems clear, therefore, that one of the small-scale industries undertaken by the inhabitants at Qumran was date agriculture and processing. These products—dates, date wine, and date honey—would have provided them goods with which to trade. Now we will turn to other types of manufacture that took place at Qumran, and ask whether or not these products were traded. We will begin with the pottery.

---

32. Magen and Peleg, "Back to Qumran," 68, 70, Fig. 3.17; Magen and Peleg, *Final Report*, photograph on xvii; Pfann, "Table," 177n62. Mizzi, "Burial," 353, dates the jars to the first century BCE.

33. Magen and Peleg, *Final Report*, 123; Magness, "Review Article," 651.

34. Mizzi, "Burial," 355, points out that both the Temple Scroll and rabbinic literature reiterate the same position.

35. Magen and Peleg, *Final Report*, 123.

36. Mizzi, "Burial," 354.

37. Mizzi, "Burial," 355.

Part 1: Questions of Archaeology

Manufacture and Distribution of Qumran Pottery

De Vaux uncovered two pottery kilns (and the installations associated with them) in the southeast extension off the main building, in L64 and L84.[38] Therefore, we know that pottery was being produced at Qumran. As Magness has amply demonstrated, the Qumran pottery repertoire is plain, undecorated, and utilitarian, with the same limited range of types repeating over and over.[39] Most of these types are common to the regional repertoire of Judean pottery, in particular the Jericho region.[40] These include plates, cups, bowls, cooking vessels, and storage jars, in particular common bag-shaped jars. However, one type of storage jar is for all intents and purposes unique to Qumran, the hole-mouthed cylindrical jar with a flat base and a bowl-shaped lid.[41] This type of cylindrical jar is found in quantity at Qumran, both in the caves associated with the site and in the buildings. From Cave 1Q alone, the remains of forty-eight of these jars were discovered. Dozens of specimens were found in the buildings. Further, wasters of these jars were found in the dumps, indicating that they were being manufactured at Qumran.[42] This jar-type is almost exclusive to Qumran; only at Masada were sherds of this type found outside of Qumran.[43] No certain specimen

---

38. De Vaux, *Archaeology*, 116.

39. Magness, *Archaeology*[1], 73–89; eadem, "Community," 7–9. Very little evidence of "luxury types," such Eastern Terra Sigillata A, has been found, and it certainly was not produced at Qumran.

40. Bar-Nathan, "Qumran," 263–77; Magness, *Archaeology*[1], 75.

41. De Vaux, "La poterie," 8, describes the first specimens of these jars, from Cave 1Q, as follows: "un vase cylindrique, dont la hauteur varie entre 54 et 68 cm., pour un diameter de 23 à 28 cm. Le fond, très aplati, est porté sur une base en disque mince et un peu concave." There is a variant to this jar type, which has an ovoid body and may have handles. The variant type is not unique to Qumran, but is found in small numbers throughout the region, including Jericho. Magness, *Archaeology*[1], 80–81.

42. Bar Nathan, "Qumran," 275.

43. Bar-Nathan labels this type of jar M-SJ17, subtype E (Bar-Nathan, *Pottery of Masada*, 67–71). Three vessels, eight rims, and three handles were discovered in the Zealot occupation level. Bar-Nathan considers that the presence of these jar remains at Masada indicates that this type of "archive storage jar" was used by the Zealots in the first century CE (71). However, if this was a jar type used by the Zealots, we would expect to find this type in Jerusalem, which so far has not been the case. Magness, on the other hand, argues that the presence of these jars at Masada is evidence that Essenes fled south from Qumran in 68 CE and ended up at Masada. Magness, *Masada*, 178. Tov, following Talmon, makes the same suggestion on the basis of the literary remains, although he acknowledges that this is uncertain. Tov, "Qumran Origin," 57, 61–62.

of this specific sub-type has been found elsewhere, including in Jericho or in Jerusalem.[44] The inhabitants at Qumran were evidently manufacturing the hole-mouthed cylindrical jar in large quantities, but they do not seem to have been selling or bartering them outside of the settlement.

This evidence contradicts Magen and Peleg's thesis that Qumran was a pottery production center in what they label "Phase B."[45] An actual pottery production center, such as operated during the Second Temple period in the Galilee and outside of Jerusalem, requires an abundant water supply, an ample source of fuel, and a good local source of clay, as well as a major road for trade traffic.[46] Qumran lacks all of these attributes. In fact, the inhabitants of Qumran appear to have been importing their clay.[47] Neutron Activation Analysis and petrographic analysis[48] both indicate that a major clay source for Qumran pottery was the Motza clay formation located between Jerusalem and Hebron. A second source, shared with Jericho, probably came from somewhere in Jericho's vicinity. Qumran mud was unsuitable for pottery;[49] it was used for mud brick, kiln linings, oven covers, and the stucco for the plaster tables found in L30.[50] So, far from exporting their pottery for sale, the Qumran residents were importing the clay to make it, including their own particular hole-mouthed cylindrical storage jar.

Other Small Finds, Including Coins

Beyond its pottery, the artefacts from Qumran (excluding the manuscripts), its caves, and ʿEin Feshkha give no indication of local manufacture and must have been imported into the site; that is, they were purchased or bartered. Iron implements, such as pruning hooks, sickles, and axes, used in normal daily activities, were found in small quantities. The glassware, most of ordinary quality free-blown glass, has much in common with the

---

44. Magness, "Connection," 187. See also Magness, "Review Article," 652, 662.

45. Magen and Peleg, "Back to Qumran," 92–94; *Final Report*, 115-22.

46. Berlin, "Jewish Life," 422. See also Magness, "Connection," 186.

47. Magness, *Archaeology*^{1}, 74; eadem, "The Connection," 184; eadem, "Review Article," 653.

48. Gunneweg and Balla, "Neutron Activation," 3-54; Michniewicz and Krzyśko, "Provenance," 59-99.

49. As first noted by de Vaux, *Archaeology*, 16.

50. Crawford, *Scribes and Scrolls*, 198; Gunneweg and Balla, "Neutron Activation," 8-10.

regional repertoire, with no peculiar features. It did not include luxury specimens. There is also no evidence for a glass workshop.[51]

Linen textiles were recovered from Caves 1Q, 3Q, 8Q, and 11Q, with some carbonized remnants at the site (L96).[52] All the textiles, with one exception, are plain and undyed; some have a decorative border of blue thread. None of them is large enough for a garment, although most of them are probably reused garments.[53] They were used as scroll wrappers, lid wrappers, and packing material. Sukenik, on the basis of their manufacture, argues that these linen textiles must have come from the same fabric workshop.[54] Given the absence of loom weights, spindle whorls in any quantity, or any other evidence of cloth manufacture at Qumran, the textiles must have been imported into the settlement.

A small number of limestone vessels—cups, bowls, and plates—were recovered at Qumran. These also must have been imported, since the only place they were manufactured in Judaea was at limestone quarries outside Jerusalem.[55]

Finally, over one thousand coins were found at Qumran from the Second Temple period settlement. They can be divided into two groups; coins scattered throughout the site, and the silver coin hoard found in three small ceramic pots buried under the floor of L120. The scattered coins, both silver and bronze, date from the Seleucid period to the second year of the First Jewish Revolt (67–68 CE).[56] This coin evidence does not indicate any level of commercial activity, but is simply the ordinary detritus found at any archaeological site.

The buried coins are a hoard, consisting of 561 silver coins. Mizzi and Magness have characterized it as a "savings hoard," while Ariel suggests that it may be a foundation deposit placed during the restoration of a building

---

51. Mizzi, "Glass," 109–11, 117.

52. Bélis, "Unpublished Textiles," 123–36; Crowfoot, "Linen Textiles," 18–38; Shamir and Sukenik, "Qumran Textiles,"; Sukenik, "Wrapper,"; Sukenik et al., "Textiles and Strings," 97–118. No wool textiles, common in other sites around Judea, were recovered from the site of Qumran or its caves.

53. Shamir and Sukenik, "Qumran Textiles," 218.

54. Sukenik, "Wrapper," 347.

55. Leibner, "Arts and Crafts," 274. See also Adler, *Origins*, 66–71.

56. Murphy, *Wealth*, 308–9; Crawford, *Scribes and Scrolls*, 201. For more recent coin discoveries, see Farhi, "Numismatic Finds," 210–25, and Ariel, "Coins," 403–30. These discoveries do not change the overall picture.

Economic Activity, Trade, and Manufacture at Qumran

after the 31 BCE earthquake.[57] The pots in which the coins were buried give no indication of ownership. Ariel states that the latest coin dates to 9/8 BCE, which would then make the foundation deposit hypothesis plausible. However, Lönnqvist reports that at least one of the coins from the hoard was countermarked in 52/53 CE, while another might date to as late as 65/66 CE.[58] If his evidence is correct, then it would seem most likely that the pots were buried for safekeeping not long before the Roman attack on the site in 68 CE, rather than as a foundation deposit.[59] In any case, these coins do not point to any accumulation of wealth at Qumran.

In sum, the archaeological evidence from Qumran and its environment, including the manuscript caves and 'Ein Feshkha, leads inexorably to the conclusion that Qumran was a small, poor site, engaged in date processing and pottery production on a modest scale. Its date industry surplus probably enabled the inhabitants to trade or barter for goods and foodstuffs, such as grain, olive oil, and wine.[60] The inscriptions found in the *khirbeh* and the small quantity of documentary texts found in Cave 4Q, as we shall see, support this conclusion.

The Inscriptions and Documentary Texts

The inscriptions from Khirbet Qumran were inked or inscribed on ceramic remains, both on intact vessels and on ostraca. There are also a small number of inscribed stone seals or weights. The languages represented are Hebrew/Aramaic, Greek, and possibly Latin.[61] The inscriptions were scattered across the buildings, with some concentrations in cisterns, dumps, or

---

57. Mizzi and Magness, "Was Qumran Abandoned," 310; Ariel, "Coins," 404.

58. Lönnqvist, *Report*, 9-10, 23-24.

59. Crawford, *Scribes and Scrolls*, 210. Mizzi and Magness, "Was Qumran Abandoned," 305, raise several doubts about Lönnqvist's evidence, presenting the possibility that coins from other excavations were mixed with the Qumran coins kept in Amman. The chain of provenance for the Qumran coins is not well-documented.

60. It is interesting in this regard to note that no wine amphoras were found at Qumran. Magness, "Community," 6-7.

61. Crawford, *Scribes and Scrolls*, 189. The inscriptions excavated by de Vaux have been published by Lemaire, "Inscriptions," 341-88. The readings presented here are taken from Lemaire, although I have not always followed his details. Eleven fragmentary inscriptions were discovered by Magen and Peleg, which have been published by Misgav, "Ostraca," 431-42. The nine inscriptions which are legible contain a few Jewish male names and fragments of words.

PART 1: QUESTIONS OF ARCHAEOLOGY

fills. There were also a few inscriptions found in the manuscript caves. Four inscriptions were found at 'Ein Feshkha.

The content of the inscriptions, which are very broken and poorly preserved, include Jewish male names, most written singly, three student exercises, and a few inscriptions having to do with economic activity. It is on these latter inscriptions that I will focus.

Four inscriptions, KhQ2553, 2554, 2661c, and Gr4Q1, contain the word לאפך (only KhQ2553 and Gr4Q1 have the complete word). This word is an Aramaic by-form of the Hebrew הפך, "to turn," in the sense of "to return [to its owner]."[62] If the understanding of this reading as "to return to" is correct, it may indicate some sort of import/export arrangement; the vessel would have been full when received, and then returned when empty. This is possible but uncertain.

The four inscriptions are as follows:

KhQ2553 top of a broken jar L124	ש○○○ לבית קוס דרום לאפך "? For the house of Qos south to return"[63]	This inscription may indicate that the jar and its contents came from the south, i.e., the Negeb or Idumea. Qôs, normally spelled with ש but also found with ס (cf. ברקוס, Ezek 2:53, Neh 7:55), is the name of the Edomite national deity.[64] Thus בית קוס may be referring to the "temple of Qôs." L124 is composed of fill supporting the wall of a storeroom on the western edge of the western industrial complex, which indicates that this jar, whatever its origin, was discarded.
KhQ2554 ostracon L124	שנים ו/ילי ל[○[65] "two and to me[66] to["	This ostracon was also found in the fill of L124, indicating that it was discarded.

62. Lemaire, "Inscriptions," 273.

63. On the opposite shoulder of this jar is a second inscription of four lines: שמען בר יונתן//מתתיה//בר יסף//ו/י, "Shimon son of Yonatan//Mattitiah//son of Joseph//and. . ." Are Shimon and Mattitiah the owners of the jar? The relationship of this second inscription to the first is uncertain.

64. Knauf, "Qôs," 674.

65. Lemaire, "Inscriptions," 368, suggests לא]פך on the basis of KhQ2661c (see below).

66. Lemaire, "Inscriptions," 368, suggests the Greek name ילי, ιουλια, "Julia." This reading is possible, depending on whether one reads a waw or a yod as the first letter.

Economic Activity, Trade, and Manufacture at Qumran

KhQ2661c shoulder of a broken ovoid jar L124	שנים ולי לאפ]ך "two and to me to retu[rn"	As Lemaire remarks, "l'inscription semble pratiquement identique à KhQ2554 trouvée dans le même locus 124."⁶⁷ It was also discarded in fill.
Gr4Q1 on the shoulder of an incomplete ovoid jar Cave 4Q	ל[?] [ם יאיר לאפדך] "? Yair to return"	Here we find the proper name Yair, followed by "to return." Its presence in Cave 4Q probably indicates that the jar was being used for a purpose unrelated to its inscription.

Two inscriptions, KhQ2416 and KhQ2417, found on fragments of broken jugs, are made from clay that has been shown by Neutron Activation Analysis to belong to the same chemical group, "Edom/Nabatea."⁶⁸ Both were found in L130, an open area bordered by the wall of the aqueduct channel to the immediate north of the structures of the western industrial complex. De Vaux noted that most of the ceramic remains found in this locus were broken and mixed with ash, which includes these two inscribed ostraca.⁶⁹ The inscriptions are:⁷⁰

KhQ2416 fragment of a broken jug L130	גרף מ XX III III	The first word may be a proper name. The single *mem* might be a monetary notation, followed by the Roman numerals 20, 3, 3.
KhQ2417 fragment of a broken jug L130	זמרי? מ XX X	Lemaire very hesitantly suggests the proper name Zimri, followed again by *mem* and the Roman numerals 20, 10.⁷¹

They are not easily distinguished.

67. Lemaire, "Inscriptions," 371.

68. Gunneweg and Balla, "Neutron Activation," 19–20; Lemaire, "Inscriptions," 363–64.

69. De Vaux, *Archaeology*, 55–56; Lemaire, "Inscriptions," 363. Magness has argued that these deposits of ash mingled with potsherds and animal bones are indicative of sacrifice taking place at Qumran. She posits an altar in L130. A discussion of her thesis is beyond the scope of this paper. See Magness, "Sacrifices," with responses in the same volume, and, most recently, Magness, *Archaeology*², 142–64.

70. Lemaire, "Inscriptions," 363, notes that his readings are very uncertain for both inscriptions.

71. Lemaire, "Inscriptions," 364.

Part 1: Questions of Archaeology

What can be made of these two enigmatic inscriptions? Both jugs were small, approximately 18 cm in height,[72] indicating that they were used for an expensive liquid. Their chemical group reflects an origin in the southeast of the Dead Sea; therefore, it is most likely that they were imported into Qumran, probably not directly from Nabataea but indirectly through Jericho or ʿEin Gedi. Their inscriptions may indicate price or units of measurement. However, the fact that these jars were broken and discarded in the ash/pottery/bone debris of L130 makes certainty as to their original purpose difficult.

KhQOstracon 1 was found by Strange in 1996 beside the "long wall" on the southeast of the Qumran plateau.[73] This broken ostracon is a draft of a gift deed, dated paleographically to the middle of the first century CE. It was first published by Cross and Eshel in 1997,[74] followed by a final publication in DJD 36 in 2000.[75] Some of Cross and Eshel's readings have been disputed by Yardeni and Puech,[76] most importantly in line 8, as will be seen below. All agree, however, that this ostracon is a draft of a gift deed.

The draft opens with a date formula, "in year two." Cross and Eshel suggest that this is the second year of the reign of a Jewish king, either Agrippa I or possibly Agrippa II.[77] In line 2, Jericho is given as the location of the execution of the official deed of gift. The giver is Ḥonî, who gives (נתן) certain property to Eleazar son of Naḥmani (line 3). The property is itemized in lines 4–8. Included are a house (הבית; line 6), and fig and olive trees (והתאנים הזי]תים; line 7). The disputed readings are in lines 4 and 8. In line 4, Cross and Eshel read]את חסדי מחולון, "Ḥisday from Ḥolon," and argue that Ḥisday is Ḥonî's slave and is part of the property the latter is gifting.[78] Yardeni reads את הסקים, "the sacks" or "the sackcloth," which as Cross observes is an awkward reading followed as it is by house boundaries.[79] Regardless, it is part of the property that Ḥonî is giving to Eleazar.

---

72. Lemaire, "Inscriptions," 364.
73. Strange, "Excavations," 41–54.
74. Cross and Eshel, "Ostraca," 17–28.
75. Cross and Eshel, "Ostraca from Khirbet Qumran," 497–512.
76. Yardeni, "Draft," 233–37; Puech, "L'ostracon," 1–29.
77. Cross and Eshel, "Ostraca from Khirbet Qumran," 501.
78. Cross and Eshel, "Ostraca from Khirbet Qumran," 502.
79. Yardeni, "Draft," 236–37; Cross and Eshel, "Ostraca from Khirbet Qumran," 505–6.

Economic Activity, Trade, and Manufacture at Qumran

More importantly, in line 8 Cross and Eshel read לכמלותו ליחד, "when he fulfills (his oath) to the community;" on the basis of this reading they interpret the document as the gift of the prospective member Ḥonî to the Essene *yaḥad* residing at Qumran.[80] This seems to me to be an overinterpretation of this draft. Yardeni (followed by Puech) proposes the more mundane reading וכולאילנ אח[, "and every oth[er?] tree," more in keeping with the list of trees in line 7. This is the more banal, and therefore more probable, reading.[81] In any case, this deed of gift witnesses to an economic transaction taking place in the vicinity of Qumran.

There are a few other ostraca that may give some indication of economic activity and/or trade at Qumran, but they are too small to draw firm conclusions. They include:

KhQ461 ostracon L29	מעו/ירבת "from Arabat," or related to Hebrew root ערב I, "to stand surety for, to pledge"	
KhQ2538 fragment of a jar L124	בת "bath"	liquid measurement

In addition, five ceramic fragments—KhQ386 (L23), KhQ680 (West Trench), KhQ1095 (L59), KhQ2115 (L111), and KhQ3759 (L4)—displayed lines or incisions, most likely counting devices.[82]

We will now turn to the few documentary texts purported to come from Qumran Cave 4Q. Their provenience, however, is uncertain, since

---

80. Cross and Eshel, "Ostraca from Khirbet Qumran," 504.

81. Yardeni, "Draft," 236. See Cross's counterargument in Cross and Eshel, "Ostraca from Khirbet Qumran," 506-7.

82. Two other inscriptions deserve mention here. Gr7Q6 is an ovoid jar with four pierced ledge handles on the shoulder, similar in type to jar Gr4Q1 (see above). Its inscription, רומא, was interpreted by de Vaux as a personal name, "Ruma," common in Nabataean but unattested in contemporary Jewish contexts. See de Vaux, "Archéologie²," 30. Lemaire, "Inscriptions," 376, citing O'Callaghan, raises the possibility that it refers to the city of Rome. Mizzi explores this possibility, suggesting very hesitantly that the goods stored in the jar might have been set aside for Roman taxes, but concludes that that is unlikely. Mizzi, "'Rome," 351-74.

Gr6Q1 was purchased by Milik on the antiquities market. Its provenance is supposedly 100 meters south of Cave 6Q. See Milik, "Appendice," 37. The inscription on this whole round jar reads II II III לג II ס. A לג is a liquid measure, while ס is an abbreviation for סאה, a measurement for dry goods. These marks thus indicate the capacity of the jar. Unfortunately, because it was purchased on the antiquities market, we cannot be certain that its provenance was Qumran. Crawford, *Scribes and Scrolls*, 147-48.

they were all purchased from the Bedouin in the 1950s and not excavated *in situ*. Yardeni has demonstrated that some of these texts in fact came from Naḥal Ḥever/Wadi Seiyal.[83] She concludes that, therefore, all of these documentary texts must be considered non-Qumranic. However, on the basis of their paleographic dates, Lange and Mittman-Richert argue that some of them may be from Qumran.[84] We will briefly consider those that, on the basis of paleography, date to the time of the Qumran settlement and may therefore have originated in the Qumran caves.[85]

4Q345 is a double deed of sale. On its recto, line 1, it contains a date formula mentioning the month of Elul, and on line 5 a price: "for 30 silver q(uarters)/*d(enarii)*." On the verso, lines 20-21, appear the names of the parties to the sale: Hoshaʻyah and Yishmaʻel. 4Q346 is a very fragmentary deed of sale, containing the names Shimʻon and Menashe. 4Q351, 4Q352, 4Q352a, 4Q353, 4Q354, 4Q356, and 4Q357 are all accounts of or receipts for cereal or some other commodity, probably imported into the settlement.

4Q350 is a special case, since it is an opsisthograph, a reuse of a scrap of parchment, 4Q460 frg. 9.[86] The recto, 4Q460, has a Narrative Work and Prayer in Hebrew, while the verso, 4Q350, has a list or receipt for cereals in Greek. Because the fragment of 4Q460 contains the Divine Name, the editors argued that the scrap would not have been reused by the inhabitants of Qumran, but instead was reused by Roman soldiers who had entered 4Q after they occupied the site. However, there is no evidence for Roman tampering in 4Q, and it is difficult to understand why a Roman soldier would extract a fragment of parchment, use it for an ephemeral list, and then redeposit it in the cave. Even if the scrap was not found in the cave by the hypothetical Roman, but was found drifting in the ruins after the Roman takeover, why would it then be placed in the cave after being used for a list, along with the other fragments of 4Q460? It seems better to understand the reuse of 4Q460 frg. 9 as made by an inhabitant of Qumran, who needed to make a quick list of foodstuffs being brought into the settlement and used the back of one of their own manuscripts for that purpose.[87]

83. Yardeni, "Appendix," 283-84.

84. Lange and Mittman-Richert, "Annotated List," 209. Their list consists of 4Q345, 4Q346, 4Q350, 4Q351, 4Q352, 4Q352a, 4Q353, 4Q354, 4Q355, 4Q356, 4Q357, and 4Q358.

85. For all of these documents, with the exception of 4Q350, see Yardeni, "Appendix," 283-318.

86. Cotton, "4QAccount gr," 294-95. Larsen, "4QNarrative," 369-86.

87. Crawford, *Scribes and Scrolls*, 145n109, and bibliography there.

As we found with the inscriptions, the documentary texts, if they did belong to Qumran, tell us very little about economic activity at the settlement, except that it was taking place on a small scale, as expected at any settlement.

Conclusions

We catch a glimpse of economic life at Qumran/ʿEin Feshkha through its archaeological remains. As we have demonstrated, the settlement was connected to the wider region of the Dead Sea, but access to and from Qumran was limited, and import/export depended on pack animals and foot traffic.[88] By these means the inhabitants took their surplus commodities to market and brought back their necessities.

Two small-scale industries were undertaken at Qumran, date farming and processing, and pottery manufacture. Dates and their products probably made up the bulk of the inhabitants' saleable products and would have been traded at the nearest local markets, ʿEin Gedi and Jericho. The inhabitants might also have ventured as far as Jerusalem to purchase goods. The pottery produced at Qumran, for which the clay was imported, seems to have been for use only in the settlement and not for sale or barter; at least we do not see the iconic hole-mouthed cylindrical jar with bowl-shaped lid so common at Qumran at other sites around the region, the presence of which would indicate that the Qumran inhabitants were trading or selling them.

Other small-scale trade or barter probably also took place. Wool from the small flock of sheep and goats kept at ʿEin Feshkha could have been traded for finished cloth, whether wool or linen (recall that only linen remains were found in the caves and at the site). Cereals for bread had to have been imported (the scanty documentary remains from Cave 4Q with their lists of grains and some of the inscriptions may testify to this), although the actual bread preparation took place at Qumran.[89] The inhabitants probably raised enough vegetables at ʿEin Feshkha to supply their own needs.

In sum, the economic life revealed by the archaeological remains at Qumran/ʿEin Feshkha is in keeping with the small size of the site, its

---

88. These would also be the means by which scrolls were brought into the settlement from the outside.

89. The remains of grinding mills and ovens were found in the ruins, indicating bread preparation. See Pfann, "Table," 175.

connectivity to the wider region, and its ability, in a harsh climate, to produce desirable commodities for trade.[90]

---

90. It will be noted that I have said nothing concerning the scrolls found in the Qumran caves and their contribution to the economic life of the site. This is because I do not believe that the work of scribes surrounding the scrolls, including their copying, repair, and preservation and storage, or the intellectual activity associated with the manuscripts, contributed to the economic life of the settlement. Rather, the economic activity at the settlement supported the scribal activity taking place there. For a different view, see Stegemann, *Library*, 52–55.

Part 2

Questions Concerning Women

5

Not According to Rule
Women, the Dead Sea Scrolls, and Qumran

UNTIL THE LAST QUARTER of the twentieth century, the juxtaposition of the words "women," "Dead Sea Scrolls," and "Qumran" in the same title would have seemed like an oxymoron. From the beginning of Dead Sea Scrolls research, the people who lived at Qumran and stored the manuscripts in the eleven surrounding caves were identified with the ancient Jewish sect of the Essenes.[1] This identification was based on the descriptions of the Essenes provided by the classical authors Josephus, Philo, and Pliny the Elder. Philo (*Apol.* 14) and Pliny (*Nat. Hist.* 5.17) are unequivocal in their description of the Essenes as an all-male, celibate group. Josephus also focuses his description of the Essenes on those members who shunned marriage and embraced continence (*War* 2.120–121). Thus, it was almost uniformly assumed that the Qumran site, identified as an Essene settlement, housed an all-male, celibate community. This assumption was aided by the fact that one of the first non-biblical scrolls to be published, the Community Rule or Serekh ha-Yaḥad, contains no references to women.[2] Further, the ruins of Qumran did not disclose a settlement organized around normal family life, and the graves excavated in the adjoining cemetery had a larger proportion

---

1. The first scholar to do so was Sukenik in 1948; see Silberman, "Sukenik, Eleazar L.," 902–3.

2. With the exception of the formulaic phrases לבן אמתכה, "for the son of your handmaid" (1QS 15:16) and וילוד אשה, "and one born of woman" (1QS 11:21), which are actually variant ways to describe a male human being.

of men than women and children.³ Although it was acknowledged in the scholarly literature that Josephus describes a second group of Essenes that practiced marriage for the sake of procreation (*War* 2.160–161) and that many of the Qumran scrolls, e.g., the Damascus Document, in fact do contain material concerning women, the picture of Qumran as a celibate, quasi-monastic community dominated the first forty years of research.⁴

This situation began to change in the early 1990's through the work of such scholars as Hartmut Stegemann, Lawrence Schiffman, Elisha Qimron, and especially Eileen Schuller.⁵ The change came about not so much because new evidence came to light, although certainly the pool of evidence became deeper and wider as more and more manuscripts were published, but because these scholars broadened their focus to acknowledge the references to women in the Qumran literature and to try to understand these references in the wider context of Dead Sea Scrolls scholarship.

In this article I take a systematic look at what information the Qumran scrolls can give us about women, both generally in Second Temple Judaism and in the wing of Judaism represented in the Qumran collection.⁶ This attempt is fraught with several methodological difficulties. First, the corpus of the Qumran Scrolls is not complete. Rather, the scrolls are the fragmentary remains of the library of the group of Jews that inhabited Qumran from the first quarter of the first century BCE until its destruction by the Romans in 68 CE.⁷ The fact that I identify it as a library indicates a certain coherence; these scrolls are a deliberate collection that betrays a particular group identity within the broad spectrum of Judaism of the period. It is mainly a collection of religious documents; there are very few business documents that have so far surfaced among the scrolls stored in the caves, as there were at Masada, Naḥal Ḥever or Wadi Murabbaʿat.⁸ The caves in

---

3. De Vaux, *Archaeology*, 45–48, 57–58, 127.

4. See, e.g., Vermeš, *Dead Sea Scrolls*, 96–97, 128–30; for a popular interpretation, see Wilson, *Scrolls from the Dead Sea*.

5. Stegemann, *Library*, 193–98; Schiffman, *Reclaiming*, 127–43; Qimron, "Celibacy," 287–94; Schuller, "Women," 115–31; Schuller, "Women²," 117–44; Schuller and Wassén, "Women," 981–84.

6. I identify that wing of Judaism as the Essenes. Crawford, *Scribes and Scrolls*, 269–308.

7. Broshi, "Qumran: Archaeology," 737. Magness, *Archaeology*², 63.

8. For the economic or business documents found at Qumran and the other Judean Desert find sites, see Yardeni and Cotton, DJD 27; in particular, see Yardeni, "Appendix," 283–318. Yardeni does not believe that any of the documentary texts alleged to be from

which manuscripts were discovered were not refugee caves, but storage caves.[9] The majority of the non-biblical scrolls, and particularly the compositions that were unknown prior to the discoveries at Qumran, betray certain traits and biases that identify them as the property of a particular Jewish group or movement, not a random sampling of the broader Judaism of the period. These include an adherence to the solar calendar, a particular style of biblical interpretation, a distinctive vocabulary, and a discrete set of legal regulations.[10] Further, the collection is also defined by what is not there: there are no works identified as Pharisaic (e.g., Psalms of Solomon), no "pagan" compositions, and no early Christian works.[11] Thus, there is an intentional collection to examine. But the fact that it is fragmentary means that at best we have only a partial picture, and the picture we do have is an accident of preservation.

Another methodological peril is that we are dealing with a literary corpus. The literature within this corpus is written (composed, redacted, copied) by men for a male audience; therefore, what they do have to say about women is primarily prescriptive and presents what is to them the ideal situation. This may have very little to do with the reality of women's lives in the Second Temple period.[12] It is also important to bear in mind the social location of this literature. It is the collection of a Jewish group that had the time and means to write about, meditate on and practice a particular way of life without, evidently, major concerns about day-to-day existence.[13] Further, it presupposes an androcentric social order. In other words, it is the product of a social elite. Thus, the slice of Jewish life in the

---

Qumran were from Qumran (283). Lange and Mittmann-Richert, however, argue on the basis of the paleographical dates of the manuscripts that at least some of them came from Qumran. Lange and Mittman-Richert, "Annotated List," 144. For a more comprehensive discussion, see Crawford, *Scribes and Scrolls*, 258-59, and Crawford, "Economic Activity," 50 in this volume. Inscriptions found in the buildings also indicate economic activity occurring at Qumran during its main habitation period. Crawford, *Scribes and Scrolls*, 188-94, and "Economic Activity," 50 in this volume.

9. See Mizzi, "Miscellaneous Artifacts," 152-53, for a discussion of the evidence.

10. See Crawford, *Scribes and Scrolls*, 11-14.

11. Some early scholars did attempt to identify some of the fragmentary Greek papyri from 7Q as from the New Testament, but those identifications have been disproven. O'Callaghan, "New Testament," 1-14; Thiede, "Earliest."

12. Bernadette Brooten warns against this methodological pitfall in her programmatic essay "Early Christian Women," 67-73.

13. For a discussion of quotidian life and economic activity at Qumran, see Murphy, *Wealth*, 293-400, and Crawford, "Economic Activity," 50 in this volume.

Second Temple period that we are investigating through this literature is a very narrow slice. However, keeping these problems in mind we may at least begin to sketch in the presence of women described by the Qumran scrolls.

We will begin first with the legal texts dealing with marital relations and women's biology and sexuality. Following this we will examine those texts which either discuss or assume the participation of women in the ritual and/or worship life of the community, paying particular attention to the roles that women could play and the rank, if any, that they could attain.[14] The second major section of the paper will investigate the archaeology of Qumran, especially the small finds and the gender of the skeletons in the excavated graves, for evidence of the presence of women in that particular place during the approximately two centuries in which the settlement at Qumran existed. Finally, I will attempt to put all this evidence in a wider context and discuss the question of the identification of the Qumran community with the Essenes.

Legal Texts Concerning Women

Marriage and Sexuality

There are a large number of manuscripts that deal with legal prescriptions in one way or another. For our purposes "legal prescriptions" or "regulations" refer to legislation that has a strong scriptural[15] base, is generally applicable to all Jews (whether or not all Jews followed a particular regulation), and does not refer to a specific organized community structure.[16] For example, legislation in the Qumran scrolls concerning Sabbath observance (binding on all Jews) would fall under the rubric "legal prescription," while the initiation procedure for entrance into the community would not.

---

14. There are two sources of texts about women in the Qumran scrolls that we will not discuss here. The Wisdom compositions portray in more general, less prescriptive terms Jewish society and women's place within it. The "literary" compositions (e.g., the Genesis Apocryphon) present a fictionalized view of women and are therefore only marginally relevant to determining the actual place of women in the community portrayed in the Qumran collection.

15. When using the term "scriptural" or "biblical" I am referring to those Hebrew texts from the Persian period or earlier that were part of the literary heritage of ancient Israel, their "classic" texts. Most of these texts became part of the later Jewish canon of scripture.

16. This definition follows that of Hempel, *The Laws*, 25–26.

Not According to Rule

One difficulty that immediately arises concerns the distinction that is usually made between sectarian and non-sectarian documents. How is a "sectarian" text defined?[17] Does the simple fact that a text was discovered in the Qumran caves make it sectarian? For example, the book of Deuteronomy was found at Qumran in multiple copies; however, it is not considered to be the exclusive property of the community there, proclaiming their own distinct ideology, but to be an authoritative book for all Jews of the period. On the other hand, most scholars agree that the Community Rule is the exclusive property of the wing of Judaism of which Qumran was a settlement, proclaiming its distinct ideology over against other Jewish groups of the period. Thus, the question of "sectarian" vs. "non-sectarian" is important in determining the particular stance of the community referenced in the texts, concerning women or anything else. Since I view the Qumran scrolls as a deliberate and particular collection,[18] my assumption is that, overall, the scrolls labeled as "sectarian" are ideologically in agreement (although it is always possible to discover internal contradictions). Happily, the legal texts found in the Qumran caves are largely compatible with each other and betray a bias of interpretation that often contrasts with that found in other legal systems, most prominently that of the later rabbis.[19] Therefore it is methodologically appropriate to treat them systematically.

As might be expected, much of the legislation that specifically applies to women has to do with marriage, sexuality, and women's biological functions that impinge on ritual purity (e.g., menstruation and childbirth). We will begin with the regulations concerning marriage. It is important to emphasize from the beginning that the texts containing regulations concerning marriage regard marriage as a normal state for both men and women. The Damascus Document, which contains the bulk of the marriage regulations, states, "And if they live in camps, according to the rule of the land, taking wives and begetting children, they shall walk according to the Law . . ." (CD 7:6–7). This passage, which begins with the adversative clause ואם ("and if"), differentiates between those who dwell in camps and marry and have children from others who do not; that is, marriage does not seem to be considered the only legitimate path to follow for the members of the sect. This would imply that there are those who choose not to marry.[20]

---

17. For a good discussion of this problem see Newsom, "'Sectually Explicit,'" 167–87.
18. See Crawford, "Qumran Collection," 109–31.
19. Harrington, "Purity," 726.
20. See Qimron, "Celibacy," 289–91, who argues that "those who walk in the

Part 2: Questions Concerning Women

For those who do marry, the Damascus Document declares that marriage should be governed according to the Torah. In another example, the Rule of the Congregation specifies that a man is eligible to marry at the age of twenty, although no comparable age is given for the female partner.

The legal regulations do, however, place restrictions on marriage. There are forbidden unions outside of those enumerated in the Torah. 4QMMT B 48-49 enjoins male Israelites to shun "any forbidden unions" (ת[ע]רובת [ה]גבר) and be full of reverence for the sanctuary (המקדש).[21] The Damascus Document (CD 5:9-11; 4QD^e 2 ii 16), 4QHalakhah A (frag. 12) and the Temple Scroll (11QT^a 66:15-17) forbid uncle-niece marriage; the prohibition is based on Lev 18:12-14, in which sexual relations between a nephew and his aunt are forbidden. The exegetical position of the three documents cited above is that "the commandment concerning incest, written for males, is likewise for females" (CD 5:9-10). Therefore, a niece is prohibited from marrying her uncle.[22] The Damascus Document (4QD^f 3, 9-10) also contains the statement that a woman's father should not give her "to anyone who is not fit for her," evidently referring to forbidden degrees of marriage, or perhaps some overt incompatibility. The regulation is based on Lev 19:19, which forbids "mixing" (כלאים) improper kinds of animals, seeds or cloth. This prohibition of "mixing" is also used to condemn marriage between the priestly and lay orders (4QMMT B 80-82). All these statements about forbidden unions appear to be polemical; that is, they are inveighing against the practices of other Jewish groups of the period.

The Qumran documents also betray a strict attitude toward polygamy and divorce. Both polygamy and divorce are allowed according to the Torah (Deut 21:15-17; Deut 24:1-4). However, according to the Damascus Document, polygamy is a form of זנות (usually translated as "fornication"):

---

perfection of holiness" (CD 7:5) abstained from sexual relations because of purity concerns. See also Hempel, "Earthly Essene," 266, who states "the protasis clearly presupposes that an alternative lifestyle from the one in the camps with wives and children did exist."

21. Strugnell, "More on Wives," 541. The tie between proper marriage (= sexual purity) and reverence for the sanctuary is a theme that also is found in the Temple Scroll and the Damascus Document.

22. This ruling is in active contrast to the rabbis, who promoted uncle-niece marriage. See Ilan, *Jewish Women*, 76. The exegetical principle explicated by the Damascus Document, that what is written concerning males likewise applies to females, opens many doors for women to obey Torah prescriptions written from a male perspective. Unfortunately, we do not have any other specific examples from Qumran literature of another legal regulation which applies this exegetical principle.

> The 'builders of the wall'... are caught twice in fornication: by taking two wives in their lives, even though the principle of creation is 'male and female he created them' and the ones who went into the ark 'went in two by two.' And concerning the prince it is written 'he shall not multiply wives for himself...' (CD 4:19—5:2)

The prohibition of polygamy is made by reference to the stories of creation and the flood, as portrayals of God's real intentions for humanity, and capped by the citation from the Law of the King (Deut 17:17).[23] The Temple Scroll also prohibits polygamy for the king (11QT^a 57:17–19).

The evidence on divorce is mixed. There are various statements that indicate that divorce was tolerated (e.g. 4QD^a 9 iii 5; 11QT^a 14:4). However, the "Law of the King" in the Temple Scroll prohibits divorce for the king: "and he shall take no other wife in addition to her, for she alone will be with him all the days of her life" (11QT^a 57:17–18).

This rule does permit remarriage after the wife's death. The passage, however, only applies to the king; it is possible that it should be extrapolated to apply to all Jews, but that may be a risky assumption. The passage from the Damascus Document discussed above may also be understood to prohibit divorce, but it may simply support serial monogamy. The interpretation of the passage hinges on the understanding of the word בחייהם ("in their lifetime") which, with a 3mpl suffix, refers to men. Are men prohibited absolutely from having more than one wife (thus precluding any second marriage, including one following divorce),[24] or does it only prohibit having two wives at the same time?[25] The most that can be said is that divorce is nowhere forbidden for all Israelites, although (in light of the prohibition of divorce for the king) it may have been less frequent among the Qumranites than among Jews outside their movement.[26] This is, however, speculation.

The impact of these marriage regulations on the actual lives of women is difficult to gauge, but the regulations, if followed, would have resulted in fewer marriage partners for women, since more types of marriage (including polygamy) were forbidden. There is not, to my knowledge, any specific

---

23. Vermeš, "Sectarian," 200.
24. Isaksson, *Marriage*, 59–60.
25. Vermeš, "Sectarian," 197.
26. Although it is beyond the scope of this article, it should be noted that the gospels record a logion of Jesus prohibiting divorce and remarriage (Matt 5:32 [except for fornication], 19:9; Mark 10:11–12; Luke 16:18). Paul likewise prohibits divorce and remarriage (1 Cor 6–7).

discussion of the duty of levirate marriage[27] in the Qumran scrolls, but a prohibition of polygamy would have made its fulfillment more difficult.

Closely related to the regulations concerning marriage are the rules concerning sexual relations, since for all Jews in this period marriage was the only legitimate venue for sexual intercourse. Many of the statements in the Scrolls concerning sexuality reflect general Jewish morality at the time: women must be virgins at the time of their first marriage, sexual activity for women outside of marriage was forbidden, with adultery considered especially heinous, and the main purpose of sexual activity was procreation. However, the Qumran scrolls do betray a strict attitude toward sexual activity even within marriage. The Damascus Document declares: "And whoever approaches his wife for זנות ("fornication"), which is not according to the rule, shall leave and not return again" (4QD^b 9 vi 4–5; 4QD^e 7 i 12–13). The meaning of זנות in this context is enigmatic; does it mean intercourse during pregnancy or menstruation, some form of "unnatural" sexual activity such as anal or oral intercourse, or simply sex for pleasure?[28] The Damascus Document elsewhere specifically prohibits intercourse during pregnancy (4QD^c 2 ii 15–17; the prohibition also includes homosexual intercourse). It is possible that the Damascus Document (4QD^c 2 i 17–18) also forbids intercourse on the Sabbath (reading [ביום השבת] as restored by Baumgarten) or perhaps during the daylight hours.[29] Both the Damascus Document (CD 12:1–2) and the Temple Scroll (11QT^a 45:11–12) forbid sexual intercourse within the city of the Temple for purity reasons.[30] Thus, the legal regulations of the Qumran scrolls place restrictions on sexual expression for both women and men that are more severe than those of the Torah. These rules, combined with the greater restrictions on marriage, polygamy, and possibly divorce, may have resulted in a greater proportion of unmarried persons in the community at any given time; marriage may not have been so attractive or easy to contract for this group.[31]

27. The duty of a deceased husband's brother to marry a childless widow in order to produce an heir for the dead husband's estate (Deut 25:5–10).

28. Baumgarten, DJD 18:164–65.

29. Understanding ביום as an absolute; so Brin, *Concept*, 366. Jub. 50:8 forbids intercourse on the Sabbath; Jubilees was an important text in the Qumran collection and especially for the Damascus Document, which cites it by name (CD 16:3–4). See also Wassén, *Women*, 95.

30. See also 4QMMT B 48–49, which enjoins reverence for the sanctuary within the context of forbidden marriages.

31. Qimron, "Celibacy," 287–94; Stegemann, *Library*, 193–98.

Purity Regulations

Purity regulations are of great significance for the investigation of legal regulations concerning women in the Qumran Scrolls. Since many of the purity regulations concern bodily secretions, women (who experience the regular flow of menstruation as well as the secretions of childbirth) are particularly subject to the rules of purity.

4QTohorot A (4Q274) places stringent restrictions on a menstruating woman or one with abnormal bleeding.

> And she who has a discharge of blood, during the seven day period shall not touch a man with a discharge or any of the utensils [wh]ich the man with gonorrhoea has touched, upon which he has l[ain], or upon which he has sat. And if she does touch, she shall wash her clothes and bathe, and afterwards, she may eat. And she must not mingle in any way during her seven day period, lest she contaminate the camps of the holy [ones of] Israel. (1 i 4–6)

Menstruating women are not to "mingle" in any way because they contaminate others; anyone who touches another person who is impure through bodily flows likewise contracts impurity for the full seven days (see also 4QD^a 6 ii 2–4). This extends the commandment in the Torah, in which the person who is touched becomes impure only until sundown (Lev 15:21–23). The practical implications of the heightened consequences of touching an impure person are seen in the Temple Scroll, which calls for special quarantine areas for menstruants and postpartum women (as well as those men with genital flux or anyone with skin disease) outside every city in Israel (11QT^a 48:14–17),[32] and in the War Scroll, where women (and children) are banned from the war camp in order to prevent impurity due to ejaculation in sexual intercourse,[33] as well as the impurity of menstruating women (1QM VII, 3–4; based on Num 5:1–3).

Although pregnancy itself does not cause ritual impurity, the death of a fetus in utero did, according to the Temple Scroll.

> And if a woman is pregnant and her child dies within her womb, all the days which it is dead within her she shall be impure like a

---

32. The עיר המקדש ("city of the sanctuary") does not have these quarantine areas because menstruating and postpartum women were barred from the Temple City all together. See Crawford, *Temple Scroll*, 47–49; Crawford, "Meaning," 250.

33. Men rendered impure through involuntary ejaculation are also banned from battle (1QM VII, 6).

grave; every house which she enters will be unclean with all its utensils for seven days; and everyone who comes into contact with her shall be impure up to the evening . . . (11QT^a 50:10–12).

This ruling comes from an analogy from the Torah: if a person finds a human bone in an open field or a grave, they become impure (Num 19:16); according to the Temple Scroll a woman is like an open field or a grave, therefore the dead thing inside her conveys corpse uncleanness.[34] All of these purity regulations would have placed a heavier burden on women in the community than would adherence only to the injunctions of the Torah.

Community Rules

We have been dealing with legal regulations that, while found only in the Qumran Scrolls and betraying their exegetical position, were meant to apply to all Jewish women. The Scrolls also present us with statements concerning women's participation in the life of the community that presumably adhered to those legal regulations.

Rituals and Prayers

There are several texts that preserve prayers and blessings applicable only to women, indicating that women participated in the ritual life of the community, at least in a limited way.

4QPurification Liturgy (4Q284) contains a purification ritual for a woman following menstruation (2 ii and 3). The text mentions "food" and "seven days"; presumably the woman abstained from the pure food of the community during her period. Following mention of sunset on the seventh day (the time of the ritual bath), 2 ii 5 preserves the beginning of a blessing evidently spoken by the woman: "Blessed are you, God of Israel . . ." Frg. 3 contains a response from a male officiant (a priest?).[35]

---

34. This ruling is in direct contradiction to the rabbinic ruling in m. Hul. 4.3, which states that the womb makes the fetus a "swallowed impurity"; that is, it does not convey corpse uncleanness until it leaves the womb. See Crawford, *Temple Scroll*, 45.

35. 4Q512, another purification liturgy, contains a series of blessings spoken by a male thanking God for purification after various types of uncleanness. However, 41 2 inserts above the line איש או אשה, thus implying that women as well as men participated in these rituals.

Not According to Rule

4Q502 is an intriguing text belonging to the Qumran community that its editor identified as a Ritual of Marriage,[36] although others have suggested that it is a "golden age ritual" or a New Year festival.[37] In it, men and women are paired together by age group, and the names assigned to these age groups at least sometimes have the function of titles, such as "daughter of truth," (2 6), which is parallel to the epithet "sons of truth" in 1QS 4:5–6; "adult males and adult females," (34 3); "brothers," (9 11); "sisters," (96 1); "male elders," (19 5); "female elders," (19 2; 24 4); "virgins," (19 3); and "young men and young wo[men]," (19 3). The ritual is a community rite which thanks and praises God. In 24 4 a woman is described as follows: "[and] she will stand in the assembly of male elders and female elde[rs] . . .," clearly identifying "female elders" (זקנות) as a title for certain women in the community.[38] Whatever the true purpose of this ritual, it describes women participating in the worshipping life of the community, and belonging to particular defined groups within the community.

Another defined group of women appears in the Cave 4Q fragments of the Damascus Document, which indicates that at least some women in the community were given the honorific title "Mothers." The text in question reads "[and whoever murmu]rs against the Fathers (אבות) [shall be expelled] from the congregation and never return, [but if] it is against the Mothers (אמות), he will be punished te[n] days, because the Mo[th]ers do not have authority (?) (רוקמה)[39] in the midst [of the congregation]" (4QD^f

---

36. Baillet, DJD 7:81–105. 4Q502 is most likely a sectarian text, since it contains a passage from the sectarian "Treatise Concerning the Two Spirits" found in the Community Rule (1QS 4:4–6).

37. Baumgarten, "4Q502," 125–35; Satlow, "4Q502," 57–68. See also Davila, *Liturgical Works*, 184, who argues that the work's identification as a wedding ritual is the "least speculative" of the three.

38. Davila, *Liturgical Works*, 197. "Male elders" (זקנים) is used as a title for a distinctive group elsewhere in Qumran literature. See 1QS 6:8–9, where the זקנים are ranked behind the priests, or CD 9:4, where the זקנים function as judges. If the זקנים are a distinctive group, it is reasonable to suppose that the זקנות were as well. See also Josephus' and Philo's use of the term πρεσβυτεροι as honored members of the Essene community (*War* 2:146; *Prob.* 87). Crawford, "Mothers, Sisters," 94 in this volume.

39. Translations of רוקמה vary; the root רקם means "variegated, multi-colored," and the noun form usually means "embroidery" or "multi-colored fabric." It occurs elsewhere in the Qumran literature with that meaning (e.g., 4QShirShabb, 1QM, 4QpIsa^a). That meaning does not appear to fit the context here; hence the variety of translations in the literature. Brooke has argued that the primary meaning of the root רקם should be taken seriously, so that רוקמה would denote a tangible thing, possibly "a piece of embroidered cloth associated with priestly status" (Brooke, "Between Qumran," 168). Elwolde, on the other hand,

Part 2: Questions Concerning Women

7 i 13–15). Two things are clear from these lines: women could attain the status of "Mother," and that status, although acknowledged and honored, was of less consequence than the status of "Fathers."[40]

Women also had particular roles to play within the life of the community. The Damascus Document gives women the responsibility of examining prospective brides whose virginity prior to marriage had been questioned. These "trustworthy and knowledgeable" women were to be selected by the Overseer (מבקר), the chief officer of the community (4QD^f 3 12–15). According to the Rule of the Congregation (1QS^a), after marriage a woman "shall be received to bear witness (תקבל לעיד) concerning him [her husband] (about) the commandments of the Torah . . ." (1QS^a 1:11). Although there is dispute about the precise nuances of the woman's responsibility,[41] it is clear that women were considered eligible after marriage to give testimony. However, she is not eligible to give testimony generally, but only concerning her husband.[42] That would imply that the testimony concerned matters that were private between a husband and wife. Perhaps her responsibility lay in the area of sexual purity, in which a woman would by necessity need to be fully instructed.[43]

Several texts indicate that women were expected or allowed to be present during the rituals of the community, and to participate in its daily life. The Rule of the Congregation 1:4–5 gives instructions for the assembly of the congregation:

> When they come they will assemble all who come, including children and women, and they will recite in [their hear]ing [a]ll the

---

has focused on the Septuagint rendering of two words from the root רקם in Ezek 17:3 and Ps 139:15 (LXX 138:15), where the Greek words ἥγημα ("leadership") and ὑπόστασις ("essence") are used respectively. Therefore, he argues for a secondary meaning of רקם as "essential being," "authority," or "status," based on "the metonymy of expensive clothing/covering and the power represented by it." (Elwolde, "*rwqmh*," 72). Elwolde's argument appears more convincing to the present author, hence the translation given above.

40. See also Crawford, "Mothers, Sisters," 94 in this volume.

41. The history of the interpretation of this phrase is in itself a lesson in gender bias. The original editors took it at face value, understanding it to mean that women could give testimony (Barthelemy, "Régle," 112). A second generation of (male) scholars, however, proposed emending the text to a masculine verb, on the grounds that women in Judaism could not give testimony (e.g., Baumgarten, "Testimony"). Most recently the text as it stands is generally accepted without emendation (e.g., Schuller, "Women^2," 133).

42. Davies and Taylor, "Testimony," 227.

43. Isaksson, *Marriage*, 57, notes a rabbinic saying that a wife can be heard on sexual matters concerning her husband, e.g., impotence (b. Ned. 90b–91b).

statutes of the covenant and instruct them in all their commandments lest they stray in their errors."

The Rule of the Congregation appears to be describing actual assemblies during the history of the community and not merely an assembly at some projected "end of days."[44] Therefore I would argue that women and children participated in these assemblies, as they did also in the public liturgy in 4Q502.

Finally, we should be mindful of falling into the trap of silence. Just because a text does not specifically mention women, or portray women as participating in particular aspects of community life does not mean that they were not there. As Schuller states, "many regulations, though expressed in the masculine, apply also to women, and in that sense form part of the corpus of texts about women."[45] If we shift our focus to include women in the life of the community described in the Qumran sectarian scrolls, our picture of that community is radically changed.

To summarize the evidence of the texts: women were present in the community life regulated by the legal prescriptions in the Scrolls. This is indicated by the number of regulations pertaining to women, especially in the areas of marriage, sexual conduct, and biological causes of impurity. That these prescriptions were not simply the general laws in force in Judaism at this time (and thus can tell us nothing about this particular community) is evidenced by the fact that some of them embrace positions in opposition to other groups within Judaism of the period (e.g., the bans on uncle-niece marriage and polygamy).

The regulations for community life also indicate the presence of women; in fact, women had particular roles to play in the governance of community life, and could attain special honored positions (e.g., "Mothers," "female elders"). Finally, although the hierarchy of the community was male-dominated and the viewpoint of the texts androcentric, there is nothing in the texts themselves that indicates that women were deliberately excluded or that this was a male-only community.

---

44. See also Hempel, "Earthly Essene," 254–56, who argues that 1QS^a 1:6—2:11a refers to actual, not eschatological, community legislation. She also suggests that that community legislation emerges from the same social situation as the Damascus Document, which I also believe is the case.

45. Schuller, "Women^2," 122.

Part 2: Questions Concerning Women

Archaeological Evidence

Let us now turn to the site of Qumran itself, in the vicinity of which the Scrolls were found. At Qumran's lowest level its excavator, Roland de Vaux, discovered a small Iron Age II settlement, but the more important and extensive settlement was dated to the late Second Temple period. De Vaux distinguished three phases of the Second Temple period settlement: Period Ia, which began, according to de Vaux, around 135 BCE, Period Ib, which was a seamless outgrowth of Period Ia, and Period II, which began after an earthquake in 47 BCE. Period II ended when Qumran was destroyed by a Roman legion in 68 CE. A short period followed during which the site was used as a Roman army camp.[46] Since de Vaux's time, the archaeological strata of Qumran has been reevaluated; the consensus now holds that a small Iron II farmstead was located at Qumran; after a long period of desertion a Jewish community settlement was founded c. 100–75 BCE; this settlement was in continuous existence until its destruction by the Romans in 68 CE; finally, there was a short phase of Roman occupation and possible squatters' camps, which petered out in the second century CE.[47]

De Vaux's excavations revealed an anomalous site from the Herodian period. In de Vaux's own words,

> Khirbet Qumran is not a village or a group of houses; it is the establishment of a community. We must be still more precise: this establishment was not designed as a community residence but rather for the carrying on of certain communal activities. The number of rooms which could have served as dwellings is restricted as compared with the sites designed for group activities to be pursued . . . there is only a single large kitchen, a single large washing-place, and one stable. There are several workshops and several assembly rooms.[48]

De Vaux found at Qumran evidence for a communal lifestyle, including a common assembly hall used for dining (L77) and a "scriptorium," a room in which he claimed manuscripts were copied (L30). There was also a large cemetery, separated from the buildings by a low wall, which contained approximately 1200 graves. The graves had an unusual orientation, with the corpses buried in a north-south direction, rather than the

---

46. De Vaux, *Archeology*, 1–45.
47. Mizzi and Magness, "Was Qumran Abandoned."
48. De Vaux, *Archaeology*, 10.

usual east-west orientation.[49] Finally, de Vaux connected the Scrolls found in the eleven caves with the site of Qumran, based on the date and type of pottery found in the caves and in the ruins, as well as the proximity of the caves, especially Caves 4Q-10Q, to the site of Qumran.[50] Although in recent years there have been many challenges to de Vaux's interpretation of the archaeological remains,[51] none of these theories have gained more than a handful of adherents. The scholarly consensus still centers on de Vaux's interpretation of Qumran as a site inhabited by a particular group of Jews pursuing a communal lifestyle, who collected, preserved, and copied the Qumran scrolls, stored some of them in the caves during the life of the settlement, and eventually deposited the remainder of their library in the marl terrace caves before the site was destroyed by the Romans in 68 CE.[52]

With that context in mind, we may turn to the evidence for women at the site of Qumran. On the face of it this question is a strange one. Women make up half of the human race, and most archaeological remains are gender neutral; that is, architectural remains such as buildings are used by both sexes, and the same is true for most small finds, objects like lamps, coins, or cups. There are artifacts that are "gendered"; those for women would include hairnets, combs, mirrors, cosmetic containers, female jewelry, and, above all, spindle whorls, the ubiquitous evidence of the female activity of spinning.[53] Male gendered objects are weapons, male jewelry, tefillin cases,[54] and tools associated with male activities such as plowing or blacksmithing. Usually, the evidence for the presence of women at any given archaeological site is the same as that for men.[55] But Qumran, as stated above, is an anomalous site. First, the architectural configuration of the site does not support

---

49. De Vaux, *Archaeology*, 46-48. See also Hachlili, "Qumran Cemetery,"; Norton, "Reassessment"; and Eshel, "New Data."

50. De Vaux, *Archaeology*, 97-102. See also Crawford, *Scribes and Scrolls*, 123-24, 130-37, 149-54.

51. See Broshi, "Qumran: Archeology," 737-39; and Crawford, *Scribes and Scrolls*, 168-70, for summaries of these views.

52. Magness, "Qumran Archaeology," 53-57; Crawford, *Scribes and Scrolls*, 318-20.

53. Taylor, "Cemeteries," 318.

54. The supposition that only men used tefillin (phylacteries) is based on later Jewish practice. We do not actually know whether or not women in the Qumran community used phylacteries. Tal Ilan notes that *Mekhilta de-Rabbi Ishmael* states that women are exempt from wearing phylacteries, but also mentions a woman by the name of Mikhal b. Kushi who did don phylacteries. Ilan, "Attraction," 27.

55. See Magness's comparison of Qumran with other archaeological sites in the Judean Desert. "Women at Qumran?," 126-31.

the normal features of family, village, or city life in the Second Temple period. If women were living at Qumran, they were not living in the usual family arrangements presumed as the norm by the vast majority of Second Temple literature (and supported by archaeological evidence), including the Qumran documents themselves. Second, the material artifacts indicate that if women were at Qumran, they were there in much smaller numbers than men. The evidence for that statement comes from a study of the small finds and the excavated graves.

The term "small finds" refers to objects that were used or owned by individuals. Most of these objects, as stated above, are "gender neutral"; that is, we cannot determine the gender of the user from the object itself (e.g., coins or lamps). However, there are objects that are associated only with women, which, if women were physically present at Qumran, should be found there.

A survey of the records of the small finds at Qumran yields a startling discovery: there is only one spindle whorl (found in locus 7, the stratum of which is unrecorded) and four beads.[56] Recall that these finds cover a period of almost two hundred years! Further, the caves in which the scrolls were found yielded three beads and two fragments of a wooden comb.[57] This compares, for example, with the Cave of Letters at Naḥal Ḥever, inhabited by refugees during the Bar Kokhba Revolt in 132–35 CE. In this cave there were balls of linen thread, two mirrors, five spindle whorls, comb fragments, eighteen beads, a cosmetic spoon, a cosmetic box and a hairnet.[58] The differential between these finds, coming from a period of months, and those at Qumran, coming from a period of 150 years, is striking. However, we must be careful of how we interpret this "small find" evidence; to claim that the lack of female-gendered objects shows that women were not present at Qumran is to make an argument from silence. The lack of female-gendered objects does not positively prove that women were absent from Qumran, but it does make their presence more difficult to assert. One other possible avenue of positive evidence is the gender of the corpses exhumed in the cemetery. Of the ca. 1200 graves in the cemetery, de Vaux excavated only forty-three. Steckoll excavated nine more graves in 1966–67, but those

---

56. Magness, "Women at Qumran?," 125. Taylor ("The Cemeteries," 318n117) notices a spindle whorl found in L20, but L20 is only from the post-settlement Roman encampment. Her identification of the so-called sundial as a spindle whorl is not convincing (see also Magness, "Women at Qumran?," 123n45).

57. Magness, "Women at Qumran?," 125.

58. Yadin, *Finds*, 34–36; also cited by Magness, "Women at Qumran?," 128–29.

remains have apparently disappeared.[59] The parts of the skeletons preserved from de Vaux's excavations are now housed in Munich, Paris and Jerusalem.[60] Röhrer-Ertl identified the twenty-two skeletons in the Munich collection as nine males, eight females and five children.[61] The remains of the Paris and Jerusalem collections have been identified by Sheridan as sixteen males, one female (Tomb A), and one male with a question mark.[62] However, Zias has challenged the antiquity of some of the skeletons from the Munich collection, arguing that six of the female skeletons (T32–36, South T1) and all of the children (South T2–4) are recent Bedouin burials and not from the period of the Qumran settlement at all.[63] Zias notes that five of the tombs (T32–36) were oriented along an east-west axis, in accordance with Muslim burial practice; the graves were particularly shallow; and the grave goods found in T32–33 and South T1 are anomalous in the Qumran cemetery.[64] If Zias is correct (and his evidence is compelling), that would reduce the number of positively identified females buried at Qumran in the Second Temple period to three (Tombs A, 22, and 24II).[65] It is important to emphasize that forty-three (or even fifty-two, including Steckoll's tombs) graves out of 1200 are not a statistically compelling sample.[66] We are left again with an argument from silence: the percentage of women from the exhumed graves from the period of the Qumran settlement is not as large as we would otherwise expect.[67]

59. Steckoll identified five of the burials as male (G3, 4, 5, 9 and 10), three as female (G 6, 7, 8), and one as a child (G6, buried together with the female). Steckoll, "Preliminary," 335. Steckoll's identifications are regarded with suspicion by other osteo-anthropologists. See Sheridan, "Scholars," 206n22.

60. For a history of the post-mortem journeys of these skeletons, see Taylor, "The Cemeteries," 296n38, 298.

61. Röhrer-Ertl et al., "Über die Graberfelder," 3–46.

62. Sheridan, "Soldiers," 225–34.

63. Zias, "Cemeteries."

64. Zias, "Cemeteries," 225–30. Zias argues that the jewelry found in those tombs resembles that found in Bedouin burials that have been identified with certainty.

65. For a critique of Zias's arguments, see Zangenberg, "Bones," 52–76.

66. Since this article was written, in 2015–16 a salvage excavation in the northern extension of the main cemetery was conducted by Nagar et al. for the Israel Antiquities Authority. Thirty-three skeletons were unearthed and studied before being reburied. The excavators report that all the skeletons were of adult males; no women or children were found. As they state, "These results are markedly different from the expected demography of a regular, civilian, historic cemetery." Nagar, "Conclusive," 31–32.

67. Magness, "Women at Qumran?," 118.

Part 2: Questions Concerning Women

What conclusions can be drawn from this scanty evidence? I think the argument can be made that the demographic profile of the Qumran settlement, based on the available evidence, is overwhelmingly male. If women were present there, it was only in small numbers and for short periods of time. That is, individual women may have been there long enough to die there, but women as a group were not there in large enough numbers or for a long enough period of time to leave discernible evidence in the archaeological record. Thus, the evidence of archaeology seems to be at odds with the textual evidence presented above. I will propose a solution to this problem in the final section.

Conclusions

Sukenik's early proposal, subsequently adopted by Cross, Milik et al.,[68] that the community that collected the Qumran scrolls should be identified with the ancient Jewish sect of the Essenes, became the consensus position in Dead Sea Scrolls scholarship for the following reasons. 1) The location of Qumran fits with the information of Pliny the Elder, who locates the Essenes "on the west side of the Dead Sea ..." and to the north of the oasis of Engedi (*Nat. Hist.* 5.73).[69] 2) Several of the theological concepts that Josephus and Philo attribute to the Essenes appear in the Qumran scrolls, such as determinism and a belief in the afterlife. 3) Essene practices as described by Josephus, Philo, and Pliny seem to be reflected in both the Qumran scrolls and the archaeological record, e.g., communal property, common meals, particular initiation procedures and special purity regulations.[70] Further, it is clear from the descriptions in Josephus, Philo, rabbinic literature, and the New Testament that the sectarian compositions do not reflect Pharisaic beliefs and practices.[71] Finally, although some of the legal positions embraced by the sectarian compositions are the same as those

---

68. See Cross, *Ancient Library*², 51–53; and Milik, *Ten Years*, 56.

69. Pliny's use of the term *infra hos* has been the cause of some controversy. Pliny could mean that the Essene settlement was located in the hills looking down over the oasis of Ein Gedi (hence "above"). However, Pliny is naming towns and settlements along the shores of the Dead Sea beginning in the north and proceeding southwards: Jerusalem/Jericho > Essenes [Qumran] > Ein Gedi > Masada. Thus, the Essenes would be located to the north of ("above") Ein Gedi. This is the way in which I understand Pliny's description. See Beall, *Josephus'*, 5.

70. VanderKam, *Dead Sea Scrolls*, 71–87; Crawford, *Scribes and Scrolls*, 273–308.

71. See, e.g., Schiffman, *Reclaiming*, 87–89.

attributed to the Sadducees in rabbinic literature, and the "sons of Zadok" are an important leadership group in some of the texts,[72] the group who collected the Qumran scrolls is not identical with the aristocratic Sadducees who controlled the Temple and the High Priesthood in the late Second Temple period.[73] Thus, the identification of the Qumran group with the Essenes (understanding the Essenes as originating in a Zadokite or "proto-Sadducee" movement) has much merit.

There are, however, difficulties with this Essene identification. The evidence of Josephus and Philo and the information attainable from the sectarian compositions do not always line up precisely. For our purposes the greatest difficulty with the Essene identification is that Philo and Pliny both declare that the Essenes were celibate males. Philo says, "they banned marriage at the same time as they ordered the practice of perfect continence" (*Apol.* 14); and Pliny states that they are "without women, and renouncing love entirely . . . and having for company only the palm trees" (*Nat. Hist.* 5.73).[74] Josephus' evidence is more nuanced; he does say in his main discussion concerning the Essenes that "they disdain marriage for themselves" (*War* 2.120) and "take no wives" (*Ant.* 18.21), but he also discusses a "marrying" group of Essenes (*War* 2.160–162). As we have seen above, although the Scrolls ban polygamy, only tolerate divorce, expand the number of forbidden marriages, and evidently restrict the expression of sexual intimacy within marriage, nowhere do they advocate celibacy. This is a seemingly irreconcilable contradiction.

However, we also noted above that according to the archaeological evidence women lived at Qumran in very small numbers, if at all. Pliny is the only ancient source who places the Essenes at a specific geographical location (a location that seems to fit the site of Qumran); Josephus and Philo

---

72. Schiffman, *Reclaiming*, 83–89.

73. Schiffman, *Reclaiming*, 73–76.

74. Both Philo and Josephus claim that the Essenes avoid marriage for misogynistic reasons, considering women to be "selfish, excessively jealous, skilful in ensnaring and seducing" (*Apol.* 14) and being "convinced that none of them is faithful to one man" (*War* 2.121). This misogyny betrays the bias of Philo and Josephus and may not at all reflect the Essene attitude. Pliny makes no such claim, only remarking that the Essenes' sexual abstinence is "admirable" (*Nat. Hist.* 5.73). The classical sources' emphasis on Essene celibacy may stem from a desire to present them as if they were similar to Hellenistic associations such as the Pythagoreans, who also practiced sexual self-restraint. Vermeš and Goodman, *Essenes*, 13; and Taylor, *Essenes*, 43–45.

Part 2: Questions Concerning Women

locate them more generally in the towns and villages of Judaea.[75] Further, as mentioned above, Josephus also states that

> there exists another order of Essenes who, although in agreement with the others on the way of life, usages, and customs, are separated from them on the subject of marriage. Indeed, they believe that people who do not marry cut off a very important part of life, namely the propagation of the species; and all the more so that if everyone adopted the same opinion the race would very quickly disappear. (*War* 2.160)

In other words, some of the Essenes married. Josephus goes on to say that this group of Essenes eschewed intercourse with their pregnant wives, a practice that accords with the legal regulations from the Damascus Document discussed above. Although Josephus presents the "marrying Essenes" almost as an afterthought, his notice may give us the clue we need to reconcile the seeming contradictions of the various sources.

If one removes the word "celibacy" from the discussion concerning the identification of the Qumran community with the Essenes, then it is possible to suggest that most Essenes married and lived a family life, but that some Essenes avoided marriage primarily for purity reasons.[76] Qimron has proposed that the phrase in the Damascus Document "those who walk in the perfection of holiness" (CD 7: 4-6), describes community members who avoid marriage for purity reasons.[77] These community members are contrasted with ordinary community members, who pursue marriage: "And if (ואם) they reside in camps in accordance with the rule of the land, and take wives and beget children . . ." (CD 7:6-7). The adversative clause indicates a demarcation of those described in the previous lines and those described in the following lines; in other words, two groups, one of which married, the other of which did not. It is possible that the latter group included the widowed and/or divorced, as well as those who either chose not to marry or could not find suitable marriage partners; therefore, abstention from marriage would not necessarily have been a lifelong choice, but more

---

75. Philo, *Prob.* 76: "fleeing the cities . . . they live in villages." *Apol.* 1: "They live in a number of towns in Judaea, and also in many villages and large groups." There is an internal contradiction in Philo. Josephus, *War* 2.124: "They are not in one town only, but in every town several of them form a colony."

76. This solution was evidently first proposed by Marcus, who suggested that Josephus reversed the actual situation of the Essenes, in which most were married, but a few were celibate. As cited by Cross, *Ancient Library*[1], 96-7n101.

77. Qimron, "Celibacy," 289-90. See also Baumgarten, "Qumran-Essene," 23n23.

limited in scope.[78] This proposal accounts for Josephus' evidence regarding the two groups of Essenes.

Could women become members of the Essenes through marriage? While it is clear from Josephus and Philo that men took the leading roles in the community, Josephus notes that before marriage "they observe their women for three years. When they have purified themselves three times and thus proved themselves capable of bearing children, they then marry them" (*War* 2.161). The two halves of the last sentence have both been taken to refer to proving a woman's fertility before marriage.[79] However, the time frame in that regard makes no sense. The women "purify themselves three times"; this must refer to three menstrual cycles, a matter of months, not years! To what then do the "three years" refer? It would seem to be a period of initiation, similar to that undergone by men.[80] In fact, according to Josephus elsewhere, the Essene initiation process took three years. Perhaps only married or betrothed women were eligible to join the community;[81] certainly women could not attain the same status as men in the organization. That is, they could not serve as judges or other officers or take part in the deliberations of the community and they could only serve as witnesses in the limited way described in the Rule of the Congregation (see above). But it is plausible that women were admitted to some form of membership. In fact, Josephus goes on to say "the women bathe wrapped in linen, while the men wear a loincloth. Such are the customs of this order. (*War* 2.161)" This statement seems to presume that the women of the group observed the same purification rituals as the men (as witnessed by 4QPurification Liturgy discussed above), implying membership in the order.

The proposal concerning two groups of Essenes also helps to account for the paucity of evidence regarding women's presence at Qumran. Stegemann observed that although Pliny limits the Essenes to one geographical location, Philo and Josephus do not,[82] but instead locate them in

78. Baumgarten, "Qumran-Essene," 19, has suggested that the community contained those who never married or at a later stage in life renounced sexual relations in an effort to "walk in the perfection of holiness."

79. Dupont-Sommer, *Essene Writings*, 35n3; Beall, *Josephus'*, 112. Kister, "Notes," 281, suggests that the three-year period of observation took place after marriage, to see if procreation would occur. If no pregnancy resulted from the marriage, presumably it would be dissolved.

80. Schuller and Wassén, "Women," 983.

81. Davies and Taylor, "Testimony," 226–27, suggest that women could only be part of the community by virtue of attachment to a man, specifically a husband.

82. Stegemann, "Qumran Essenes," 84.

settlements throughout Judaea. Josephus, in fact, implies a community of Essenes in Jerusalem itself (*War* 5.145). How can these contradictions be reconciled? If Qumran is understood as a scribal center for the Essenes,[83] then the settlement of Essenes Pliny describes can continue to be identified with Qumran, while positing other groups of Essenes living among the Jewish population of Judea. Pliny, who was a non-native and used sources when composing his work, simply had no awareness of other Essene settlements. Josephus and Philo, who were both Jewish, had better information. It can also be argued that as a scribal center Qumran would have housed a large collection of manuscripts and would have been populated mainly by males, although it is possible that a very small number of women lived there as well. Thus, to outsiders, the community would have indeed looked "celibate."[84] The dwellers at Qumran, whether they lived there permanently (a small number) or temporarily, would have adhered to a rigorous degree of purity, the same degree required for the Temple in Jerusalem.[85] If this is correct, it would be impossible for women in their childbearing years or for married women or men to reside permanently at Qumran, since those groups are periodically rendered impure by bodily flows. Thus, only men abstaining from marriage (and perhaps older women; the "Mothers" or "female elders"?) could reside permanently at Qumran. This would account for the disproportionate number of males in the excavated graves, but also leave space for a small percentage of women.

The foregoing proposal also solves another dilemma of scrolls scholarship, the relationship of the Damascus Document and the Community Rule. Both documents exist in multiple copies at Qumran, legislate for a particular community, betray evidence of editing and redactional growth, and may mutually influence one another, e.g., in the parallel sections of their penal codes.[86] However, there are also clear differences in the type of com-

---

83. Crawford, *Scribes and Scrolls*, 315–19.

84. Qimron, "Celibacy," 288.

85. Magness, "Communal Meals," 15–28. Magness argues that the archaeological layout of the Qumran settlement indicates that the inhabitants organized their space into ritually pure and impure zones. She sees a parallel between the layout of Qumran and the purity regulations of the Temple Scroll, which bar the ritually impure (including menstruants) from the sacred zone of the Temple City. Magness has recently argued, based on archaeological evidence, that the inhabitants of Qumran were performing sacrifices there. If she is correct, this would be a further argument in favor of an all-male, ritually pure group at Qumran. Magness, "Sacrifices."

86. See Hempel, *Qumran Rule Texts*, 1, 123–52.

munity for which they legislate, the most pertinent difference being that the Damascus Document legislates explicitly for women, while the Community Rule has no overt information about women at all. One proposal concerning their relationship is that the Damascus Document was the rule for all Essenes living throughout Judaea, while the Community Rule applied only to those permanent dwellers at Qumran, who have chosen to pursue "the perfection of holiness."[87] Thus, the two documents existed side by side, because the two groups of Essenes existed at the same time. These groups would not have been separate or isolated, but in constant dialogue and communication.[88] This would account for the mutual influence of the Damascus Document and the Community Rule on one another, as evidenced by the 4Q copies of the Damascus Document penal code, as well as documents like Miscellaneous Rules (4Q265), which contains material found in both the Community Rule and the Damascus Document. Baumgarten points out that an "extensive pericope" from the 4QD penal code closely parallels that of 1QS. However, the 4QD penal code includes offenses such as זנות with a wife and murmuring against the Mothers, which presume the presence of women in the community. The Community Rule does not contain these offenses (either in 1QS or in the 4QS manuscripts), which points to a community without women.[89] I am suggesting that Qumran housed this special Essene community.

To summarize, the Qumran documents are the library or collection of the Jewish Essenes in the late Second Temple period. The Essenes included women, and its members married, but a subgroup within the Essenes eschewed marriage for purity reasons. Qumran was a scribal center for the Essenes, inhabited mostly by males pursuing a rigorous standard of purity and, perhaps, adhering to some form of the Rule of the Community, while the majority of the Essenes lived throughout Judea, most likely following regulations like those found in the Damascus Document. This thesis allows us to place women back into the frame of Qumran studies and resolves the question of so-called Essene "celibacy."

---

87. Qimron, "Celibacy," 288-92.

88. The idea that the ascetic desert community (יחד) and the less ascetic communities throughout Judea were contemporaneous is also suggested by Cross in *Ancient Library*[3], 186. See also Schofield, *From Qumran*, esp. 274-80; and Collins, *Beyond*, esp. 207-8.

89. The relation between the penal codes of the Damascus Document and the Community Rule is more complex than I am able to discuss here. See Baumgarten, DJD 18:7-9; and Hempel, "Penal Code," 338-43, 348.

6

Mothers, Sisters, and Elders
Titles for Women in Second Temple Jewish and Early Christian Communities

THIS ARTICLE CONCERNS TWO fragmentary texts from the Qumran scrolls, each of which gives us a tantalizing glimpse of women, first as part of the community presupposed by each text, and second as having a particular role or status within that community. That role or status is indicated by the appearance of a particular title, which, according to their grammatical forms, applied only to women. The later use of these same titles is then traced in Jewish inscriptions and texts, in order to suggest a wider context in which the Qumran titles might be understood. Finally, I will look at the use of these titles in the early Christian community as illustrated by certain passages in the New Testament. The appearance of these same titles in the three different contexts demonstrates a continuity of usage among Jewish communities in the Second Temple period, from the late second century BCE to the early second century CE.

For the purposes of this article I will assume that (but not argue for) the Qumran scrolls belonged to the Essene movement as described by Josephus, Philo, and Pliny. However, contrary to the testimony of both Philo and Pliny, I believe from the evidence of the Qumran scrolls that the Essene movement as a whole included women, as Josephus indicates in his discussion of the "marrying Essenes" (*War* 2.164).[1]

1. See Crawford, "Not According to Rule," 71 in this volume, and *Scribes and Scrolls*, 299–302.

Mothers, Sisters, and Elders

The Qumran Texts

The first text comes from the Cave 4Q fragments of the Damascus Document, which have revealed that the Damascus Document contained a much more extensive legal code than was evident from the Cairo Genizah manuscripts.[2] While there is much new legislation in the 4QD fragments concerning women, the lines discussed below do not legislate for women *per se*, but rather reveal the presence in the community for which the Damascus Document is legislating of a group of women singled out for special honor, the "Mothers." The lines in question occur in 4QD^e, 7 i 13–15.[3]

ואשר ילו[נ] על האבות
ישלח[] מן העדה ולא ישוב [ואם] על האמות וענש עשר[ת] ימים
כי אין לאמ[ו]ת רוקמה בתוך[העדה

> And whoever murmu]rs against the Fathers [shall be expelled] from the congregation and shall not return; [but if] against the Mothers, then he shall be punished te[n] days, because the Mo[th]ers do not have "authority" in the midst of [the congregation].

From the parallelism of the terms "Fathers" and "Mothers" it is evident that the term "Mothers" does not simply refer to biological mothers (as is common in biblical Hebrew) but to a special group within the congregation. The command to honor fathers and mothers is found, of course, in the Fifth Commandment (Exod 20:12; Deut 5:16), and is constantly emphasized in Wisdom literature, including Wisdom literature from Qumran (e.g., Prov 23:22; 4Q416 2 iii 15–16). Already in biblical Hebrew the word "father," אב, is used not only for the biological father or even for the head of an extended family household (the בית אב), but as a term of respect and honor for a master (2 Kgs 5:13), a priest (Judg 17:10, 18:19), a prophet (2 Kgs 2:12, 6:21, 13:14) and a counselor (Gen 45:8). That extended meaning is applied here to a specific group of (older?) men in the congregation. The term "Fathers" occurs elsewhere in Qumran literature indicating a venerable group, for example in the War Scroll, 2:1, 3, 7, in which the אבות העדה, "fathers of the congregation," as a group are serving in the sanctuary (note the recurrence of the term העדה, "the congregation"). If the "Fathers" are an organized group, then it is methodologically sound to assume that the "Mothers" are as well. The term "mother," אם, is used once in the Hebrew Bible as a term

---

2. Baumgarten, DJD 18:2–6.

3. Baumgarten, DJD 18:162–66. Baumgarten dates the manuscript to the first half of the first century CE on paleographic grounds.

of honor, when Deborah is called "a mother in Israel" in Judg 5:7.[4] In 4QD[e] the meaning is obviously parallel to the honorific "Fathers" and refers to a specific group of (older?) women in the congregation.

What the functions of these "Mothers" were within the congregation cannot be determined with certainty. The word רוקמה seems to refer to some kind of function or honor that the Mothers do *not* have. Translations of רוקמה vary; Baumgarten suggests "authoritative status"; other translations include "distinction," "mingling," and "esteem."[5] The root רקם means "variegated, multi-colored," and the noun form usually means "embroidery" or "multi-colored fabric." It occurs elsewhere in the Qumran literature with that meaning (e.g., 4QShirShabb, 1QM, 4QpIsa[a]). That meaning does not appear to fit the context here; hence the variety of translations. Brooke takes the primary meaning of the noun seriously, so that רוקמה would denote a tangible thing, possibly "a piece of embroidered cloth associated with priestly status."[6] Thus the רוקמה would be a mark of authority not worn by women. Elwolde, however, has focused on the Septuagint rendering of two words from the root רקם in Ezek 17:3 and Ps 139:15 (LXX 138:15), where the Greek words ἥγημα ("leadership") and ὑπόστασίς ("essence") are used respectively. Thus, he argues for a secondary meaning of רקם as "essential being," "authority," or "status," based on "the metonymy of expensive clothing/covering and the power represented by it."[7] Elwolde's argument appears most convincing to the present author, hence the translation given above.

This lack of authority would explain why the punishment for murmuring against the Mothers was lighter than that for murmuring against the Fathers. Fathers were highly respected members of the community, while Mothers had a less exalted station, as exemplified in the difference between permanent expulsion and ten-day punishment. But the very presence of a penalty for "murmuring" against the Mothers indicates some kind of status and authority.[8]

---

4. Cities are often referred to as "mothers," evidently to denote their important status, e.g., Abel-beth-Maacah in 2 Sam 20:19.

5. Baumgarten, DJD 18:164; Vermeš, *Dead Sea Scrolls in English*, 152; García Martínez and Tigchelaar, *Study Edition*, 1:617; Wise et al., *Dead Sea Scrolls*, 73.

6. Brooke, "Between Qumran," 168.

7. Elwolde, "*rwqmh*," 72.

8. Hempel, "Penal Code," 347n54.

MOTHERS, SISTERS, AND ELDERS
4Q502

The second text which contains titles or epithets for groups of women is 4Q502, originally published by Baillet under the rubric "Rituel de mariage."[9] This papyrus document clearly belongs to the same group that produced the Community Rule, since it contains a quotation from the Doctrine of the Two Spirits (frag. 16; 1QS 4:4-6). Baillet noted that the manuscript contained praise addressed to the deity, and suggested that the themes of at least the first group of fragments fit best the context of a marriage ceremony.[10] Baillet's characterization of the text as a marriage ritual has not received universal acceptance, although Davila has tentatively supported it.[11] Baumgarten has suggested it was a "Golden Age Ritual,"[12] while Satlow has argued that it may represent a Spring New Year Festival,[13] and Wise et al. have stated that 4Q502 was "intended to accompany the entrance of youths into the Yahad when they came of age."[14] None of these identifications have yet completely resolved the question, but nevertheless we can say that 4Q502 is a liturgical work for a joyous occasion of thanksgiving and praise, in which different groups within the community participate.

For the purposes of this article, it is important that, according to the extant text, the participants in this ritual are male and female, grouped together in worship by age and gender. In some cases, the titles appear in male and female pairs (e.g., בנים ובנ[ות, 14, 6 or נערים ונע[רות, 19, 3). I would argue that the names affixed to these groupings (זקנים וזק[נות, "elders and [female] eld[ers," 19, 2, etc.) are not simply age designations but titles for recognized groupings within the community, like the titles "Fathers" and "Mothers" in 4QD^e.[15] That titles are being used is evident from the use of בת

---

9. Baillet, DJD 7:81-104. 4Q502's paleographic date is the beginning of the first century BCE.

10. Baillet, DJD 7:81, compared these fragments to the marriage rituals found in the book of Tobit (Tob 8:1-8).

11. Davila, *Liturgical Works*, 184.

12. Baumgarten, "Golden Age Ritual," 99-106.

13. Satlow, "4Q502," 59.

14. Wise et al., *Dead Sea Scrolls*, 518.

15. I thus disagree with Baumgarten's emphasis on the elderly age of the participants in the ritual (Baumgarten, "Golden Age," 129). Groups of all ages are present, and it is difficult to pinpoint precisely the age difference between, for example, אשישים ("seniors") and זקנים ("elders"). They could be men of the same age, but with different statuses and roles to play in the ritual. See also Elder, "Woman Question," 230-32.

אמת, "daughter of truth," in 2, 3; this epithet must be the female equivalent to the term בני אמת, "Sons of Truth," found in, e.g., 1QS 4:6.[16] Thus women are being given official epithets or titles in this document, not simply being referred to by age.

The first group with a title that I would like to investigate is זקנות, "female elders," mentioned in 19, 2: זקנים וזק]נות (partially restored); 24, 4: ו]עמדה בסוד זקי[ם] וזקנו]ת (the letters of זקנות are very broken, but the *qof* seems certain); and possibly 107, 1: זק]נ, where the ending, either a masculine or a feminine plural, is missing.

The meaning of זקן in biblical Hebrew is two-fold; its primary meaning is "old in years." When the root זקן is applied to females in biblical Hebrew it carries this primary meaning, e.g., Gen 18:3, concerning Sarah, and Ruth 1:12, concerning Naomi. However, its secondary meaning in the masculine plural is a technical term referring to a leadership group in ancient Israel (e.g., Gen 50:7, Exod 3:16, etc.). This technical usage continues in the Qumran literature, where the elders are a leadership group (see, e.g., 1QS 6:8; CD 9:4; 1QM 13:1).[17] In 4Q502 I would argue that זקנים is being used in its secondary meaning of a leadership group, given that frag. 24 places the זקנים in a council (סוד), in front of which a female worshipper (!) stands. Frag. 19, 1 also contains the word סוד; Baillet suggests that the text should be restored as בסוד ק]דשים, i.e., a heavenly council, but Davila argues, and I agree, that an earthly council fits the overall context better.[18] In that case it is possible to connect the זקנים in l. 2 with the סוד in l. 1. Since the זקנים and the זקנות (partially restored) in l. 2 are connected by the conjunction, we can assume that they form one group (as in the other examples given above). Further, since frag. 24 mentions a סוד זקנים, "council of male elders," it can be tentatively argued, given reading of frag. 19, that this council included female elders as well. This strengthens the argument for Baillet's restoration of the last word on 24, 4 as זקנו]ת. If the arguments above are accepted, then we may conclude that since the זקנים form a leadership group in the community performing this liturgy, then this must be true as well for the זקנות, with whom they are paired.[19] Thus, we find a recognized group of women who played some kind of role in the community, at least as organized participants in its worship life.

---

16. Baumgarten, "Golden Age," 128.
17. The term can also refer to old men; see CD 14:14 and 1QpHab 6:11.
18. Baillet, DJD 7: 86–87; Davila, *Liturgical Works*, 196.
19. Davila, *Liturgical Works*, 197.

The second possible title for women that occurs in 4Q502, albeit in a very fragmentary context, is אחיות, "sisters," found on 96, 1. The word אחים, "brothers," also occurs in 9, 11, although unfortunately the two terms are not found together. The terms אח/אחות in biblical Hebrew can refer to a literal brother or sister (e.g., Gen 4:2, 30:8), any kind of relative (e.g., Gen 13:8; 24:60), or a member of the same tribe or nation (e.g., Exod 2:11; Num 25:18). The use of the term "brother" to refer to fellow Israelites or simply people affiliated with the speaker in some way is widespread in the Hebrew Bible. A specialized use of the term אחות as "beloved" occurs in Cant 4:9, and in Tobit the term is used to indicate a wife who is also a fellow Israelite (Tob 5:21; 7:15; 8:4, 7).

In Qumran literature "brother" is used to indicate fellow community members (e.g., CD 6:20; 7:1–2; 1QS 5:25; 6:10).[20] If this is the usage meant for אחים here in 4Q502, the same may be true for אחיות as well; that is, the "sisters" are fellow female members of the community. Unfortunately, the contexts are too broken to be certain. The word אחיות occurs in the first line of frag. 96, followed by words for "blessing" and "joy," but whether the text is referring to blood sisters, fellow Israelites or even brides or wives is completely unclear. Baumgarten speculates that the "Mothers" and "Fathers" of 4QD^e may be related in some way to the "Sisters" and "Brothers" of 4Q502;[21] this is entirely possible (see the discussion concerning the early Christian evidence below) but difficult to prove.

In conclusion, we have two texts from the Qumran collection that contain two, and possibly three, terms that were used as titles or epithets for recognized groups of women in the communities reflected by the documents. Although these texts are not directly related to each other, they are indirectly related through their mutual relationship to the Community Rule. Therefore, I would argue that the communities reflected in the two texts are one and the same, and that that community group is the Essenes, who certainly contained women in their "marrying" manifestation (Josephus, *War* 2.160) and in their ascetic, chiefly male manifestation may have included a small number of women.[22] These texts make clear that these

---

20. Davila notes the use of the term "brothers" to refer to the followers of Bar Kokhba in 5/6Hev 12:4. This secular document dates to the second century CE. Davila, *Liturgical Works*, 193.

21. Baumgarten, "Laws," 54–55.

22. Magness, *Archaeology*, 177–78; Crawford, *Scribes and Scrolls*, 202.

female Essenes, although not in any way equal to the male Essenes, were active, honored and organized participants in their community life.

Jewish Sources Outside Qumran

The two texts we have just discussed, 4QD^e and 4Q502, are not just important pieces of evidence for reconstructing the place of women in the organizational and communal life of the Essene/Qumran community. The use of the epithets "Mothers," "Sisters," and "Female Elders" in these documents may be the earliest attestation for the use of these titles for women in a Second Temple period Jewish community, making 4QD^e and 4Q502 extremely valuable for reconstructing the social history of women in Second Temple Judaism. I will now survey the evidence for the use of these titles in Jewish sources outside the Qumran literature, in order to demonstrate that their appearance in the Qumran scrolls is not an anomaly, but part of a more widespread practice in which women attained both honored stations and leadership roles in various Jewish communities of the late Second Temple and post-70 CE periods.

The most compelling evidence comes from Jewish inscriptions from the Hellenistic and Roman diaspora communities. These inscriptions, collected by Brooten and Kraemer,[23] appear both in Greek and Latin and date from the first century BCE to the sixth century CE. Their provenances reach from Italy to Asia Minor, Palestine and Egypt.[24] These inscriptions give the titles "Mother of the Synagogue" (μητηρ συναγογη, *mater synagogae*) and "elder" (πρεσβυτερα, *presbutera*) to women. As Brooten has argued, there is no reason to assume that these titles do not reflect a leadership role for the women so designated.[25]

Brooten lists seven Greek inscriptions that contain the epithet πρεσβυτερα, and Kraemer adds one more.[26] The women called πρεσβυτερα appear to have been members of a synagogue council of elders;[27] recall that the זקנות in 4Q502 19 are paired with the זקנים in relation to a סוד and may appear with them in a סוד on frag. 24. Although caution is in order when drawing any connection between these two disparate bodies of evidence,

---

23. Brooten, *Women Leaders*; Kraemer, *Maenads*.
24. Brooten, *Women Leaders*, 1.
25. Brooten, *Women Leaders*, 7–10.
26. Brooten, *Women Leaders*, 57; Kraemer, *Maenads*, #89.
27. Brooten, *Women Leaders*, 54–55.

the linguistic parallels are intriguing. Does 4Q502 reflect a mixed-gender council of elders, a practice which became more common in the diaspora?

There are three Greek and two Latin inscriptions in which the title "Mother" appears.[28] There is also one intriguing inscription with the title *pateressa*, "fatheress," indicating without doubt that the woman named in the inscription, Alexandra, was a female *pater*.[29] It is difficult to determine whether or not the title "Mother of the synagogue" (or indeed "Father of the synagogue") was only an honorific bestowed upon prominent synagogue members, or denoted an actual function. Brooten argues for a use of the term as an honorific title of respect in the first centuries CE based on rabbinic use of the titles "Father" and "Mother" for esteemed persons, although later the title may have indicated a civic function.[30] To her argument we may add the earlier evidence from 4QD^e, according to which the "Mothers" are held in esteem but lack "authority."

There is some literary evidence in Greco-Roman Jewish literature for the inclusion of women in the term *presbuteroi*, but it is less clear-cut than the inscriptional evidence given above. Philo and Josephus both use the term when discussing the Essenes, but there are two problems. One is that Philo describes the Essene movement as exclusively male. If we assume that in fact the Essene movement contained women (as Josephus indicates in *War* 2.160 and as we find in the Qumran sectarian texts), then it is possible to understand *presbuteroi* as including women as well as men. The second is that the ambiguity of the meaning of *presbuteroi* makes it difficult to be certain whether they mean "elders" in the technical sense, or (as is more likely) simply "old people." Philo makes it clear that the *presbuteroi* were held in honor by the Essenes:[31]

> The aged (πρεσβυτέρων), for their part, are surrounded with respect and care; they are like parents (γονέων) whose children lend them a helping hand in their old age with perfect generosity and surround them with a thousand attentions (*Quod omnis* 87).
>
> As for the aged (δι πρεσβύτεροι), even if they have no children, they are as father not only of many children but of very good ones. They usually quit life in extremely happy and splendid old age,

---

28. Brooten, *Women Leaders*, 57.
29. Brooten, *Women Leaders*, 61.
30. Brooten, *Women Leaders*, 62–68.
31. All translations of Philo and Josephus are taken from Vermeš and Goodman, *Essenes*.

honored by privileges and by the regard of so many sons who care for them spontaneously rather than as a result of natural necessity (*Hyp.* 13).

Note that in these passages Philo observes that the *presbuteroi* are treated like fathers. Josephus states that the Essenes make it their duty to obey the *presbuteroi* (*War* 2.146); he might mean "old people," but Hippolytus (*Refutation* 9.25), who is adapting Josephus, says that the Essenes are taught to obey τοῖς ἄρχουσι καὶ πρεσβυτέροις ("rulers and elders"), which may imply the more technical sense of "elders."

Philo also uses the term *presbuteroi* in his description of the Therapeutae, a Jewish mixed-gender community of contemplatives near Alexandria.[32] He says regarding the hierarchy of the Therapeutric community:

> Elders (πρεσβυτέροι) are, in their regard, those who from their earliest age have passed their youth and maturity in the contemplative branch of philosophy . . . (*Vita* 2.67).

Thus, the *presbuteroi* are not simply old, or may not be old at all; they have reached a certain stage in the contemplative life. This implies that *presbuteroi* here carries its more technical meaning, also found in the Qumran literature.

Philo also compares the older Therapeutae to "fathers" (πατράσι) and "mothers" (μητράσιν), claiming that the younger members of the group wait upon them like "true sons." It may be that the older Therapeutae held the honorifics "Father" and "Mother," but this is speculation.

Outside Philo and Josephus the literary evidence is very sparse. 4 Macc 16:14 refers to the woman who is martyred along with her seven sons as a πρεσβῦτι: "O mother, soldier of God in the cause of religion, elder and woman!" There is no reason to think the text is calling attention to the mother's age. She is being honored with the title "elder." The fact that the author adds "and woman" (καὶ γύναι) indicates that "elder" would normally refer to a man.

Brooten cites a fifth century CE Christian document, *De Altercatione Ecclesiae et Synagogae*, in which the title *matres synagogae* occurs, referring

---

32. I do not identify the Therapeutae with the Essenes, even though Philo mentions the Essenes in the first line of *De Vita*. Philo is contrasting the life of action as practiced by the Essenes with the contemplative life of the Therapeutae. The two groups are therefore two sides of the same coin, comparable but not identical. Therefore, it is methodologically permissible to use the description of the Therapeutae as a comparison to the Essenes. See also Taylor and Davies, "So-Called Therapeutae."

to a Jewish office holder.³³ Thus the title is known (at least among Christians) beyond its immediate Jewish context. There are to my knowledge no uses of the term "sister" as a title for a female member of a Jewish community outside of Qumran. The term is used in some Second Temple literature to denote wives or prospective wives; for example, Joseph uses the term for Aseneth in *Joseph and Aseneth*. If 4Q502 is a marriage liturgy, then this connotation may be appropriate for the אחיות mentioned in frag. 96.

Evidence from the Early Christian Communities

The early Christian communities also contain evidence for the use of the epithets πρεσβυτέρα, ἀδελφή and possibly μήτηρ as titles for women in positions of leadership and authority in the early Christian community.³⁴

Ἀδελφός and ἀδελφή were common terms for fellow Christians (i.e., as members of the same community, a use inherited from the Jewish community) and as such are ubiquitous in the various books of the New Testament. The plural term ἀδελφοί, "brethren," may be understood to include both men and women (as, for example, in the translation of the *NRSV*). This understanding is certain, since ἀδελφή is used on its own to signify female members of the early Christian community(ies) (e.g., 1 Cor 7:15; Rom 16:1; Jas 2:15). It is also used in the more technical phrase "sister wife" (ἀδελφὴν γυναῖκα; 1 Cor 9:5). Paul may use this phrase simply to mean "believing wife," since he claims that the other apostles, including James the brother of Jesus and Cephas (Peter), were accompanied by their wives. These wives may have participated in various leadership roles in the communities they visited, but Paul does not say this.³⁵ In fact, Paul does not use the term "sister wife" to describe the female member of the two missionary couples mentioned by name in his letters: Prisca and Aquila (Rom 16:4-5; 1 Cor 16:19) and Junia and Andronicus (Rom 16:7). Neither of these women are called "sister wives," although Prisca is identified as the wife (γυναῖκα) of Aquila in Acts 18:1. Both women are active as missionaries and leaders in the early Christian movement; Paul credits Junia with being "prominent

---

33. Brooten, *Women Leaders*, 63-64.

34. There have been many discussions of women's roles in the early church, which have established that, contrary to traditional views, women did play active roles in missions and the founding and leadership of early Christian communities. An early important study is that of Schüssler Fiorenza, *In Memory*. See also Eisen, *Women Officeholders*.

35. Clark Wire, *Corinthian*, 102.

among the apostles," while Prisca travels with Paul and has a house church (1 Cor 16:19). A certain Nereus and his "sister" (τὴν ἀδελφὴν αὐτοῦ) are mentioned in Rom 16:15; it is possible that they are a missionary couple.[36]

It seems reasonable to assume that the term אחיות in 4Q502 is parallel to the general use of the term "sister" in the New Testament, that is as a fellow (female) member of their respective communities. If 4Q502 is a marriage ritual, then it is possible that אחיות has a similar meaning to "sister wife," that is, a wife who is also a member of the particular community behind the text (as the term "sister" is also used in Tobit; see above).

The use of the term "sister" as "fellow Christian" also fits in with the creation in early Christianity of "fictive kin groups," in which the believer's relationship with the newly formed Christian community supersedes that with his or her actual blood relatives.[37] It is in this context that the term "mothers" is used in the New Testament when it does not simply mean "biological mother." In the Gospel of Mark, Jesus (Mark 3:31–35 // Matt 12:46–50, Luke 8:19–21) rejects his biological family in favor of a new family of fellow-believers: "Whoever does the will of God is my brother (ἀδελφός) and sister (ἀδελφή) and mother (μήτηρ)."[38] This notion continues in the early Christian movement: Thecla, in *The Acts of Paul and Thecla*, rejects both her biological family and her fiancée in favor of a new ascetic life after being converted by Paul. She finds a new mother in her protectress Tryphena, whom she converts to Christianity. In I Timothy, in which the structure of the Christian community is being subsumed into the Roman patriarchal family structure, the readers are urged "Do not speak harshly to an older man (Πρεσβυτέρῳ), but speak to him as to a father (πατέρα), to younger men as brothers (ἀδελφούς), to older women (πρεσβυτέρας) as mothers (μητέρας), to younger women as sisters (ἀδελφάς)—with absolute purity" (5:1–2). In other words, these women are to be considered the same as biological mothers and sisters; thus, a fictive kin group is formed. It is possible that in this new kin group "Father" and "Mother" were honorifics used for revered older members of the church. Certainly, a parallel can be drawn with Philo's description of the Therapeutae, who "like true sons" wait upon "their fathers and mothers" (*Vita* 2.72); in other words, they create a fictive kin group. According to Philo, the aged Essenes are also treated like fathers by the younger members (*Hyp* 11.13). Philo asserts that this occurs

---

36. Schüssler Fiorenza, *In Memory*, 180.
37. Levine, "Women," 159.
38. Schüssler Fiorenza, *In Memory*, 147.

even if they have no biological children; that is, the Essenes too formed a fictive kin group. I would argue that this notion of a "new family" in the community is at least part of what is behind the terms אמות and אבות in the Damascus Document; as biological parents are to be honored, so are the new parents found in the community.

The term πρεσβυτέρα, "female elder," appears in the New Testament and other early Christian sources, but with the ambiguity in meaning we have already discovered between "old person" and "senior leader." In passages such as 1 Tim 5:1–2, discussed above, the terms πρεσβυτέρῳ and πρεσβυτέρας mean "old men" and "old women." This is likewise the case in 1 Pet 5:5 (but cf. 5:1) and Titus 2:2–3 (in which older people are role models). However, the word πρεσβυτέρα also connotes one having a leadership role in the early Christian community as it formed hierarchies of leadership. This is clear from such passages as Acts 14:23, where the πρεσβυτέρους are appointed; 1 Tim 5:17, where the πρεσβύτεροι who "labor in preaching and teaching" are to receive double compensation; and Jas 5:14, where the πρεσβυτέρους τῆς ἐκκλεσίας pray over and anoint the sick. These passages originate in three very different groups within the early Christian movement, so the title was widespread. In passages such as these, we must not allow the masculine form of the noun to be misleading; it is probable that these groups of elders also included women.[39]

Women are also called *presbutera* in several early Christian inscriptions, in which the epithet signifies the holder of an office rather than an old woman. Cardman cites two Latin inscriptions: "Leta the presbyter" (Italy, 4th/5th centuries) and "the presbyter Flavia Vitalia" (Yugoslavia, 425).[40] Kraemer (## 93, 94) mentions two inscriptions, one from third century CE Asia Minor: "Diogas the bishop to Ammion (fem.) the elder (*presbutera*), in memory," and the other from Sicily in the 4th/5th century: "Here lies Kale, the elder (*pre[s]b[uti]*)."[41] Eisen adds two more, one for "Epikto the Presbytis (*presbutida*)" from Thera, 2nd–4th centuries CE, and a label for the mummy of the "*Presb[utera]* Artemidora," from 2nd/3rd century CE Egypt.[42] Some early Christian movements later condemned as heretical had women elders among their leaders (e.g. the Quintillians).[43] Further, the

---

39. Eisen, *Women Officeholders*, 4–6.
40. Cardman, "Women," 321, and Eisen, *Women Officeholders*, 129–32.
41. Eisen, *Women Officeholders*, 128.
42. Eisen, *Women Officeholders*, 123–28.
43. Kraemer, *Maenads*, #103.

Synod of Laodicea, which took place in the 4th century CE, legislated *against* the participation of women elders in ecclesiastical functions.[44] That women held other offices and bore other titles in the early church such as "deacon" (e.g., Phoebe, Rom 16:1) and "widow" (e.g., 1 Tim 5:3–16) is beyond dispute. The title "elder," however, would seem to be a specific inheritance from the parent Jewish community in Christianity, as is the use of this title (for both men and women) in its technical sense. Thus, we see a continuous use of this title for women from its appearance in 4Q502, through Diaspora Jewish communities and into the early Christian movement.

Conclusion

The appearance of the epithets זקנות, אמות, and אחיות in the Damascus Document and 4Q502 is important new evidence for the attempt to reconstruct women's roles and status in various groups within Second Temple Judaism and early Christianity. They constitute the earliest appearance of these titles in Second Temple Judaism. 4QD^e was copied no later than 50 CE, and the composition of the Damascus Document is even earlier, since its earliest manuscript (4Q266) dates to the first half of the first century BCE. Thus, some form of the Damascus Document was in existence in the second century BCE, and that form may well have included the passage in question. 4Q502's paleographic date is the beginning of the first century BCE, which means, unless it is an autograph, that it was composed even earlier. Therefore, by the first century BCE these epithets, indicating a particular role and status for women within the Essene/Qumran community, were in use. These titles are not, however, unique to the Essenes, since they also appear in Hellenistic Jewish inscriptions and early Christian works. Thus, although the particular functions attached to these titles may vary from community to community, they are indications that women were leaders and participants in community organization and worship in Second Temple Judaism, roles that continued in the early Christian movement.

---

44. Eisen, *Women Officeholders*, 121.

7

"There Is Much Wisdom in Her"
The Matriarchs in the Qumran Library

THE MATRIARCHS OF ISRAEL, Sarah, Rebekah, Rachel, and Leah, and their servants/co-wives Hagar, Zilpah, and Bilhah, play central roles in the patriarchal narratives in the book of Genesis. Feminist biblical interpretation has highlighted the importance of these women in those narratives and has emphasized God's choice of the mother (Sarah, Rebekah, and Rachel), as well as the father (Abraham, Isaac, and Jacob), for the favored son (Isaac, Jacob, and Joseph).[1]

Although the matriarchs are occasionally mentioned in post-exilic and Second Temple compositions (e.g., Ruth 4:11), it was only in the book of Jubilees that, prior to the discovery of the Qumran library, the matriarchs and their servants/co-wives achieved any prominence.[2] Within the Qumran library, fourteen or fifteen copies of Jubilees were discovered, as well as several previously unknown works that mention the matriarchs and their co-wives. These texts present us with a group of compositions preserved by the community of Jews at Qumran and offer us a window into

---

1. See, for example, Niditch, "Genesis," 32–40.
2. See especially Halpern-Amaru, *Empowerment*. Jubilees is preserved in its entirety only in Ethiopic; however, its original language was Hebrew, and that Hebrew text was preserved in the Qumran collection. For the Qumran manuscripts, see VanderKam and Milik, "Jubilees." For the Ethiopic text, see VanderKam, *The Book of Jubilees*. A convenient translation is found in Wintermute, "Jubilees." Most scholars agree that the book of Jubilees dates to the mid-second century BCE. See most recently VanderKam, *Jubilees*[2], 28–38.

how the figures of the matriarchs and their servants/co-wives were viewed in the late Second Temple period.

This article will examine the textual evidence for each generation of the matriarchs and their co-wives in turn, beginning with Sarah and Hagar, continuing with Rebekah, and ending with Leah, Rachel, Bilhah, and Zilpah. I will then draw together the common themes and explicate the specific role the matriarchs and their servants/co-wives play in this collection of texts.

Sarah and Hagar

Sarah plays a prominent role in two texts found in the Qumran caves, Jubilees and the Genesis Apocryphon, both of which fall into the category of rewritten scripture texts.[3] However, Hagar, an important character in Genesis, practically disappears in both texts. Since Jubilees is an earlier text than the Genesis Apocryphon,[4] I will begin with Sarah's characterization (and Hagar's disappearance) in Jubilees.

Jubilees

Sarah first appears in Jubilees, as she does in Genesis, in the notice of her marriage to Abraham. "And in the fortieth jubilee, in the second week, in its seventh year, Abraham took a wife and her name was Sarah, daughter of his father, and she became a wife for him" (Jub. 12:9//Gen 11:29). While in Genesis Sarah's genealogy is not directly mentioned, Jubilees makes it clear that Sarah is Abraham's (half-)sister. This agrees with Gen 20:12, where Abraham claims that Sarah is his half-sister via his father. This tradition in Jubilees

---

3. The Rewritten Scripture texts have been identified as a particular category of texts within Second Temple Jewish literature. A short definition of the category is as follows: rewritten scriptures constitute a category or group of texts, which are characterized by a close adherence to a recognizable and already authoritative base text (narrative or legal), and a recognizable degree of scribal intervention into that base text for the purpose of exegesis. Further, the rewritten scriptural text will often (although not always) make a claim to the authority of revealed scripture, the same authority as its base text. The receiving community will not necessarily accept such a claim. For a complete discussion of this category, see Crawford, *Rewriting*, 2–15. See also now Zahn, *Genres*, 98–136.

4. For the dating of both texts, see Crawford, *Rewriting*, 62, 106. Not all scholars agree that the Genesis Apocryphon is later than Jubilees; see the discussion in Machiela, *Genesis Apocryphon*, 13–17, for various theories concerning its date.

disagrees with that of Josephus, the rabbis, and Pseudo-Philo, all of whom identify Sarah with Iscah, the daughter of Haran, making her Abraham's niece.[5] As we know from elsewhere in their library, the Qumran community specifically forbade uncle-niece marriage.[6] Thus it is no surprise that Jubilees, an important text for the community who owned the Qumran library, clarifies any possible vagueness in the Genesis text by identifying Sarah as not the niece, but the half-sister of Abraham. Although brother-sister incest is, of course, strictly forbidden in the Torah (Lev 18:9), Jubilees creates a genealogical pattern in which the founders of a line marry their sisters, removing any question of impure antecedents.[7] Thus Seth, the son of Adam and Eve born after the murder of Abel, marries his sister Azura (Jub. 4:11), founding a line not tainted with the blood of Cain. Later descendants of the chosen line marry their cousins (e.g., Enoch, Noah), thus practicing first-degree endogamy.[8] This important theme of endogamy in Jubilees will continue in its presentation of Rebekah, Rachel, and Leah.

The continuing narrative of Jubilees demonstrates a concern to remove from the Genesis narrative any possibility of less than exemplary behavior by the ancestors of Israel. In the case of Sarah, this concern especially manifests itself in Jubilees' treatment of the two "endangered wife" stories. The second episode with Abimelech in Gerar (Genesis 20) is omitted altogether.[9] The first episode in Egypt is rewritten to present both Sarah and Abraham as innocent victims of the Pharaoh: "And Abraham went into Egypt, in the third year of the week, and he stayed in Egypt five years before his wife *was taken by force* from him" (Jub. 13:11; emphasis mine). God protects Sarah and gets her (and Abraham with her) safely out of Egypt (Jub. 13:15).[10]

The rest of the events concerning Sarah in Jubilees also concern her Egyptian maid, Hagar. The driving problem behind the narrative in Genesis

---

5. Halpern-Amaru, *Empowerment*, 35n4.

6. See CD 5:9-11 and 11QT^a 66:15-17, and the discussion in "Not According to Rule," 71 in this volume.

7. Halpern-Amaru, *Empowerment*, 18-19, 35-36. Halpern-Amaru points out that Jubilees uses the expedient of brother-sister marriages in the founding pairs of important lines (Seth/Azura, their son and their grandson; Abraham/Sarah) to avoid marriage into a rejected familial line (i.e., Cain, Haran).

8. Halpern-Amaru, *Empowerment*, 19.

9. The author of Jubilees certainly knew this episode, since he uses Abraham's excuse that Sarah is his half-sister in his genealogical notice concerning Sarah.

10. Halpern-Amaru, *Empowerment*, 48-49.

15–18, 21, is Sarah's barrenness, which is introduced in Genesis with her first mention: "Now Sarai was barren; she had no child" (Gen 11:30). As a result, Sarah attempts to procure children through the fertility of her maid Hagar: "and Sarai said to Abram, 'You see that the LORD has prevented me from bearing children; go in to my slave-girl; it may be that *I* shall obtain children by her'" (Gen 16:2; emphasis mine). This attempt, Genesis implies, is misguided, and leads to hostility and the eventual expulsion of Hagar and Ishmael. Further, Genesis portrays both Sarah and Abraham as skeptical of God's promise that they will have a miraculous child (Gen 17:17–18, 18:10–12). Jubilees attempts to sanitize the Genesis narrative; while the author cannot entirely remove the hostility of Sarah towards Hagar, he does remove the first account of the pregnant Hagar running away from Sarah, as well as giving Sarah the motive of trying to realize the promises of the covenant. He does this by having Abraham inform Sarah of God's promises (Jub. 14:21), something that never explicitly happens in Genesis. Thus, Sarah's actions with Hagar are not selfish, but an attempt to obtain descendants for Abraham: "It may be that I will build seed *for you* from her [emphasis mine]" (Jub. 14:22). Sarah's character is rehabilitated in Jubilees to become the ideal wife for Abraham.

Hagar is almost invisible in the Jubilees narrative. When she is mentioned, she is consistently identified as Sarah's *Egyptian* maid, emphasizing that her union with Abraham is exogamous, outside the line of approved Jubilees unions. Her ability to act on her own initiative, demonstrated in Genesis 16, and her special status as the first woman in Genesis after Eve to receive a theophany, is totally removed from Jubilees. The only point in the narrative when she speaks is after she and Ishmael are banished from Abraham's household, and her words are entirely concerned with her child, the child of Abraham. Hagar and her son, by virtue of her unacceptable lineage, are almost completely eliminated from Jubilees.

Genesis Apocryphon

The second composition from the Qumran library in which Sarah plays a major role is the Genesis Apocryphon. An Aramaic work, the Genesis Apocryphon, like Jubilees, belongs to the category Rewritten Scripture. It uses as its base text the book of Genesis in its proto-Samaritan recension, but it also uses the books of Enoch and Jubilees as source material.[11] In its

---

11. Crawford, *Rewriting*, 106; Machiela, *Genesis Apocryphon*, 12–13, 16–17.

version of the Abraham and Sarah story, the Genesis Apocryphon greatly expands the characterization of Sarah, so that she appears as a more fully rounded character, rather than as simply (as in Genesis and Jubilees) the ideal wife for Abraham.

The episode in which Sarah appears is in the Genesis Apocryphon's retelling of Abraham and Sarah's (Abram and Sarai in the Aramaic) sojourn in Egypt (Genesis 12; compare Jubilees 13). After some geographic detail concerning the trip from Canaan to Egypt, Abram narrates the following dream:

> And I, Abram, had a dream in the night of my entering into the land of Egypt, and I saw in my dream that there was a cedar tree and a date-palm, very beautiful. Some men came, seeking to cut down and uproot the cedar and leave the date-palm by itself. Now the date-palm cried out and said, "Do not cut down the cedar, for we are both sprung from one stock." So the cedar was spared by the protection of the date-palm, and it was not cut down. Then I started from my sleep while it was still night, and said to Sarai, my wife, 'I have had a dream and now I am fearful because of it.' She replied, 'Tell me your dream so I may understand.' So I began to explain it to her, and I also explained its significance. I said, 'Men will come intending to kill me while sparing you. Notwithstanding, this is the kindness that you can do for me. In every place we shall go, say concerning me, "He is my brother." Thus I may live because of you and my life be spared owing to you. They will attempt to separate us and to kill me.' Then Sarai wept at my words that night. (19:14–21)

This dream is unique to the Genesis Apocryphon, and its purpose is clear: to vindicate the dubious actions of Abram in Genesis 12, when he allowed Sarai to be taken into the Pharaoh's household to save his own skin. Instead, the text claims that his actions were guided by a prescient dream sent by God.

The symbolism of the dream itself seems to come from older traditions concerning Abram and Sarai. The cedar tree is meant to be identified with the patriarch Abram. This cedar, however, is in danger. As Gevirtz notes, "the motif of a tree being cut down occurs as a metaphor for disaster, destruction and death in the Hebrew Bible."[12] If the cedar is Abram, then the date palm must be Sarai. In fact, the pairing of these two trees, and the understanding that they symbolize Abram and Sarai, seems to be an old exegetical tradition. The pairing of the trees also occurs in Ps 92:12, "The righteous flourish like the palm tree, and grow like a cedar in Lebanon." Rabbinic exegesis

---

12. Gevirtz, "Abram's Dream," 234.

Part 2: Questions Concerning Women

understood the pair to stand for Abram and Sarai (m.Tanh Lek Lekha 5; Zohar to Genesis 12; GenR 40, 1). In the case of the Zohar and Genesis Rabbah, the rabbis tie the psalm verse to the episode of Abram and Sarai in Egypt (Gen 12:10–20). That is exactly the identical point in the Genesis narrative where the author of the Genesis Apocryphon uses the same symbolism in the dream vision. The Genesis Apocryphon and the rabbinic literature stem from two different exegetical traditions; thus, the fact that the same tradition appears in both corpora indicates its age.

It should be noted that the Genesis Apocryphon reverses the form of Abram's request in Gen 12:13. Rather than "say you are my sister," as in Genesis, Abram instructs Sarai to say, "he is my brother," thus putting the onus for the deception on Sarai. After hearing the dream and Abram's interpretation, Sarai weeps, emotion that we do not see either in Genesis or in Jubilees. The display of emotion by Sarai is typical of late Second Temple narrative literature, which, under the influence of the Hellenistic novel, places much more emphasis on the thoughts and feelings of characters than was characteristic of earlier Israelite literature.

After five years in Egypt (following the Jubilees chronology), representatives of the Pharaoh come to Abram and finally catch sight of Sarai. A long description of her beauty, unique in Second Temple literature, follows:

> How splendid and beautiful the form of her face, and how pleasant and soft the hair of her head; how lovely are her eyes, and how graceful is her nose; all the radiance of her face . . . ; how lovely is her breast, and how beautiful is all her whiteness! Her arms, how beautiful! And her hands, how perfect! And how attractive all the appearance of her hands! How lovely are her palms, and how long and dainty all the fingers of her hands. Her feet, how beautiful! How perfect are her thighs! There are no virgins or brides who enter a bridal chamber more beautiful than she. Indeed, she greatly surpasses in beauty all women; and in her beauty she ranks high above all of them. Yet with all this beauty there is much wisdom in her; and whatever she has is lovely.

This description is a long addition to the text of Gen 12:15, which, like other scriptural passages, is remarkably laconic about physical description. This description is part of a trend toward greater interest in female beauty in Second Temple literature; many of these descriptions are remarkably prurient, given their location in religious literature. For examples, see the description of Judith's toilet in Jdt 10:3–4 and the description of Susannah in her bath and at her trial in Sus 15–18, 31–33, as well as the descriptions of the female lover in the Song of Songs. This description of Sarai, which lingers on all the parts of her body, is part of that general trend.

Pharaoh's response confirms the divine nature of Abram's dream, for he takes Sarai as a wife (a non-biblical detail that gives Sarai a more honorable position) and seeks to kill Abram; this differs from Gen 12:16, where he is well treated. Sarai is thus justified in her falsehood, which the Genesis Apocryphon has her stating directly (*contra* Gen 12:18, where Pharaoh accuses Abram after the fact of saying that Sarai is his sister).

Sarai's abduction triggers another substantial addition in the Apocryphon, which is prompted by the absence of any reaction by Abram in the Genesis text to his wife's perilous situation. The author portrays Abram (and Lot) as weeping and mourning, and then as praying to God for help to prevent Sarai from being defiled by illicit intercourse.

> but I wept bitterly—I, Abram, and Lot, my nephew, along with me—on the night when Sarai was taken from me by force. That night I prayed, I entreated, and I asked for mercy. In sorrow I said, as my tears ran down, "Blessed are you, O God most high, my Lord, for all ages . . . Now I lodge my complaint with you, my Lord, against Pharaoh Zoan, the king of Egypt, because my wife has been taken away from me by force. Mete out justice to him for me, and show forth your great hand against him and against all his house. May he not be able to defile my wife tonight. (20:10–15)

The afflictions God brings upon Pharaoh and his household become the result of Abram's prayer, rather than a unilateral action on God's part. Abram's praying is a detail again common to different strands of interpretation; it is found in Philo (*de Abr.* 95), Josephus (*War* 5.380), and rabbinic midrash.[13] God responds to Abram's prayer by afflicting Pharaoh and his household with an "evil spirit," as in Gen 12:17. Genesis Apocryphon makes sure to state explicitly what is only assumed in Genesis; Pharaoh is not able to approach Sarai for sexual intercourse (20:17).

At the end of the two years (again following the Jubilees chronology) Pharaoh seeks the aid of his wise men, magicians and healers, who are unable to cure him. This detail, which is not part of Genesis 12, seems to anticipate the plague and passover narrative in Exodus, in which the magicians of Egypt are unable to stop the plagues of gnats or boils (Exod 8:19; 9:11). Finally, the Egyptian official Hyrcanus returns to Abram seeking his aid to heal the Pharaoh because he had seen Abram in a dream.

13. Fitzmyer, *Commentary*, 201.

PART 2: QUESTIONS CONCERNING WOMEN

These details of the dream and healing anticipate the parallel account to this Pharaoh/Sarai episode, the Abimelech/Sarah episode in Genesis 20. In that episode, God sends a dream to Abimelech in which he tells Abimelech that Sarah is Abraham's wife, not his sister. God then advises Abimelech to seek healing from Abraham. Abimelech is healed in response to Abraham's prayer. The same result is obtained here in 20:19–20. Further, once Sarai returns to Abram, Pharaoh assures Abram that he has not touched her (20:30), as does Abimelech in Gen 20:6. These anticipations indicate that the author of the Genesis Apocryphon knew the Abimelech/Sarah episode and was attempting to harmonize the doublet. Whether or not the Genesis Apocryphon contained that Abimelech/Sarah episode is impossible to say.[14]

When Pharaoh does return Sarai to Abram he also gives her gifts: "The king gave her much silver and gold, many garments of fine linen and purple, which he laid before her, and Hagar too" (20:31–32). This largesse is based on Gen 12:16, but the Apocryphon has changed the sequence and the recipient: in Genesis, Abram is given gifts when Sarai is taken, whereas here Sarai is given the gifts once she is restored to her husband. Thus, Abram does not benefit from Sarai's narrowly averted defilement, nor is his wealth the result of Pharaoh's generosity, since the gifts are given to Sarai. An anticipation occurs here with the mention of Hagar: in Genesis she suddenly appears in 16:1 with no explanation of how she came to be a part of Sarah's household; the author of the Apocryphon explains that by making her part of Pharaoh's gifts at this point in the narrative.[15] This detail is the only mention of Hagar in the extant Genesis Apocryphon.

After the Egypt sojourn, there are no further scenes involving Sarai (or Hagar) in the Apocryphon. The manuscript breaks off at its rewriting of Gen 15:1–4, the narrative of God's promise to Abram. While it is probably safe to assume that the text continued on at least through Genesis 16, given the mention of Hagar at the end of the Egypt episode, we are left to speculate as to Sarai's or Hagar's portrayal in subsequent events.

There remains one brief passage in the Qumran manuscripts mentioning Sarah outside the received text of Genesis. In 4Q364, one of the Reworked Pentateuch manuscripts,[16] an exegetical comment is added to Gen 25:19: "These are the generations of Isaac, son of Abraham. Abraham

---

14. Bernstein, "Re-Arrangement," 49–50.

15. Bernstein, "Re-Arrangement," 44. Bernstein notes that this anticipation is evidence that the Apocryphon continued at least through the Hagar stories.

16. For 4Q364, see Tov and White, "4Q364," 197–254.

begat Isaac, *whom Sarah his wife bore to him*" (emphasis mine; 4Q364 1a–b, 1–3). This exegetical addition betrays the same concern as Jubilees: that the chosen sons have the proper mothers as well as the proper fathers; they are the products of a divinely sanctioned, endogamous union.

Finally, Hagar may be mentioned on a small fragment of 4QCommentary on Genesis C, if the editor has correctly restored her name.[17] The text is too fragmentary to draw any conclusions.

Already certain themes are emerging. Jubilees is at pains to portray Sarah as the ideal, divinely sanctioned marriage partner for Abraham. Her lineage is impeccable, their union is endogamous, and she is privy to and understands God's promises to Abraham. Neither Sarah nor Abraham is at fault in the episode with Pharaoh, nor is Sarah condemned (even indirectly) for her treatment of Hagar. The Genesis Apocryphon also absolves Sarah of any guilt in the Pharaoh episode, while emphasizing her beauty and the emotional partnership she shares with Abraham. Hagar, on the other hand, is greatly diminished, both in Jubilees and the Apocryphon; of improper lineage, her exogamous union with Abraham cannot result in a chosen heir, and so she disappears from the story.

Rebekah

Like Sarah, Rebekah is most prominently featured among the texts found in the Qumran caves in the book of Jubilees. Before investigating her portrayal in Jubilees, however, I wish to turn to two brief mentions of Rebekah in other Qumran texts that throw light on her portrayal in Jubilees.

Qumran Texts

The first mention of Rebekah occurs in the Reworked Pentateuch manuscript 4Q364, introduced above. In 3 ii 1–6, Isaac and Rebekah react to the departure of Jacob for Canaan (Gen 28:5).[18]

> 1. him you shall see [
> 2. you shall see in peace [
> 3. your death, and to [your] eyes[lest I be deprived of even
> 4. the two of you. And he called[to Rebekah his wife and he told

---

17. Brooke, "Genesis C," 221.
18. Tov and White, "4Q364," 206–7.

5. to her all the wo[rds
6. after Jacob her son[

The lines appear to contain a dialogue between Isaac and Rebekah, in which Rebekah grieves over Jacob's departure and Isaac attempts to comfort her. As in the Genesis Apocryphon's portrait of Sarah, 4Q364 emphasizes the emotional responses of the characters.

This additional material is paralleled in a variety of sources available in the Second Temple period. The first is the text of Genesis itself; the phrase "the two of you" echoes the identical phrase in Gen 27:45, in which Rebekah, while sending Jacob away, says to him, "Why should I lose even the two of you in one day?"[19] If this had been the only line extant, it could be surmised that a simple harmonization had occurred. However, the remainder of the lines does not contain echoes of Pentateuchal passages, but rather other texts from the period. Jubilees 27, which narrates the same scene as Genesis 28, contains the lines "The spirit of Rebecca was grieved after Jacob her son" (Jub. 27:14) and "we see him in peace" (Jub. 27:17). The texts are not exact copies of one another, but certainly point to the same interpretive tradition, manifest in slightly different ways in the two works. Since it is likely that the scribal tradition manifest in 4Q364 is older than composition of the book of Jubilees, we can date this tradition no later than the mid-second century BCE.

Further, the text in 4Q364 is similar to the scene in the book of Tobit in which Tobit and his wife Anna bid farewell to their son Tobias. Anna weeps over Tobias's departure, but Tobit comforts her, promising her "your eyes will see him on the day when he returns to you in peace" (Tob 5:21). The similarities between the two texts, in vocabulary and scenario, are striking.[20] A common exegetical tradition seems to be at work among these three texts; as we will see, this exegetical tradition, at least as concerns Rebekah, reaches its apotheosis in Jubilees.

The second brief mention of Rebekah is found in 4QNaphtali (4Q215).[21] In line 1 of fragments 1–3, Rebekah is mentioned as the nursling of Deborah, a tradition known from Gen 35:8. As we shall see in the discussion of

---

19. Hence, in DJD 13 Tov and I filled out line 3 of the fragment with למה אשכל גם from Gen 27:45; see Tov and White, "4Q364," 206.

20. Five manuscripts of Tobit, four in Aramaic and one in Hebrew translation, were discovered in the Qumran caves.

21. 4QNaphtali (4Q215), a Hebrew composition, is preserved in one small group of fragments. Its paleographical date is 30 BCE to 20 CE. See Stone, "Testament of Naphtali."

Bilhah and Zilpah below, the relationship of Deborah and Rebekah is used by the exegetical tradition reflected in the Qumran library as a "hook" on which to hang an important genealogical reconstruction.

Jubilees

In Jubilees Rebekah emerges as a major character in her own right, acting as Abraham's partner and agent in assuring the promises of the covenant are passed on to the chosen heir, Jacob. While this role is certainly based on her role in Genesis as Jacob's mentor and ally against Isaac and, especially, Esau (Gen 25:19-28; 27:1—28:5), any hint of deception or wrongdoing found in the Genesis narrative is erased from Rebekah's portrayal in Jubilees.

The lovely narrative of Rebekah's betrothal and marriage to Isaac found in Genesis 24 is omitted from Jubilees; Jubilees is only interested in Rebekah's lineage, which is unblemished. She is Isaac's first cousin once removed, thus a proper endogamous spouse for the child of Abraham and Sarah (Jub. 19:10). The story of the birth of Jacob and Esau is also truncated; Rebekah is not given a prescient dream (although she is the recipient of such a dream later, as will be seen), and does not automatically favor Jacob (Gen 25:19-28). Rather, in Jubilees she acts in response to and in concert with Abraham, who recognizes Jacob as the correct heir of the Promise:[22]

> And Abraham loved Jacob, but Isaac loved Esau. And Abraham saw the deeds of Esau and he knew that in Jacob a name and seed would be named for him. And he called Rebekah and he commanded concerning Jacob because he knew that she loved Jacob more than Esau. (Jub. 19:15-16)

Rebekah carries out Abraham's commission in several ways. First and foremost, she makes sure that Jacob enters into a proper endogamous marriage. In a scene not found in Genesis, she instructs him to take a wife from "my father's house and my father's kin" (Jub. 25:3). She then follows this with a direct blessing of Jacob, a blessing he receives *before* he receives Isaac's blessing (Jub. 25:11-22).

Rebekah plays her expected role in the deception of Isaac (Genesis 27), and afterwards, she plays the pivotal role in Jacob's escape from Esau. However, while in Genesis she simply hears that Esau intends to kill Jacob (Gen 27:42), in Jubilees she receives a prescient dream warning her of

---

22. Halpern-Amaru, *Empowerment*, 81-83.

Esau's threat (Jub. 27:1). Rebekah is the only woman in Jubilees to receive a dream from God, which were normally reserved for the chosen males.

Rebekah does not play a narrative role again in Genesis after Jacob's departure for Paddan-Aram. This is not the case in Jubilees. Rebekah recurs repeatedly in Jubilees' version of Jacob's life in Canaan after his return, in which he is portrayed as the ideal son to both his father and his mother (Jubilees 29–35). She blesses Levi and Judah, the sons of Jacob singled out, according to Jubilees, for special roles (*contra* Genesis); she accompanies Jacob to Bethel, where Levi is installed as priest; and right before her death she attempts to broker a peace treaty between Jacob and Esau. In all of these actions she is presented as a bridge between the founding patriarch, Abraham, and the later generations of Jacob and his sons.[23]

Once again, the theme of correct endogamous marriage is prominent in the portrait of Rebekah in Jubilees. Although the other fragmentary texts mentioning Rebekah do not directly support this theme, their parallels with the traditions of Jubilees indicate that this concern was shared elsewhere in the exegetical tradition of the wing of Judaism of which Qumran was a part. Her actions throughout Jubilees indicate that she (and not Isaac) is the conduit of God's Promise from Abraham to Jacob, and hence to the twelve tribes.

Rachel and Leah

Rachel and Leah are both prominent in the book of Jubilees. Rachel also appears in two other Qumran texts, 4QNaphtali and 4QText Concerning Rachel and Joseph (4Q474). Leah does not figure elsewhere in the Qumran library. We will investigate the two fragmentary texts in which Rachel appears, before turning to Jubilees.

Qumran Texts

In 4QNaphtali Rachel is mentioned briefly in line 9: "] and one to Rachel. And when Rachel could not bear children [." The text refers to two passages in Genesis: 29:29, in which Laban gives Bilhah to Rachel as a servant, and 30:1–3, where the barren Rachel gives Bilhah to Jacob as a surrogate. This

---

23. Halpern-Amaru, *Empowerment*, 90.

text gives us no new information about Rachel, since its focus, as we shall see below, is on Bilhah, the mother of Naphtali.

4QText Concerning Rachel and Joseph (4Q474) is a Hebrew work surviving in only one fragment.[24] As its name implies, the characters mentioned are Rachel and her elder son Joseph. The text reads as follows:

> 2. she rejoic]ed in a son loved by hi[s fath]er above all[his brothers
> 3. he pr]ided [himself] on a dear son[
> 4. to] ask the Lord, that[He g]i[ve her another]son[
> 5. the L]ord [lo]ved Rachel highly[. . .]to[show her mer]cy[
> 6.] her from all tha[t

The incident on which the composition builds is found in Gen 30:22–24:

> Then God remembered Rachel, and God heeded her and opened her womb. She conceived and bore a son, and said, "God has taken away my reproach"; and she named him Joseph, saying, "May the LORD add to me another son!"

The most remarkable statement in 4Q474 is that the Lord loved *Rachel* highly, not (as is usual) Jacob.[25] This mark of divine favor is not assigned to any of the other matriarchs anywhere else in the tradition. Unfortunately, because the text is fragmentary, we do not know why Rachel was singled out in this way.

Another interesting feature of this brief text is the restoration in line 5, לרחם, "to have mercy." If this restoration is correct, then the language parallels Jub. 28:24, "And the Lord had mercy upon Rachel and opened her womb."[26] The verb רחם does not occur in the base text of Gen 30:22, although the word for "womb" uses the same root. The composers of 4Q474 and Jubilees are using a play on words to emphasize Rachel's favored status as a matriarch of Israel, not just with Jacob but with God.

---

24. The paleographical date of the manuscript is mid-first century BCE. See Elgvin, "4QText."

25. See, e.g., Gen 29:20, 30, and T. Benj. 1:4–5.

26. Unfortunately, this passage is not preserved in the Qumran manuscripts of Jubilees.

PART 2: QUESTIONS CONCERNING WOMEN

Jubilees

Jubilees attempts, as it does with all the stories of the matriarchs, to expurgate from the Genesis story of Rachel and Leah any negativity, being especially concerned with the rivalry between the two sisters. The author does this in two ways; first by softening Jacob's love for Rachel and dislike of Leah, and second by creating a positive portrayal of Leah.[27]

The narrative begins in chapter 28 with Jacob's arrival at Laban's household. The author does not have to linger over Rachel and Leah's genealogical credentials; as Jacob's maternal first cousins, they are the perfect spouses in the Jubilees schema for Jacob. The text moves right to the marriage, omitting the romance between Rachel and Jacob (Gen 29:9–12, 17–20). Laban's deception of Jacob, substituting Leah for Rachel, is left in place. Both sisters are described as very beautiful, although Leah has "weak eyes." More importantly, Jubilees justifies Laban's deception of Jacob by declaring that it is a heavenly law that the elder sister must be married before the younger:

> And Laban said to Jacob, "It does not happen thus in our land, to give the younger woman before the elder." And it is not right to do this because thus it is ordained and written in the heavenly tablets that no one should give his younger daughter before the elder because he should first give the elder and after her the younger. And they will write it down as sin in heaven concerning the man who acts thus. And no one who does this thing will be righteous because this deed is evil before the Lord. And you command the children of Israel so that they will not do this thing: "Let not the younger woman be taken or given without the elder one being first, because that is very evil." (28:6–7)

Therefore, Jubilees implies that Leah's marriage to Jacob is divinely ordained.[28]

The birth of Jacob's children by their various mothers is narrated swiftly, almost without comment. The scene in which Rachel bargains Jacob's sexual favors to Leah in exchange for mandrakes, which reflects poorly on all three protagonists, is omitted (Gen 30:14–21). When Jacob seeks his wives' support to return to Canaan, their bitterness against their father is left out (Gen 31:14–16), and their consent is given as a result of

---

27. Halpern-Amaru, *Empowerment*, 64–72.
28. Halpern-Amaru, *Empowerment*, 45.

their understanding of Jacob's status as heir to the Promise (Jub. 29:2–4). Rachel's theft of her father's idols (Gen 31:19) is not mentioned until 31:2, when their destruction, as part of the purification ritual before the pilgrimage to Bethel, is applauded.

Finally, although Rachel's death is reported as in Genesis, without embellishment, Leah is given a warm eulogy, emphasizing her excellent qualities and Jacob's love for her:

> And Leah, his wife, died in the fourth year of the second week of the forty-fifth jubilee. And he buried her in the cave of Machpelah near Rebekah, his mother, and north of the tomb of Sarah, his father's mother. And all of her children and his children went out to weep with him for Leah, his wife, and to comfort him concerning her because he was lamenting her. For he loved her very much after Rachel, her sister, died since she was perfect and upright in all of her ways, and she honored Jacob. And in all of the days which she lived with him he never heard a harsh word from her mouth because she possessed gentleness, peace, uprightness, and honor. And he remembered all of her deeds which she had done in her life, and he lamented greatly for her because he loved her with all his heart and all his soul. (36:21–24)

This is the ultimate elevation of Leah, who, after all, is the mother of Levi and Judah, the two leading sons of Jacob in Jubilees.

As with the other matriarchs, the Qumran texts that feature Rachel and Leah emphasize their fitness as ideal spouses for a patriarch. Most strikingly, Rachel is portrayed as loved by God (4Q474), and Leah as loved by Jacob (Jubilees).

Bilhah and Zilpah

In Genesis, Bilhah and Zilpah, the maids of Rachel and Leah respectively, are almost entirely characterless. They have no genealogy; Laban simply gives each one to his daughter on her wedding night (Gen 29:24, 29). Assigned as surrogate child-bearers for Jacob by their mistresses, they differ from Hagar in that their surrogacy is successful; their mistresses accept the children as their own and their four sons are counted among the eponymous ancestors of Israel. They are numbered among Jacob's household, but no detail of their lives or their deaths are recorded. The only exception is the incident of Reuben's incest with Bilhah, which is narrated in one verse:

Part 2: Questions Concerning Women

"While Israel lived in that land, Reuben went and lay with Bilhah his father's concubine; and Israel heard of it" (Gen 35:22).

As we have already noted, there is a concern in the Qumran texts, especially in Jubilees, for the purity of the genealogies of the matriarchs. The texts are at pains to show that the matriarchs are the proper endogamous spouses for the patriarchs, and that their sons are the chosen heirs of the Promise. Hagar, the Egyptian mother of Ishmael, is an improper exogamous spouse, and so she and her descendants are rejected from the Promise. Therefore, Bilhah and Zilpah, whose sons are among the chosen heirs, must have the proper genealogical credentials and take their places among the righteous matriarchs of Israel.

Qumran Texts

These two concerns are highlighted in the Qumran texts in which Bilhah and Zilpah appear: 4QNaphtali, 4QCommentary on Genesis A (4Q252), and Jubilees. 4QNaphtali is the most important of these texts in this regard. The relevant lines are:

1. with Aḥ'iyot, Bilhah's father [. . .], Deborah who nursed Reb[ekah
2. And he went into captivity. And Laban sent and redeemed him, and he gave him Hannah, one of [his] maidservants[
3. first Zilpah. And he made her name Zilpah, after the name of the city to which he was taken captive[
4. And she conceived, and she bore Bilhah, my mother. And Hannah called her name Bilhah, for when she was born[
5. hastening to nurse, and she said, 'How my daughter hastens!' And she called (her) Bilhah again[

In these lines Zilpah and Bilhah are given proper Aramaean genealogies. They are the daughters of Aḥ'iyot, the brother of Deborah, whom we know from Genesis as Rebekah's nurse. Their mother is Hannah, one of Laban's servants. Thus, they are sisters.[29] They may also be related to Laban's family; in line 2 Laban redeems Aḥ'iyot from captivity. According to Lev 25:47–50, a person is obligated to redeem a relative who has fallen into slavery.[30]

---

29. An alternative rabbinic tradition found in Genesis Rabbah and Targum Pseudo-Jonathan makes them sisters as well, as the daughters of Laban by an unnamed concubine. Stone, "Genealogy," 28; Halpern-Amaru, *Empowerment*, 105n7.

30. Stone, "Testament," 81.

"There Is Much Wisdom in Her"

Thus, the text infers that Aḥ'iyot was somehow Laban's kin, therefore making Bilhah and Zilpah part of the extended family of Abraham. This strengthens their genealogical credentials. That this inference was accepted is shown from the parallel passage in the later (Christian) Testament of Naphtali, which almost certainly knew 4QNaphtali:[31]

> But my mother was Bilhah, daughter of Rotheos, Deborah's brother, nurse of Rebecca; she was born the very day on which Rachel was born. Rotheos was of Abraham's tribe, a Chaldean, one who honored God, free and well-born, but he was taken captive and bought by Laban, who gave him Aina, his servant girl, as a wife. She bore a daughter and called her Zelpha from the name of the village in which he had been taken captive. After that she bore Bilhah, saying, 'My daughter is ever eager for new things: No sooner had she been born than she hurried to start sucking'. (T. Naph. 1:9–12)

Bilhah and Zilpah are thus acceptable, both as spouses for Jacob and as mothers of his sons.

The second issue raised by the Genesis account with which this interpretive tradition, with its concern for the righteousness of the matriarchs and patriarchs, has to contend, is the incest of Reuben with Bilhah. This incident is a clear violation of the laws of incest in Lev 18:8 and 20:11. The violation is the focus of the text of 4QCommentary on Genesis A (4Q252), which discusses it in a citation from the Blessing of Jacob (Gen 49:3–4):

> *Reuben, you are my firstborn and the first fruits of my strength, excelling in dignity and excelling in power. Unstable as water, you shall no longer excel. You went up onto your father's bed. Then you defiled it.' 'On his bed he went up!'* Its interpretation is that he reproved him for when he slept with Bilhah his concubine.

This is a simple exegetical explanation of a gap in the Genesis narrative. The interpretation clarifies the incident alluded to in the quotation, referring to Reuben's violation of Bilhah narrated in Gen 35:22. In the Genesis narrative Jacob "finds out" that Reuben has violated Bilhah, but appears to do nothing about it. However, Reuben's punishment is revealed in his later (non-) blessing, where Jacob takes away Reuben's status as firstborn. The interpretation is meant to make the connection between the earlier narrative and the later blessing clear.

---

31. Stone, "Genealogy," 32.

PART 2: QUESTIONS CONCERNING WOMEN

Jubilees

Jubilees also knows of this tradition and uses it, briefly mentioning that Bilhah and Zilpah were sisters (Jub. 28:9).[32] In addition, Jubilees notes the death of Bilhah; she dies (with Dinah) lamenting for the supposed death of Joseph (Jub. 34:15).

Jubilees gives much more attention to Reuben's violation of Bilhah than either Genesis or 4QCommentary on Genesis A:

> And Reuben saw Bilhah, the attendant of Rachel (and his father's concubine), washing in the water privately, and he desired her. And hiding at night, he entered Bilhah's house at night and found her sleeping in her bed, alone in her house. And he lay with her. And she woke up and looked, and behold, Reuben was lying with her on the bed. And she uncovered the hem of her (skirt) and seized him and screamed and recognized that it was Reuben. And she was ashamed because of him and released her hand from upon him. And he fled. And she lamented greatly concerning this matter. And she did not tell anyone at all. And when Jacob came and sought her, she said to him, "I am not clean for you since I have become polluted for you because Reuben has defiled me and lay with me at night, but I was sleeping and I was unaware until he had uncovered my skirt and lain with me." And Jacob was very angry with Reuben because he had lain with Bilhah, for he had uncovered his father's robe. And therefore Jacob did not draw near her since Reuben had defiled her. And the deed of any man who uncovers his father's robe is very evil because he is despicable before the Lord (33:1-9).

Jubilees' treatment owes something to the story of David and Bathsheba (2 Sam 11:2-4); Bilhah is innocently bathing when Reuben sees her. However, unlike David, Reuben rapes Bilhah by stealth; she screams and recognizes Reuben. Bilhah, the righteous matriarch, acts in accord with Deut 22:25-27, which expects a rape victim to scream. There are also parallels with the account of Joseph and Potiphar's wife (Gen 39:6b-18); Potiphar's wife grasps Joseph's garment, he flees, and she screams. Another influence on the Jubilees account is the rape of Tamar by her brother Amnon (2 Sam 13:1-9).

Bilhah does not report Reuben until Jacob approaches her for sexual intercourse, when she informs Jacob that she is defiled, and the cause. She

---

32. Halpern-Amaru, "Bilhah," 4.

pays the consequence in the loss of her conjugal relations with Jacob. In all her actions she is completely righteous, as becomes a matriarch of Israel.[33]

Zilpah and Bilhah are brought into the family circle of Abraham in these Second Temple period texts; their lineage is correct and their conjugal relationships with Jacob entirely proper. Further, in the case of Bilhah, her conduct emphasizes her status as a righteous matriarch of Israel.

Conclusion

Two concerns resonate throughout all the extra-biblical texts concerning the matriarchs and their co-wives found in the Qumran library. The first concern is to demonstrate that the matriarchs and their servants/co-wives have the proper genealogical credentials; that is, that they are all part of the extended family of Abraham. In Jubilees, the only completely preserved text of those we have investigated, the reason for the emphasis on Abrahamic genealogy is explained: Abraham is the chosen descendant of Noah, who is in turn the favored descendant of Enoch, the antediluvian patriarch who is the righteous recipient of heavenly knowledge (Gen 5:21–24).[34] That Enochian ancestry is implied in all the genealogical tidbits presented in the Qumran texts. Only those women and men with pure lineage can be the recipients of God's promises.

The second concern emphasizes the righteous behavior of the women who are the wives and mothers of Israel's patriarchs. Over and over again, any questionable elements (e.g., sexual compromise, deception) found in Genesis are either expunged or justified in the later compositions. Israel's matriarchs must be wholly righteous, their conduct without taint of wrongdoing.

Both these themes, in more general terms, are broadly located in the Qumran library. Proper marriage and pure sexual conduct are emphasized in many of the Qumran documents.[35] And righteous behavior is the mark of the Qumran sectarians, those chosen by God to receive his knowledge and to carry out his will. The treatment of the matriarchs and their servants/co-wives indicates that women, although they maintain a subordinate status to men, are important actors in God's plan for salvation.

---

33. Halpern-Amaru, *Empowerment*, 110–11. The later Testament of Reuben knows the Jubilees narrative, but changes it into a polemic against the seductiveness of women; when Reuben enters Bilhah's tent, she is drunk and naked!

34. VanderKam, *The Book of Jubilees*, 118–19, 137–38.

35. See further "Not According to Rule," 71 in this volume.

8

Traditions about Miriam in the Qumran Scrolls

THE LITERATURE OF SECOND Temple Judaism (c. late sixth century BCE to c. 70 CE) contains many compositions that focus on characters and events known from the biblical (aka "scriptural" or "classical") texts. The characters or events in these new compositions are developed in various ways: filling in gaps in the biblical account, offering explanations for difficult passages, or simply adding details to the biblical personages to make them fuller and more interesting characters. For example, the work known as *Joseph and Aseneth* focuses on the biblical character Aseneth, the Egyptian wife of Joseph, mentioned only briefly in Gen 41:45, 50.[1] This work attempts to explain, among other things, how Joseph, the righteous son of Jacob, contracted an exogamous marriage with the daughter of an Egyptian priest. In an elaborate scene, Aseneth rejects her ancestral religion and converts to the worship of the God of Israel (10:2—17:10).

Further Second Temple period compositions focus on other biblical characters, most of them from Israel's ancient past: the patriarchs and matriarchs Abraham and Sarah, Isaac and Rebekah, Jacob, Rachel, and Leah, and their descendants.[2] The collection of manuscripts recovered from the

---

1. Burchard, "Joseph and Aseneth," 177–248.
2. See "There is Much Wisdom in Her" 107 in this volume.

caves surrounding Khirbet Qumran, popularly known as the Dead Sea Scrolls, contains a wealth of previously unknown literary compositions from the Second Temple period, many adding to our knowledge of the traditions surrounding these familiar biblical characters. There is new material concerning female biblical characters to be gleaned from the fragmentary remains of the Qumran collection.

This article focuses on two or possibly three Qumran texts that mention the biblical character Miriam, the sister of Moses and Aaron, who, with her brothers, was a leader of the Israelites during the sojourn in the wilderness.[3]

Biblical References

Miriam appears in seven passages in the Hebrew Bible. In Exod 15:20–21 Miriam, identified as a prophet, is portrayed leading the Israelite women in a victory celebration following the rout of the Egyptians at the Reed Sea:

> Then the prophet Miriam, Aaron's sister, took a tambourine in her hand; and all the women went out after her with tambourines and with dancing. And Miriam sang to them: "Sing to the LORD, for he has triumphed gloriously; horse and rider he has thrown into the sea."[4]

As it stands, Miriam's song is only a repetition of the first verse of Moses' Song of the Sea (Exod 15:1); one might ask if Miriam sang anything else.

Num 12:1–15 contains the story of Miriam and Aaron's complaint against Moses, with Miriam's subsequent punishment with a form of skin disease:

> While they were at Hazeroth, Miriam and Aaron spoke against Moses because of the Cushite woman whom he had married (for he had indeed married a Cushite women); and they said, "Has the LORD spoken only through Moses? Has he not spoken through us also?" And the LORD heard it ... Suddenly the LORD said to Moses, Aaron, and Miriam, "Come out, you three, to the tent of meeting." So the three of them came out. Then the LORD came down in a pillar of cloud, and stood at the entrance of the tent, and called Aaron and Miriam; and they both came forward. And he

---

3. Since this article was written, a comprehensive study of the figure of Miriam in Second Temple Judaism has been written by Hanna Tervanotko. See Tervanotko, *Denying Her Voice*, especially chaps. 2 and 3.

4. Brooke, "Long-Lost," 62–65.

said, "Hear my words: When there are prophets among you, I the LORD make myself known to them in visions; I speak to them in dreams. Not so with my servant Moses; he is entrusted with all my house. With him I speak face to face—clearly, not in riddles; and he beholds the form of the Lord. Why then were you not afraid to speak against my servant Moses?" And the anger of the LORD was kindled against them, and he departed. When the cloud went away from over the tent, Miriam had become skin-diseased, white as snow. And Aaron turned towards Miriam and saw that she had skin disease. Then Aaron said to Moses, "Oh, my lord, do not lay sin upon us for a sin that we have so foolishly committed. Do not let her be like one stillborn, whose flesh is half-consumed when it comes out of its mother's womb." And Moses cried to the LORD, "O God, please heal her." But the LORD said to Moses, "If her father had but spit in her face, would she not bear her shame for seven days? Let her be shut out of the camp for seven days, and after that she may be brought in again." So Miriam was shut out of the camp for seven days; and the people did not set out on the march until Miriam had been brought in again. (Num 12:1–2, 4–15)[5]

It should be noted that although Miriam is punished in this passage, she is clearly a leader of the people; it is implied in verse 6 that she is a prophet of visions and dreams, and her skin disease and subsequent quarantine cause the journey through the wilderness to be delayed seven days. Miriam's skin disease is recalled in Deut 24:9.

The death of Miriam is recounted in Num 20:1: "The Israelites, the whole congregation, came into the wilderness of Zin in the first month, and the people stayed in Kadesh. Miriam died there, and was buried there."

In the verse immediately following the notice of Miriam's death, the narrative notes that the wells dry up and the people have no water; while there is no necessary connection between these two events, later tradition creates one, by tying the abundant water to the virtue of Miriam.[6]

Miriam also appears in genealogical notices in Num 26:59 and 1 Chr 5:29 (Eng. 6:3), where she is identified as the daughter of Amram and Jochebed and the sister of Aaron and Moses. Micah, the eighth century

---

5. Since this article was written, a great deal of work has been done on this passage as an example of "color-consciousness" in the Hebrew Bible, since Moses' Cushite wife is presumably dark-skinned, and Miriam is punished by becoming "as white as snow." See, e.g., Felder, "Race, Racism."

6. Kugel, *Bible*, 363–64.

prophet, lists Moses, Aaron and Miriam as the leaders of the Exodus from Egypt (Mic 6:4).

Finally, Exod 2:4-8 portrays an unnamed sister of Moses watching over him after his mother sets him adrift on the Nile. Although later tradition identifies this unnamed sister as Miriam (for example, Jub. 47:4-9), some scholars have speculated that the tradition that identifies Moses, Aaron, and Miriam as siblings is a later P tradition, and that originally Miriam was a leader in her own right, unrelated to Moses.[7]

These few passages provide a tantalizing glimpse of a female leadership figure, a prophet whose actual role may have been far greater than recorded. Pardes suggests that "there must have been other traditions [about Miriam] which were not included in the canon."[8] It is always difficult to determine what the biblical accounts, some of which are quite ancient (e.g., Exod 15:1-18, the Song of the Sea), may have left out when they were redacted into their present form; but whether or not traditional material about Miriam was excluded from the books that now make up the biblical canon, the short passages concerning Miriam were ripe for interpretation and expansion, with the potential of forming an "extra-biblical" body of material about Miriam. In a few fragmentary manuscripts from Qumran we seem to have the oldest record of such traditions.

Qumran Evidence

The first Qumran manuscript to contain fresh information about Miriam is 4Q365, one of a group of manuscripts known collectively as 4QReworked Pentateuch.[9] 4Q365 is dated paleographically to c. 75-50 BCE but includes much older material. It contains an expanded and altered text of the Pentateuch or Torah. 4Q365 has a different text from the received text with which we are familiar (the Masoretic Text); these differences include different arrangements of passages, some omissions, and additions to the text. These differences are deliberate and usually have an exegetical purpose. One such addition occurs in the fragments that contain Exodus 15.

---

7. Setel, "Exodus," 36.

8. Pardes, *Countertraditions*, 11.

9. Tov and White, "4Q365," 255-318. Much has been written about the status of 4Q365 as an expanded Pentateuchal manuscript; see, e.g., Ulrich, "Biblical Text," 88; and Segal, "4QReworked Pentateuch," 391-99.

Part 2: Questions Concerning Women

Fragments 6a-c of 4Q365 preserve the remains of two columns. Column 1 begins with Exod 14:12 and breaks off in the midst of 15:20–21, the verses concerning Miriam's victory song at the Reed Sea: "And [Miriam the prophet, the sister of Aaron] took [the tambourine in her hand and] she lead a[ll] the women after her with [tambourines and with dancing. And she answered . . .]"

The verse presumably was completed at the bottom of colum 1 (not preserved). The next verse that we expect, 15:22, does not appear until the beginning of line 8 in column 2. In the seven preceding lines we find the very fragmentary remains of a poetic composition, presumably an expanded version of the song that Miriam sang. The preserved words are:

1. you despised [
2. for the majesty of [
3. You are great, a deliverer [
4. the hope of the enemy has perished and he is for[gotten
5. they perished in the mighty waters, the enemy [
6. And extol the one who lifts up[, a r]ansom you (fem. plural) gave[
7. [one who d]oes gloriously[[10]

As can be seen by the feminine plural imperative in line 6, this song is being addressed to a group of women, evidently those following Miriam in 15:20. The subject of the song is God, who is praised for destroying an enemy (the Egyptians). Several of the lines contain words or phrases that have already appeared in Moses' song, the Song of the Sea: גאות "majesty," and "gloriously," in lines 2 and 7, come from the same Hebrew root, גאה, already used in Exod 15:1, 7; and במים אדירים "in the mighty waters" (line 5), is found in 15:10. All this evidence allows us to say with confidence that these lines in 4Q365 are the remnant of a Song of Miriam, part of a body of traditional material that has contributed to the longer text of 4Q365. Perhaps this Song grew up in answer to the question raised above, "What did Miriam really sing?" The remnants of Miriam's Song in 4Q365 parallel other songs of triumph sung by biblical women, Deborah in Judges 5, Hannah in 1 Sam 2:1–10, and Judith in Jdt 16.[11] Miriam's role in the victory celebration at the Reed Sea is the subject of some discussion in other Second Temple literature; for example, Philo states that Moses and Miriam formed separate men's and women's choirs (*Moses* 1.180), although in another work he says that there was a single choir, with the men being led by Moses and

---

10. Brooke, "Long-Lost," 63, gives a slightly different translation.
11. Brooke, "Long-Lost," 64.

the women by Miriam (*Vita* 87). However, the content of this Qumran fragment is unique; nowhere else in Second Temple Jewish writings do we find actual words from Miriam's Song. This song cements Miriam's status as a leader of the Israelites; since she is also called a prophet in verse 20, it can be argued that the song is the product of divine inspiration.

The second work from Qumran that mentions Miriam focuses on her prophetic gifts and her membership in the family of the first high priest, Aaron. 4QVisions of Amram (4Q543–549) is an Aramaic text found in six or seven fragmentary manuscripts, which was composed, according to its editor, in the early second century BCE.[12] The text is part of a trilogy of testaments from the ancestors of the high priestly family: Aramaic Levi, the Testament of Qahat (or Kohath, the son of Levi), and the Visions of Amram (the grandson of Levi and father of Aaron).[13] Miriam appears in the Visions of Amram as the daughter of Amram and Jochebed, the grandson and daughter of Levi respectively (Exod 6:20 and Num 26:59), and thus a member of the Levitical priestly house.

Miriam is first mentioned in the opening lines of the text, when her father Amram arranges her marriage:

> A copy of the writing of the words of the visions of Amram, son of Kohath, son of Levi, all of which he declared to his sons, and which he commissioned to them on the day of his death, in the one hundredth and thirty-sixth year, that is the year of his death, in the one hundredth and fifty-second year of Israel's exile in Egypt. And then it came to him and he sent and called Uzziel, his youngest brother, and he gave him Miriam his daughter as a wife, she being thirty years old. And he made a marriage feast for seven days.[14]

Miriam is here identified as the daughter of Amram, as she is in at least some parts of the biblical tradition. However, the biblical texts make no mention of Miriam's husband; thus, we have preserved here an extra-biblical tradition. Uzziel appears in Exod 7:18 and Num 3:19, as well as T. Levi 12, as the youngest brother of Amram. It is perhaps surprising to find Amram arranging for his daughter to marry her uncle in a document preserved in the Qumran library, since uncle-niece marriage is clearly

---

12. Puech, "Visions," 285.

13. Puech, "Visions," 283. For a discussion of the family of Levi, see also Kugler, *From Patriarch*, 111–18.

14. 4Q543 1 1–7//4Q545 1A1 1–6 and 4Q546 1 1–4. The English translation is mine, based on Puech's French translation.

forbidden in certain Qumran legal texts. According to the Damascus Document, in a context that condemns the sexual activities of those outside its community:

> And each man marries the daughter of his brother or sister, whereas Moses said, "You shall not approach your mother's sister; she is your mother's near kin." But although the laws against incest are written for men, they also apply to women. When, therefore, a brother's daughter uncovers the nakedness of her father's brother, she is near kin. (CD 5:9–11)

This prohibition is also found in the Temple Scroll, 66:15–17: "A man shall not take the daughter of his brother or the daughter of his sister, for this is abominable." The same prohibition is also found in 4QHalakah A 12. The prohibition against uncle-niece marriage is quite clear in these documents. Moreover, it is based on the biblical prohibition of aunt-nephew marriage found in Lev 18:12–14:

> You shall not uncover the nakedness of your father's sister; she is your father's flesh. You shall not uncover the nakedness of your mother's sister, for she is your mother's flesh. You shall not uncover the nakedness of your father's brother, that is, you shall not approach his wife; she is your aunt.

This negative commandment is reiterated in Lev 20:19: "You shall not uncover the nakedness of your mother's sister or of your father's sister, for that is to lay bare one's own flesh; they shall be subject to punishment." According to the interpretation found in the Damascus Document, what is expressly forbidden for men (to marry an aunt) is equally forbidden for women (to marry an uncle).[15] Thus Miriam's marriage, according to the regulations of the sectarian community, is illegal. It is thus notable that they would preserve several copies of a text that so blatantly supported uncle-niece marriage.

However, the explanation may lie in the circumstances of the marriage of Miriam's parents, Amram and Jochebed. According to Exod 6:20 and Num 26:59, Jochebed was the daughter of Levi and the sister of Kohath, and therefore Amram's aunt. In other words, Amram himself contracted a

---

15. Uncle-niece marriage was also forbidden by the Samaritans, early Christians, and the Karaites. See Schiffman, "Laws Pertaining to Women," 538. Rabbinic tradition did not forbid uncle-niece marriage, but in fact actively encouraged it on the grounds that since it was not expressly forbidden in the Torah, it was approved (b. Yebam. 62b). See Broshi, "Anti-Qumranic," 596.

marriage that was explicitly forbidden according to the terms of the Torah given to his son Moses on Mt. Sinai.[16] Thus, Miriam's marriage to Amram's youngest brother is parallel to Amram's marriage to Levi's youngest daughter. Both marriages are endogamous, something applauded throughout patriarchal history.[17] Nonetheless, the forbidden quality of Amram's marriage to Jochebed forces the author of Jubilees, otherwise a polemicist in favor of endogamous marriage, to pass over this particular marriage in silence.[18] Later rabbinic tradition argues that before the revelation at Sinai only maternal relationships were considered, and that Jochebed was only the half-sister of Amram's father Kohath, through their father Levi; they had different mothers (b. Sot. 58b).

This apologetic is found more widely in Second Temple literature, which sometimes excuses the peccadilloes of the ancients on the basis of ignorance of the Law. For example, the Damascus Document excuses the fact that David had many wives, seemingly in direct contradiction to Deut 17:17, by saying "but David had not read the sealed book of the Law which was in the ark, for it was not opened in Israel from the death of Eleazar and Joshua, and the elders who worshipped Ashtoreth. It was hidden and not revealed until the coming of Zadok" (CD 5:2–4). The same argument could be applied both to Amram and Jochebed and to Miriam and Uzziel; both couples did not know the Law and therefore could not be expected to follow it. This, however, points to a different interpretive tradition than Jubilees, which argues that the patriarchs and matriarchs did observe the Law.

The second mention of Miriam in the Visions of Amram comes in 4Q546 12 3–4: "and he clung to Aaron to [. . .] and the mystery of Miriam he made for th[em . . ." The Aramaic/Hebrew word for "mystery," רז, has a divine connotation; thus, it is implied that Miriam's mystery had been revealed to her by God. As Puech notes, there are several extra-biblical traditions according to which Miriam is the recipient of divine revelation;[19] since she is called a prophet in Exod 15:20, and in Num 12:2 she makes the claim that God has spoken to her, the growth of this extra-biblical tradition is not surprising. In the *Biblical Antiquities* of Pseudo-Philo, Miriam

---

16. Aramaic Levi 12:4 amplifies the terse notice in Exodus and Numbers by stating that Jochebed and Amram were born on the same day. Greenfield et al, *Aramaic Levi*, 101.

17. Cacquot, "Les Testaments," 20.

18. Halpern-Amaru, *Empowerment*, 123.

19. Puech, "Visions," 300. For further discussion, see Tervanotko, *Denying Her Voice*, 127–31.

has a prophetic dream concerning the birth of Moses (9:10). In rabbinic tradition too, Miriam is the recipient of divine revelations (*Sifre Num* 85). The reference found here in Visions of Amram seems to be part of that same tradition, although unfortunately it is unclear what the "mystery of Miriam" was.[20]

4Q547 9 10 has a brief mention of Miriam, unfortunately in a broken context. Amram appears to be narrating his return to Egypt from the land of Canaan, perhaps followed by the birth of Miriam, the oldest of the three siblings: מרים ומן באת]רה. Nothing more can be ascertained from the fragment.

The last manuscript containing a mention of Miriam is 4Q549. This Aramaic manuscript was originally catalogued by Jean Starcky as a separate work entitled "Composition mentionnant Hur et Miriam." In his edition, however, Puech argues that 4Q549 is not a separate work, but a seventh manuscript of Visions of Amram. In support of his argument, he notes that the characters mentioned by name are either part of the family of Amram, e.g., Miriam, Aaron, and Sitri, or are associated with Moses and Aaron, e.g., Hur. Further, he finds in frag. 2 elements of the genre "testament": a meal, an announcement of the anticipated death of the patriarch, and a reunion with his sons and other male relatives. Finally, frag. 1 mentions Egypt, the setting for Visions of Amram.[21] However, Eisenman and Wise have argued that there is no connection between this manuscript and Visions of Amram, because in this text Miriam is married to Hur rather than to Uzziel.[22] As we shall see, the text itself does not clearly identify the spouse of Miriam. The lines in question are:

> 8. Ten, and he begat from Miriam, a relative (?) [[23]
> 9. and Sitri. *Vacat* and Hur took [for a wife . . .
> 10. and he begat from her Uri, and Aaro[n . . .
> 11. from her four/fourteen sons [

---

20. Puech suggests that it is a revelation concerning the birth of Moses and his mission, in the same tradition as Pseudo-Philo. "Visions," 399.

21. Puech, "Visions," 399.

22. Eisenman and Wise, *Uncovered*, 152. Tervanotko agrees with Puech against Eisenman and Wise. Tervanotko, *Denying Her Voice*, 135–36.

23. Puech, "Visions," 402–3, restores the Hebrew and translates "une parente." Caquot, "Testaments," 25, suggests that it means something like "kinsman on the father's side." Eisenman and Wise, *Uncovered*, 94, suggest a proper name, AB[?. Wise et al., *Dead Sea Scrolls*, 551, reads "a peopl[e?." García Martínez and Tigchelaar, *Study Edition*, 1097, have the same reading, but translate "aunt(?)."

These lines are clearly giving the genealogical record of the family of which Miriam and Aaron are a part, that is, the family of Amram. Sitri, according to Exod 6:22, is the son of Uzziel. In Visions of Amram, Miriam is the wife of Uzziel and, by implication, the mother of Sitri. The juxtaposition of lines 8 and 9 on this fragment, with the unnamed husband begetting children from Miriam and Sitri's name in the next line, yields the understanding that Miriam is the mother of Sitri. Hence, her unnamed spouse must be Uzziel, in agreement with the other manuscripts of Visions of Amram.[24]

The character Hur, presented as taking a wife and fathering Ur in lines 9 and 10, appears in the biblical text in two different contexts and in fact is two different characters. Hur debuts in Exod 17:10–12, where he and Aaron prop up Moses' hands during the battle against the Amalekites. In Exod 24:4 Moses leaves Aaron and Hur in charge of the people when he goes up on the mountain. Although Hur's genealogy is not given in either of these passages, his association with Moses and Aaron suggests that he is a Levite.

There is a second series of passages concerning a second Hur. This Hur is the grandfather of Bezalel, the chief craftsman of the tent sanctuary, and is a Judahite (Exod 31:2; 35:30, 38:22; 2 Chr 1:5). In 1 Chr 2:19–20 Hur is a son of Caleb by his second wife Ephrath. There would seem to be no necessary connection between these two Hurs; however, some later traditions identify the two characters and put Miriam into relationship with the second Hur.

Josephus, the late first century CE Jewish historian, knows a tradition in which the Hur of Exod 17:10–12 is married to Miriam (*Ant.* 3.53–54). He also identifies the two Hurs with one another, since he states that Bezalel is the grandson of Miriam (*Ant.* 3.105). Another literary tradition, however, identifies Miriam with Ephrath, the second wife of Caleb in 2 Chr 2:19, thus making her the mother of Hur, the grandmother of Uri, and the great-grandmother of Bezalel (Tg. Chron.; Sifre Num 78; m. Sotah 11b–12a; Exod. Rab. 1:17). Does 4Q549 belong to either of those traditions?

The Hur found in line 9 must be identified with the Judahite Hur, since he is the father of Uri in line 10, and Uri is clearly part of the Judahite ancestry of Bezalel: "Bezalel son of Uri son of Hur, of the tribe of Judah" (Exod 31:2). It might then be possible to argue that Hur is the unnamed husband of Miriam in line 8 above. We would thus have a text in line with the tradition of Josephus, which identifies the Judahite Hur with the Hur of the battle against the Amalekites and relates him to Moses and Aaron

---

24. Puech, "Visions," 404; Caquot, "Les Testaments," 25.

through his marriage to Miriam.²⁵ However, two elements militate against this solution. First, the pattern of the text seems to follow this order: Male person marries female person and begets a certain number of sons who are listed by name. Given that pattern, it is most likely that Miriam is the mother of Sitri. Since we know that Sitri is the son of Uzziel and is nowhere related to Hur, it follows that the unnamed husband of Miriam must be Uzziel. Further, there is a *vacat* in the middle of line 9, after Sitri's name and before the mention of Hur's marriage. This implies that there is no relationship between the two groups of people. Therefore, it seems more likely that 4Q549 is part of the tradition known to Visions of Amram, in which Miriam is married to Uzziel; Hur (identified with the Judahite Hur) is mentioned here because of his connection with Aaron (line 10), not Miriam. This conclusion strengthens Puech's argument that 4Q549 is a seventh manuscript of Visions of Amram.

In sum, these few fragments have added to our knowledge of the body of traditions surrounding the biblical character Miriam.²⁶ Miriam's reputation as a prophet is visible in the creation of the Song of Miriam in 4Q365 and the mention of the "mystery of Miriam" in the Visions of Amram. Miriam's status as an important member of the family of Amram is emphasized through her presence in the genealogical material in Visions of Amram. Finally, a new tradition has been discovered concerning Miriam's marriage to Amram's brother Uzziel, pointing to traditions that were neither static nor unified, but grew in different directions among different groups of Jews in the Second Temple period.

---

25. Eisenman and Wise, *Uncovered*, 93–94.

26. Another Qumran text, 4Q377, has also been identified as mentioning Miriam. The editors read 2 i 9 as יתסג[רמרים בעינו, without a space between the remains of ר and מרים. They believe this may be an illusion to Num 12. If their reading is correct, we have a further mention of Miriam in a Qumran text, but the reading does not add to our knowledge about the figure of Miriam. VanderKam and Brady, DJD 28:211. See also Tervanotko, *Denying Her Voice*, 169–72.

9

Lady Wisdom and Dame Folly at Qumran

THE FEMALE FIGURES OF "Lady Wisdom" and "Dame Folly," found in the post-exilic Wisdom literature, have always attracted much debate and speculation. The questions of who they are and what they stand for, particularly in the case of Lady Wisdom, have been hotly debated. Is she merely a literary creation, driven by the fact that the nouns for wisdom in Hebrew and Greek, חכמה and σοφία, are feminine in gender? Or is she an actual divine figure, a female hypostasis of Yahweh, the god of Israel, indicating a female divine presence in Israelite religion? These debates have yet to be resolved.[1] Now that the large corpus of sapiential texts from Qumran has been published, new light may be shed on the figures of Lady Wisdom and Dame Folly. This paper investigates these two figures in three Qumran texts: 4Q184, "The Wiles of the Wicked Woman," 4Q185, "A Sapiential Work,"[2] and 4Q525, "Beatitudes,"[3] to see whether the presentation of these figures in three otherwise unknown texts can shed any light on their function in Second Temple Jewish thought. First, however, I will begin with a

---

1. See Yoder, "Proverbs," 235–37; Tanzer, "Wisdom," 405–6.

2. Now also referred to as "Sapiential Admonitons B." See Uusimäki, *Turning Proverbs*, 6.

3. 4Q184, 185: Allegro, DJD 5:82–88. 4Q525: Puech, DJD 25:118–78.

brief overview of the wisdom texts containing these two figures, beginning with the biblical evidence.

Hebrew Bible

Lady Wisdom, or Wisdom personified as a female figure, appears in one canonical wisdom text, the book of Proverbs. Wisdom also appears in the book of Job, but less as a personified figure and more as an abstract concept. Both books are generally considered to be post-exilic, and both are found at Qumran. The parade text for the figure of Lady Wisdom (חכמות) is Proverbs 1–9, where she appears in three major pericopes: 1:20–33; 8:1–36, and 9:1–6, 10–12. In these pericopes, Wisdom speaks for herself, on her own authority. Her primary relationship is with God, since she is the first thing created by God, and she is with God during the entire act of creation. However, her chief delight and focus is men, to whom she constantly calls. It is through her that men are able to attain knowledge of God and the good life (3:13–18).[4] In Wisdom's main speech in chapter 8, she claims that she was created by God before the cosmos, dwells with God, and participated with, or at least observed, God in the creation of the world. All these attributes make her status as a divine being, at least in Proverbs 1–9, seem unquestionable.[5]

Her opposite number, Dame Folly (אשת כסילות) is, however, clearly human. She is identified with the "strange woman" (אשה זרה) the adulteress whose purpose is to lead the young man astray (the androcentric nature of the text here should not require comment). She is also the "foreign" woman (נכריה), who, like many foreign women in the Israelite tradition, leads men from the right (Israelite) path.[6] The most noteworthy thing to note about the portrayal of Folly is that, while Wisdom's gifts cover all aspects of life

---

4. I am using the term "men" advisedly here. As Carol Newsom has convincingly demonstrated, Proverbs 1–9 is written in a male voice to a male audience; women, whether as wisdom or folly, function only as the other against which men measure themselves. Newsom, "Woman," 142–44.

5. Wisdom's attributes and actions can be related to ancient Near Eastern tutelary gods such as the Sumerian Nisba and Inanna and the Egyptian Ma'at and Isis, thus reinforcing her divine status. See Fontaine, "Proverbs," 147.

6. See the condemnation of Solomon in 1 Kgs 11:1–8 for being led astray by his foreign wives. Solomon is traditionally credited as the author of the Proverbs (1:1). For further discussion of the אשה זרה in Proverbs, see Yee, "I Have Perfumed"; and Washington, "Strange Woman."

(e.g., riches, insight, a life of ease), Folly's snares are almost entirely sexual (a telling comment on male fears of female temptation). This is in spite of the fact that other parts of Proverbs 1–9 mention other types of wicked or foolish behavior (e.g., theft, lying, murder, haughtiness; cf. 1:11–19; 4:24; 6:12–19).

Thus, while Wisdom, the positive female figure in Proverbs, embraces all aspects of human life, Folly, the negative female figure, encompasses only sexual sin. In her two main speeches, 7:10–20 and 9:13–18, Folly's allure is sexual, although the consequences of heeding her are cosmic, leading to "the depths of Sheol," pointing to a dark, chthonic side of Folly.[7] This is a theme that will recur.

The wisdom poem in Job 28:12–28 is thought by many to be a separate wisdom piece incorporated by the author of Job into his book. In it, wisdom is clearly associated with God and is said to have been created by God at the time of creation. However, wisdom is not a personified figure here, and no particularly feminine characteristics are assigned to it. Interestingly, it is God who shows the way to wisdom, rather than vice-versa. A variation on this theme appears in later apocryphal and pseudepigraphical literature.[8]

Apocrypha and Pseudepigrapha

There are several passages in the apocryphal and pseudepigraphical literature in which the figure of Wisdom appears, and two distinct strands of the understanding of that figure begin to emerge. These passages draw heavily on Proverbs 1–9, although other influences also appear. The Wisdom of Jesus ben Sira, or Ecclesiasticus, opens with the praise of Wisdom, a female figure, created by God before all other things, and poured out on all flesh (Introduction:1–20). Her manifestation in human beings is the "fear of the Lord," which is the beginning, the fullness, the crown, and the root of Wisdom. In chapter 24, Wisdom describes herself as a divine being, whose home is in the heavens, seeking a dwelling place on earth, among humans. Here the relationship to Wisdom's speech in Proverbs 8 is clear.[9] Finally, God commands her to dwell with Israel, and this leads Ben Sira to his great declaration, that Wisdom is the Torah, the special possession

7. Fontaine, "Proverbs," 147; and also Camp, "What's So Strange," 31.
8. For a recent commentary on Job, see Newsom, *Job*.
9. Schuller, "Apocrypha," 237. Wisdom's speech is also similar to the self-laudatory Isis hymns from the Hellenistic period.

of Israel: "All this is the book of the covenant of the Most High God, the law that Moses commanded us as an inheritance for the congregations of Jacob" (24:23; see also 15:1–10). This important theme will recur in other literature. Finally, Sir 51:13–20 is a poem detailing the author's search for wisdom as a youth; the description of wisdom has erotic overtones (51:15), but Wisdom's overall characterization is as an abstract concept rather than a personified being.

Ben Sira does not mention Folly as a personification of wickedness; however, his book is rife with warnings concerning the dangers of women's sexuality, which he considers ready to burst out and wreak havoc at a moment's notice (e.g., 22:3–6; 25:16–26; 26:7–12). Ben Sira is found in fragmentary form at Qumran (2Q18) and Masada (MasSir), although chapter 24 has not been found either at Qumran or Masada. Chapter 51 surfaces at Qumran in an unexpected place, in 11QPsalms^a (11Q5) as a free-standing psalm, indicating that before its location in Ben Sira it was a "free-floating" composition.

The Wisdom of Solomon, which is not found at Qumran, also declares that Wisdom is a divine being, present at creation (7:22b—8:1), but the book moves in a completely different direction, heavily influenced by Hellenistic thought.[10] In the Wisdom of Solomon, Wisdom is an eternal emanation of the deity, both immanent and transcendent, that permeates all creation and makes those who seek her the friends of God. There are also erotic elements in the portrayal of Wisdom, when Solomon seeks to make her his bride and desires "intercourse" (συναναστροφή) with her (8:2–16). Nowhere, however, does the Wisdom of Solomon equate Wisdom with the Torah.[11] This portrayal of Wisdom, with its clear Greek overtones, is unique in the Apocrypha and the Pseudepigrapha.

Two other short passages are worth mentioning. Bar 3:9—4:4, which is not found at Qumran, seems to draw on Job 28 and Ben Sira for its portrayal of Wisdom. In Baruch, Wisdom is created by God, sought by humans, and, as in Ben Sira, equated with the Torah of Israel: "She [Wisdom] is the book of the commandments of God, the Law that endures forever.

---

10. Winston, *Wisdom*, 172–90. Winston also points out the parallels in the portrayal of Wisdom to the Isis aretologies of the Hellenistic period, continuing the pattern of analogy to Ancient Near Eastern goddesses.

11. However, Sanders points out that while the Wisdom of Solomon does not equate Wisdom and Torah, it does use the Torah narrative to illustrate its points about Wisdom's capacity to save and protect the one who seeks her (cf. chapters 10–11). Sanders, "Sacred Canopies," 128.

All who hold her fast will live, and those who forsake her will die" (4:1). A different interpretation of Wisdom is found in 1 Enoch 42, part of the Similitudes of Enoch (the only section of 1 Enoch not found at Qumran), which utilizes the theme of Wisdom seeking a dwelling among humans and not finding one. However, unlike Ben Sira, Enoch does not go on to say that Wisdom finds its particular dwelling among the people of Israel, and there is no equation of the divine figure of Wisdom with the Torah.[12] Rather, the figure of Iniquity, or Folly, which appears to be here a divine or semi-divine figure, goes out among humans and finds a dwelling place among them. No more is said about either figure in the Similitudes.

Several themes, therefore, are present in the apocryphal and pseudepigraphical literature which were also noted in the biblical literature: Wisdom as a divine creation, female in gender, with a particular role in creation and a particular relationship with humanity (or, more probably, men). In a separate development, Wisdom also begins to be equated with the Torah as the special possession of Israel. Folly, on the other hand, is still associated almost exclusively with sins having to do with women's sexuality (with the exception of 1 Enoch 42, where she is a more general figure). These themes are also found in the Qumran literature.

Qumran Evidence

The main sources for the figures of Folly and Wisdom at Qumran are the manuscripts 4Q184 and 4Q185, both published by John Allegro in DJD 5 and extensively commented on by John Strugnell.[13] 4Q184 is perhaps the better known text, for Allegro gave it an intriguing title, "The Wiles of the Wicked Woman,"[14] while 4Q185 merely was called "A Sapiential Work." 4Q184 discusses a female figure who can be clearly associated with Dame Folly, while 4Q185 features a female figure who is probably to be equated with Lady Wisdom. Both texts draw heavily on Proverbs 1–9, but they do not appear to utilize the apocryphal and pseudepigraphical texts discussed

---

12. Nickelsburg suggests that 1 Enoch 42 is a parody of the claim by Ben Sira 24 and Bar 4: 1 that Wisdom is gained by the study of the Torah; for Enoch, Wisdom is accessible only through divine revelation. *Jewish Literature*, 216.

13. Strugnell, "Notes en marge," 263–68, 269–73.

14. Allegro, "Wiles." Since this article was published, several important studies have been released: Puech, "4Q184," Tigchelaar, "Lady Folly," Tigchelaar, "The Poetry," and Tigchelaar, "Constructing." Tigchelaar argues that 5Q16 is part of the same composition. "Lady Folly," 380.

above. They both exist in single copies and both manuscripts date paleographically, according to Strugnell, to the first century BCE. Since 4Q184's subject, Dame Folly, is beyond doubt, I will begin with that text.[15]

4Q184

The text begins by introducing a female figure whose every action is sinful:

> She [. . .] utters futility and in [. . .
> She is always looking for depravities,
> and whets the words of her mouth, and implies insult, and is busy leading the community astray with nonsense. Her heart weaves traps, her kidneys [nets.]
> [her eyes] have been defiled with evil, her hands go down to the pit; her feet sink to act wickedly and to walk towards crimes. (1–5)

4Q184 is almost a pastiche of allusions to Proverbs 1–9, where Dame Folly's sins are sexual, and only sexual, in nature. Here in 4Q184, her wicked actions also lead to the corruption of men through illicit sexuality: "Her eyes scan hither and thither, and she raises her eyebrows impudently, to spot a just man and overtake him . . ." (13–14). The idea of the wanton woman speaking "smooth words" (17) and leading the simple astray with her sexuality occurs in Prov 2:16, 5:3, 6:24, 7:5, 21, and 9:13–18. Her paths as "paths of death" and "tracks to sin" and her gates as the "gates of death" and "entrance to Sheol" (8–11) echo Prov 2:13–15, 18–19; 5:5–6; 7:25–27; and 9:18. The idea that she sits in the city gates, where she entraps men into fornication ("In the city squares she veils herself, and stations herself in the gates of the village, and there is no-one who interrupts her in [her] incessant [fornicating.]"), is taken directly from Prov 7:10–12 and 9:13–18, and the notion that she does this to pervert a righteous man is a reversal of the role of Lady Wisdom, who cries out in the city gate in order to set the simple on the path of righteousness (cf. Prov 1:21–22; 3:23–26; 8:1–5; 9:3–6). The sin contemplated here is clearly fornication, as in Proverbs 1–9, and will lead to ruin.

The female figure of 4Q184, however, appears to be more cosmic in scope than the simple "loose woman [זונה]" of Proverbs 1–9. Her clothing is not merely flashy, as in Prov 7:10 ("decked out like a prostitute"), but are "shadows of twilight" and "diseases of corruption." Her attire has bat-like

---

15. All translations, unless otherwise noted, are taken from García Martínez and Tigchelaar, *Dead Sea Scrolls*, 377.

"wings" (4). Her dwelling is in the "heart of night," the "foundation of gloom," the "tents of silence," and "the eternal fire." One is reminded of the various divine beings associated with death in the ancient Near East: the Canaanite god Môt, whose residence is referred to as "Muck" and "Phlegm," Ereshkigal, queen of the Mesopotamian underworld, and perhaps most especially, the winged night demon Lilith, who appears, for example, in Isa 34:14 as an inhabitant of a destroyed Edom, a "land of burning pitch." Lilith goes on to a spectacular career in Hebrew folklore, and in most tales, her sin is sexual; she refuses, in one way or another, to be a proper wife to Adam, and so is driven out of Paradise; she now preys on innocent men and on women in childbirth.[16] All of these figures are associated in mythology with cosmic disorder; their counterparts (Ba'l, Inanna, Eve) are associated with the proper divine order of the world. Thus, the Wicked Woman in 4Q184 becomes the personification of chaos opposed to God's established order.[17] The chthonic qualities of Dame Folly, hinted at in Proverbs, become clear in 4Q184. In fact, as Baumgarten notes, "most pronounced is the emphasis on her association with the netherworld."[18] Dame Folly has ceased to be simply human and has become demonic.

This "catastrophization" of Dame Folly may be similar to the cosmological struggle between good and evil that one finds in some Qumran sectarian literature, particularly the Doctrine of the Two Spirits in the Community Rule, 1QS 3:13—4:26. The Spirit of Darkness, in that text, leads those who walk in its way (characterized as "paths of darkness") into, among other things, "impudent enthusiasm, appalling acts performed in a lustful passion, and filthy paths for indecent purposes" (4:9). Those who follow the Spirit of Darkness will end, like those enticed by the Wicked Woman, in the netherworld, "with the humiliation of destruction by the fire of the dark regions" (4:13).[19] Thus sin, for the Qumran community, is not simply human frailty, but part of the cosmic struggle between God and Satan. This may account for the "more than-human" quality of the Wicked Woman/Dame Folly in 4Q184.[20]

16. See Baumgarten, "On the Nature"; and Hutter, "Lilith," 520–21.
17. Moore, "Personification," 512.
18. Baumgarten, "On the Nature," 138.
19. A major factor in the Doctrine of the Two Spirits found in the Community Rule is the idea of individual predestination, a notion that does not occur in the texts so far investigated. Rather, each individual appears to be free to choose his own path, in keeping with other Wisdom texts.
20. However, it should be noted that this "demonization" is part of a larger pattern

Part 2: Questions Concerning Women

4Q185

References to Lady Wisdom are less clear in the Qumran sapiential texts, given the fragmentary nature of that material. She seems to appear in a second text published by Allegro in DJD 5, 4Q185. 4Q185 is a somewhat longer work than 4Q184, with three columns of text preserved. The portion relevant to our concerns comes from 2, 8–12.

> Blessed is the man to whom she has been given, the son of man [. . .
> The wicked person should not brag, saying:
> She has not been given to me and I [shall not look for her.]
> [God has given her] to Israel, and like a good gift, gives her. He has saved all his people, but has destroyed . . .
> Whoever glories in her will say:
> he shall take possession of her and find her.

The figure in question appears to be a personified female figure, given by God, sought (or not sought) by men, whose possession makes the good life attainable. Once again, the text is a pastiche of allusions to biblical texts. Compare, for example, Prov 3:13–18:

> Happy are those who find wisdom, and those who get understanding, for her income is better than silver, and her revenue better than gold. She is more precious than jewels, and nothing you desire can compare with her. Long life is in her right hand; in her left hand are riches and honor. Her ways are ways of pleasantness, and all her paths are peace. She is a tree of life to those who lay hold of her; those who hold her fast are called happy.

with 4Q185 2, 11–14:

> Whoever glories in her will say:
> he shall take her as po[sess]ion and find her, and ho[ld] fast to her and get her as an inheritance;
> With her [there are long d]ays, and greasy bones, and a happy heart, rich[es and honour.]
> His mercies are for her people, and his salvation [for all . . .]
> Blessed the man who does her, does not deceive her, does not slander against [her], does not [with a] fraudulent [spir]it seek her, nor holds fast to her with flatteries.

---

of the continuing denigration of human women in some of the Wisdom literature of the post-exilic period, from Dame Folly in Proverbs 1–9, through the human women who cause Ben Sira such misgivings, to Qohelet, who, in spite of his best efforts, cannot find *any* woman who is wise (7:28)!

Further, the idea that wisdom is something that is passed on from parents to children is prevalent in wisdom literature (e.g., Sir 4:16: "If they remain faithful, they will inherit her; their descendants will also obtain her."); this notion appears in 4Q185 2, 14–15 as well:

> As it was given to their fathers so will he inherit her.
> [He will grow fond of her] with all force of his strength and with all his vigour without restraint.
> And he will give her in inheritance to his descendants.

However, unlike the active figure of Wisdom found in Proverbs, this figure is an object, not a subject; she is given by God, sought by humans, and possession of her brings rewards, but, at least in the material we have, she does not act. In fact, she more closely resembles the non-personified figure of Wisdom in Job 28, where Wisdom is described as established by God, but is not active, or Bar 3:9—4:4, where Wisdom is essentially passive and, importantly, is given by God to Israel ("He found the whole way to knowledge, and gave her to his servant Jacob and to Israel, whom he loved." 3:36).[21] The notion that Wisdom is a special gift from God to Israel is also prominent in Sir 24:8, 10–12:

> Then the Creator of all things gave me a command, and my Creator chose the place for my tent. He said, "Make your dwelling in Jacob, and in Israel receive your inheritance." In the holy tent I ministered before him, and so I was established in Zion. Thus in the beloved city he gave me a resting place, and in Jerusalem was my domain. I took root in an honored people, in the portion of the Lord, his heritage.

Here, of course, Wisdom is a far more active figure; however, the result is the same: Wisdom becomes the special possession of the people of Israel. This raises the question of whether Wisdom is being equated with the Torah in 4Q185, as in Ben Sira and Baruch. A case can certainly be made for that contention. Wisdom is given specifically to Israel; she is inherited from the fathers and passed on to the descendants; possession of her brings blessing, and she is to be loved by the possessor; and, in line 13, we find the admonition, "Blessed the man who does it [her], and does not [. . . "Doing" wisdom can certainly be understood as following the Law, and this seems to be the best understanding of the female figure in this text. Thus,

---

21. Sanders, "Sacred Canopies," 126, again notes that 4Q185 also uses the Torah to illustrate its concept of Wisdom.

in 4Q185, we find the same movement toward equating wisdom with the Torah that we found in Ben Sira and Baruch.

4Q525

One other text from Qumran also contains mention of a female Wisdom figure, although the referent is not as clearly personified as in 4Q185. 4Q525 (4QBeatitudes), which is also preserved in only one copy, is dated by its editor Puech to the second half of the first century BCE.[22] The type of literature to which 4QBeatitudes belongs is Wisdom, since it contains, as de Roo notes, "striking resemblance[s] between 4Q525 and traditional Jewish Wisdom books such as Proverbs and Ben Sira."[23] However, as George Brooke has observed, 4QBeatitudes also contains eschatological language, which represents a change from Proverbs and Ben Sira, and places 4Q525 in relationship with 4Q184's cosmic description of the Wicked Woman.[24] The passages that mention the figure of Wisdom are as follows:
2 ii 2–7:[25]

> Happy are those who hold fast to her statutes and do not hold fast to the ways of injustice. *vacat* Hap[py] are those who rejoice in her and do not pour out into the ways of folly. *vacat* Happy are those who seek her with pure hands and do not search for her with a deceitful heart. *vacat* Happy is the one who attains wisdom. *vacat* He walks in torah of the Most High.
>
> He establishes his heart in her ways. *vacat* He restrains himself with her teachings and favours her chastisements const[an]tly. He does not leave her in the face of [his] affliction[s], during the time of distress does not abandon her, does not forget her [in the day] of terror, and in the humility of his soul does not despise [her.] But he reflects on her constantly, in his distress muses [on her and in al]l his being [comprehends] her. [He sets her] in front of his eyes lest he walk in the ways of[. . .

2 iii 2–3:

---

22. Puech, DJD 25:116. Since the publication of Puech's edition, Uusimäki has published a thorough study of 4Q525, including a reconstruction and English translation. See *Turning Proverbs*, 23–61. The English translations found here are based on those of Uusimäki.

23. De Roo, "Is 4Q525," 345; and Uusimäki, *Turning Proverbs*, 7–10.

24. Brooke, "Wisdom," 37.

25. All translations are taken from Uusimäki, *Turning Proverbs*.

"she cannot be obtained by gold o[r silver ... or] with any precious stone[..."

5, 11-16:

[lis]ten, do not s[eek] her with a deceitful heart and with fla[tteries do not try to grasp her. Do not] abandon your [inhe]ritance to [strangers] or your lot to foreigners, for the wise [are ... th]ey comprehend with sweetness.

Those who fear God keep her ways and they walk in [...] her statutes and her reproofs do not deny. The discerning ones attain [...] Those who walk in perfection turn aside injustice and do not deny her corrections[...]

In these passages Wisdom, which men should seek, is unquestionably equated with the Torah, most clearly in 2 ii 3-4, where the parallelism demands the equation: "Blessed is the man who attains Wisdom, and walks in the law of the Most High."[26] Wisdom/Torah, according to frag. 2, should be followed and meditated on, in order to obtain blessing (lines 12-13). According to 4Q525, Wisdom/Torah is the special inheritance of Israel, the "special path" for those who love and fear God. Thus, Wisdom has lost the special status we observed in Proverbs 1-9; Job 28; 1 Enoch 42; and the Wisdom of Solomon, and become subsumed under the Torah, as in Sir 15:1; 24:23; and Bar 4:1. This equation of Wisdom and Torah in 4Q525 and, probably, 4Q185, would be expected in the literature collected by the wing of Judaism that inhabited Qumran, which placed such emphasis on the study of and obedience to the Law.

Conclusions

What can finally be said about the figures of Lady Wisdom and Dame Folly in the Qumran literature? The development of these figures in 4Q184, 185

---

26. Brooke, "Wisdom," 36. See also Puech, "Hymne," 87. Uusimäki reconstructs more of the text, utilizing not only 4Q525 15, but 5Q16 1-2+5. These lines recall the language of 4Q184: "] gloomy [darkne]ss [...]gathers poison and in [...] serpents in [...] walk(s). To it she comes proud[ly ...]walks the fiery snake, and in [its] windo[ws] crawls the serpent. In its roof chamber[s ...] in it stand eternal curses and the poison of snakes [...] viper. In it fly the flame[s of] death, in its entrance trea[d]s [sheol, and in its ends ... lies da]rkness. Its [f]oundation is the flames of sulphur, and its base is fi[re ...] its thresholds are ... of plague/affliction, and its lintels are the reproach of shame. Its bolts are fasts of the pit[...] All those who enter shall not return, and they shall not attain the paths of life." *Turning Proverbs*, 58.

and 525 takes place along lines already discernible in non-Qumran literature. This is particularly important in the case of Wisdom, whose separate identity is lost in the growing emphasis on Torah. If she ever was a separate female divine figure, as can be argued from Proverbs 1–9, I Enoch 42 and the Wisdom of Solomon, she is no longer in Ben Sira, Baruch, and 4Q525. Equally important, this is not a sectarian phenomenon, but occurs broadly in Second Temple literature. This would lead to the conclusion that these texts are not "sectarian," but are part of the general theological trends of Second Temple Judaism, within which we continually find the elevation of Torah.[27] This trend continues to develop until it becomes "normative" in Judaism.

As for Dame Folly, she undergoes a major change, from human figure (Proverbs 1–9), to semi-divine being (1 Enoch 42), to chthonic night demon (4Q184), but in all cases her portrayal continues an unfortunate emphasis on women's sexuality as sinful. This latter development takes exceptionally strong root in Christianity, with consequences felt until the present day. Thus, we again see texts from Qumran not as isolated or unique, but as part of the general mix that we call Judaism in the Hellenistic and Roman periods.

---

27. Thomas Tobin had already reached the conclusion, on other grounds, that 4Q185 was not a sectarian text. See Tobin, "4Q185," 148–52. Puech likewise argues that 4Q525 is not a Qumran composition ("The Collection," 364). However, de Roo makes a case that 4Q525 was composed at Qumran. While the parallels she finds between 4Q525 and the so-called "sectarian" literature are provocative (see especially the parallel she draws between 4, 12, "the skillful dig her paths" and CD 6:25), it could be argued that 4Q525 affected the texts that she cites, rather than vice-versa (if Puech's paleographic date is accepted, this must be the case). There is, of course a difference between labeling a composition "sectarian," and arguing that it was composed at Qumran. A sectarian composition could have been composed anywhere, while it is difficult to determine if any text was actually composed at Qumran (as opposed to being copied). For an argument that at least some of the excerpted texts were composed at Qumran, see Crawford, "Excerpted Manuscripts," 271–73.

10

The Meaning of the Phrase עיר המקדש in the Temple Scroll

A MINOR POINT OF contention in the interpretation of the Temple Scroll has been the meaning of the phrase עיר המקדש found in the laws concerning the purity of the ideal sanctuary envisioned by the Temple Scroll. This phrase is not a biblical phrase; therefore, we cannot fall back on a biblical meaning to help us determine its significance. The problem is compounded by the fact that the Temple Scroll uses a variety of terms to refer to the Temple building itself, the various buildings and courts which surround it, and the wider area around it; these terms overlap and a clear distinction in terminology is not discernible. The terms include היכל, העיר, בית, עירי, המקדש, מקדשי, הקודש, and the phrase presently under consideration, עיר המקדש.

The phrase עיר המקדש occurs four times in the Temple Scroll (11Q19 45:11–12, 16–17; 47:9, 13), each time in the context of maintaining the purity of the Temple complex envisioned by the Scroll. All of these occurrences come from the collection of purity laws, which the redactor of the Temple Scroll has woven into the end of the Temple Source.[1] Col. 45:15–17, which outlines the procedure for purification of a man suffering from a flux, reads אחר יבוא אל עיר המקדש ("afterwards he may enter into the city of the sanctuary"). Col. 47:9–13, a section interdicting the use of vessels not

---

1. The argument that there are sources behind the composition of the Temple Scroll was first proposed by Wilson and Wills, "Literary Sources."

made from the skins of animals slaughtered in the Temple, has two occurrences of the phrase: אל עיר מקדשי לא יבואו ("to the city of my sactuary there shall not enter . . .") and וכול אוכלמה לעיר מקדשי ("and all their food to the city of my sanctuary . . .").

Finally, the phrase appears in a context which has stirred the most controversy: 45:11–12, which reads ואיש כיא ישכב עם אשתו שכבת זרע לוא יבוא אל כול עיר המקדש אשר אשכין שמי בה שלושת ימים ("and a man who lies with his wife for sexual intercourse shall not enter any of the city of the sanctuary where I have set my name for three days . . ."). This ruling is paralleled by a similar statute in the Damascus Document (CD 12:1–2; 4QD^f 5 i 17–18): אל ישכב איש עם אשה בעיר המקדש לטמא את עיר המקדש ("no man shall lie with a woman in the city of the sanctuary to pollute the city of the sanctuary"). It is evident that the subject of the two rulings is similar. In the Temple Scroll, any man who has intercourse is prohibited from entering עיר המקדש for three days, while the Damascus Document prohibits sexual intercourse בעיר המקדש. The reason for the two rulings is the same: seminal emission conveys ritual impurity (Lev 15:16–18).[2]

The question before us is the exact meaning of the phrase עיר המקדש. In the material surrounding the occurences of this phrase in cols. 45–47, we find the following terms: המקדש (46:10; 47:12, 17; 11QT^b 7:11–12); הקודש (45:8, 10); מקדשי (45:10; 46:2, 3, 8, 9, 11; 47:3–4, 11, 13, 16, 18); העיר (45:13, 17–18; 46:10, 13, 14, 16, 17; 47:3, 10) and עירי (46:15, 18; 11QT^c 3 2). Where the terms המקדש and עיר occur separately, they seem to carry their usual biblical meanings: המקדש means the sanctuary, that is the actual tabernacle or temple plus its surrounding installations (e.g., Exod 25:8; Lev 16:33; 1 Chr 22:19; Isa 63:18), while עיר is a city, i.e., a large, often fortified multi-family abode for humans. Several rulings in this section of the Temple Scroll make a clear distinction between the מקדש and the עיר: 46:9–10 declares, "And you will make a fosse around the מקדש a distance of one hundred cubits, which will separate the holy מקדש from the עיר." 47:3–4 proclaims "and the עיר which I will consecrate to set my name and my מקדש within it shall be holy and pure . . ." 47:10–11 reads, "and you will not defile the עיר in which I am setting my name and my מקדש." And in 47:17–18 we find "and you will not defile my מקדש and my עיר . . ." If this distinction is carried through to the construct phrase עיר המקדש, the plain

---

2. The ruling in the Damascus Document does not help in determining the meaning of the phrase עיר המקדש, since it is not contextualized. Hempel suggests that "CD 12, 1b–2a constitutes an interpolation in the Laws of D which seems to have originated from the same milieu as 11QT^a 45–47." Hempel, *Laws*, 156.

The Meaning of the Phrase עיר המקדש in the Temple Scroll

meaning would seem to be the עיר in which is the מקדש.[3] However, this understanding of the phrase has created certain problems for some scholars. It is not difficult to accept that a man suffering from flux would be excluded from the city; it may be inconvenient, but it would be possible. Likewise, while the prohibition on bringing the skins of animals not slaughtered in the temple into the city of the sanctuary would cause a certain amount of inconvenience and economic loss, it would not be impossible. If, however, the rulings of the Temple Scroll and the Damascus Document concerning sexual intercourse are read as complements to each other,[4] then sexual intercourse is prohibited in the city of the sanctuary, and anyone rendered impure as a result of sexual intercourse is banned from the city of the sanctuary for three days.[5] This ruling would seem to make it impossible to have normal, full-time residential family life in the city, and so commentators have taken various positions on the controversy, as we see when we turn to the history of scholarship.

History of Scholarship

Scholarship on this question actually begins before the publication of the Temple Scroll, in comments on the similar passage in the Damascus Document. Ginzberg, in 1922, noted that המקדש must refer to the temple in Jerusalem, and that עיר המקדש can mean "no other place than Jerusalem." He goes on to say that "conceivably the rigorousness of our author is dictated by a policy of making a sojourn of some time in Jerusalem very difficult for adherents of the sect..." However, he seems to reject the understanding of the phrase as coextensive with Jerusalem in favor of understanding it to correspond to the biblical עיר דוד ("the city of David," e.g., 2 Sam 5:7, 9).

---

3. Milgrom, "City of the Temple," 126.

4. It must first be accepted that the two documents stem at least from the same circles of halakhic interpretation, for which there is evidence on several counts. See Crawford, *Temple Scroll,* 80–82.

5. This three-day period of impurity, rather than the one-day period prescribed by Lev 15:8, comes from an exegesis of Exod 19:10–15, in which Moses commands the people to prepare themselves for the theophany of God on Mount Sinai. They are to purify themselves for *three* days; this purification includes abstention from sexual intercourse. The Temple Scroll understands the city of the sanctuary to be the equivalent of Mount Sinai, since God's presence resides in both.

Part 2: Questions Concerning Women

Thus, Ginzberg concludes that עיר המקדש refers to a specific area within Jerusalem, that is, the Temple Mount.[6]

Rabin, on the other hand, seems to understand the prohibition to refer to the entire city of Jerusalem. He notes that according to Josephus (*War* 5.227), a man with a flux is excluded "from the whole city" (ἡ πόλις ὅλη), and concludes concerning the D passage, "probably a 'fence' regulation to prevent defilement of the Temple, meant, like the similar Islamic law, to apply only to pilgrims..."[7] We will return to Rabin's intriguing comment below.

Yadin, the editor of 11QTemple[a], commented extensively on the use of this phrase. He noted the clear differentiation that existed between the terms מקדש and עיר and concluded that this meant that the Scroll understood the phrase עיר המקדש to mean "a city, inside of which is a sanctuary."[8] He observed that several categories of impure persons or things are banned from entering the sanctuary or the city; those banned from the sanctuary are men who have had a nocturnal emission (45:7–10), while those banned from the city are the blind (45:12–14), the man suffering from flux (45:15–17), a person with corpse impurity (45:17), lepers and other diseased persons (45:17–18), and the skins of animals not properly slaughtered in the temple (47:7–14). Since, according to Yadin, the Temple Scroll is extending the laws of purity to apply not only to the contemporary equivalent of the camp, but to other cities as well, the purity regulations become even more stringent when applied to the sanctuary and its city. Therefore, Yadin concludes "the absolute application of all the laws of purity to the Temple city led the members of the sect to forbid sexual intercourse therein, and from that to the banning of women from taking up permanent residence there was a small step. It seems that it was this edict that eventually developed into the 'abstention' of the Essenes and their celibacy."[9] And again, "Hence, according to the laws of the sect, all males residing in the Temple city must abstain from having sexual relations therein. Therefore, this ban is tantamount to ordaining complete celibacy for them."[10] In further support of his argument, Yadin notes that the Temple Scroll sets aside quarantine

---

6. Ginzberg, *An Unknown*, 73–74.

7. Rabin, *Zadokite*, 59.

8. Yadin, *Temple Scroll*, 1.280.

9. Yadin, *Temple Scroll*, 1.281. Yadin identifies the composer/redactor of the Temple Scroll with the Essenes.

10. Yadin, *Temple Scroll*, 1.288.

The Meaning of the Phrase עיר המקדש in the Temple Scroll

areas for menstruating and post-partum women in other cities in the land (49:16–17), but not for the city of the sanctuary. The Scroll does, however, mandate quarantine areas outside the holy city for those impure by reason of skin disease, flux, or noctural emission (46:17–18). Thus, he concludes "the doctrine of the sect deemed it necessary to ban women from permanent residence in the Temple city."[11]

Yadin's conclusions have been criticized on several points. Levine took issue both with Yadin's understanding of the phrase and his conclusion concerning the presence of women in the city of the sanctuary. Levine suggested that עיר המקדש referred only to the temple complex, and not to the entire city of Jerusalem, arguing that the term עיר can mean a precinct or quarter of the city, as in the phrases עיר דויד (2 Chr 8:11) and עיר בית הבעל (2 Kgs 10:25).[12] Further, Levine pointed out that the law does not prohibit the presence of women in the עיר המקדש (*contra* Yadin), but only sexual intercourse.[13] Therefore, Levine understood the ruling in 45:11–12 to prohibit sexual intercourse in the temple compound itself, but not in other parts of the city.

Schiffman has followed Levine's line of argument, maintaining that the עיר המקדש must refer only to the (vastly exapnded) temple compound, since "it is difficult to imagine that the entire city of Jerusalem was to be free of women and celibate."[14] He also makes the obvious point that ritually pure women were permitted into the outer court of the temple, and so were not permanently banned.[15]

Japhet, arguing from a different perspective, points out that Yadin's conclusions regarding the presence or absence of women in the temple city are conjectural and methodologically flawed. First, the prohibition of sexual intercourse in the "city of the sanctuary" would only affect married women, leaving whole classes of women (young girls, widows, divorced women) unaffected. Second, she notes that Yadin does not argue that married men were permanently banned from the temple city because of the ban on sexual intercourse.[16] Japhet does note the lack of quarantine areas for menstruating and postpartum women in column 46; however, she argues

11. Yadin, *Temple Scroll*, 1.289.
12. Levine, "Temple Scroll," 14, 16.
13. Levine, "Temple Scroll," 14.
14. Schiffman, "Exclusion," 313.
15. Schiffman, "Laws," 211.
16. Japhet, "Prohibition," 270–72.

that the Scroll means to subsume Jerusalem under the rubric "any city" in column 48, where quarantine areas for those categories of women are prescribed.[17] Thus, according to Japhet, all categories of women could live in the temple city; they were simply barred from the temple compound itself during times of impurity.

Milgrom, on the contrary, has followed Yadin's line of reasoning on the meaning of עיר המקדש. He argues that the Scroll explicitly states that Jerusalem is different from any other city ("and you shall not purify a city among your cities like my city," 47:14–15). Since the Scroll's aim is to strengthen the purity regulations so as to protect the holiness of the temple city, all residents who incur any impurity are banished to special areas outside the city. Since female impurities are not included in these quarantine areas, Milgrom concludes that women were prohibited from residing in the temple city.[18]

On the question of why a man who has had a nocturnal emission is barred only from the מקדש for three days, while anyone who has had sexual intercourse is barred from עיר המקדש for three days, Milgrom suggests that the reason for the difference can be explained geographically. Since nocturnal emission is involuntary, it can take place accidentally even within the temple compound, and the man affected must then go out from there. Sexual intercourse is a voluntary act; therefore, the Scroll can regulate that it must take place outside the city, and the persons affected cannot come in there for three days. They are impurities of the same degree, however, and the purification period is the same.[19]

Finally, Milgrom argues on the basis of grammar that the construct phrase עיר המקדש must mean the city that contains the sanctuary. He notes that nowhere in biblical or rabbinic literature is the sacred compound called עיר; therefore, he opts for the plain meaning of the text.[20]

The publication of 4QMMT brought new evidence into the debate. Although the phrase עיר המקדש does not occur in MMT, it does give a very clear definition of its understanding of the words המקדש and מחנה ("camp") in a discussion concerning the proper place for slaughter (4QMMT B 29–33; see Lev 17). It reads "And we are of the opinion that the sanctuary [is the tent of meeting and Je]rusale[m] is the camp, and outside the camp [is

---

17. Japhet, "Prohibition," 271.
18. Milgrom, "Studies," 513, 517.
19. Milgrom, "'Sabbath,'" 27.
20. Milgrom, "City of the Temple," 126.

outside Jerusalem . . ."[21] The definition concerns contemporary equivalents to the tabernacle and the camp in the wilderness. MMT equates the מקדש with the temple and the מחנה with Jerusalem. Further, later in the passage Jerusalem is identified as "the camp of holiness," "the chief of camps," and "the place which he has chosen from all the tribes of Israel" (4QMMT B 59–62). Thus, according to MMT, all of Jerusalem, not just part of it, is equivalent to the camp in the wilderness, and the regulations for the camp apply to all of Jerusalem.[22] Since there are important connections between the Temple Scroll and MMT on other points,[23] it can be argued that the Temple Scroll understands the meaning of עיר in the same way that MMT understands the meaning of מחנה, and that their use of מקדש is the same. However, since the language is different, and MMT specifically mentions Jerusalem while the Temple Scroll does not, the evidence of MMT is merely suggestive and not conclusive.

It seems to me that neither side has yet won the debate. The plain meaning of the phrase עיר המקדש and the grammatical arguments support Yadin and Milgrom, while Levine and Schiffman have biblical and historical precedent on their side when they argue that the Scroll could not possibly imagine a residential city without the presence of women. However, as Japhet has pointed out, Yadin's conclusions are logically flawed; the Scroll does not ban women from the temple city—on the contrary, it allows ritually pure women in the outer court of the temple. Is there a solution to this dilemma?

Proposed Solution

I would like to propose a solution that was first obliquely suggested by Rabin in his commentary on the Damascus Document. I believe that the Temple Scroll envisions the city that contains the temple compound not as an ordinary residential city, but as a sacred city that exists only to support the temple and its rites. The Scroll articulates the special status of the temple city in 47:14–15: "and you shall not purify a city from among your cities like my city . . ." If the temple city has a special, sacred status over against other

---

21. Qimron and Strugnell, DJD 10:144.

22. Isa 52:1 is relevant to this discussion as well. In Deutero-Isaiah's vision of the reconstituted Jerusalem, called the עיר הקדש, the "uncircumcised and unclean" are barred from the city. This verse states in microcosm the macrocosmic vision of the Temple Scroll.

23. Schiffman, "Miqṣat Ma'ase Ha-Torah," 435–57.

Part 2: Questions Concerning Women

cities, and a particular role as a pilgrimage city, then special regulations can be ordained for it, including a ban on sexual intercourse within the city. Those couples on pilgrimage to the holy city would be expected to refrain from sexual intercourse while there and for three days beforehand, while priests would likewise refrain during their period of service. A comparison with pilgrimage rites in other cultures shows that such a ban is not unusual. First, let us look at the internal evidence of the Scroll for our contention that the temple city is envisioned as a pilgrimage city.

The Temple Scroll does not contain architectural instructions for a residential area around the Temple compound. After the fosse, the next thing that is called for is the construction of latrines 3000 cubits outside the city. Next, the Scroll calls for the establishment of quarantine areas to the east of the city. There are no mandates concerning houses, streets, or any structures between the fosse surrounding the temple compound and the latrines 3000 cubits outside. Further, there is no provision made for the king's residence, although the Scroll clearly envisions the existence of a king in its ideal vision (columns 57–59).[24] These are strange omissions if the temple city were envisioned as a residential city, as it is in the ideal temple plans of Ezekiel and the New Jerusalem scroll, and as Jerusalem was in the historical reality of the First and Second Temples. It does not appear as if the Scroll expects permanent residences (i.e., buildings) around the temple compound. Also, the Scroll does not legislate the establishment of a cemetery for the temple city, although it is very clear about this requirement for the cities of the land (48:13–14). If the temple city was expected to be an ordinary residential city, in which people lived and died, surely a place for a cemetery would be a necessity.

Further, the quarantine areas set aside outside the temple city for those who contract ritual impurity are only for those who have had a nocturnal emission, those afflicted with skin disease, and those experiencing a discharge. Glaringly absent are quarantine areas for menstruating and postpartum women, although these categories are included for ordinary cities (49:16–17). I do not agree with Japhet's argument that the temple city is simply subsumed under the category "all cities" in regard to women with *niddah* impurity; the composer/redactor is too painstaking to ignore such an important category in regard to the temple city. Finally, although there is

---

24. Peters notes that royal and priestly powers do not easily coexist in the same city, citing as examples Jerusalem, which was dominated by the king during the period of the monarchy, and then by priests (including the Hasmonean priest-kings) in the post-exilic period, and Mecca, which was never a royal residence. *Jerusalem and Mecca*, 23.

The Meaning of the Phrase עיר המקדש in the Temple Scroll

extensive legislation for the proper purification procedures if someone dies בעריכמה ("in your cities," 49:15–21),[25] there is no mention of this in relation to the temple city. Since the Scroll's predilection is for increasing the stringency of the purity regulations as we move inward toward the temple, surely the regulations concerning the impurity of death would be more detailed for the temple city than for other cities. The Scroll's silence on the subject leads me to suspect that the Scroll did not envision death occurring in the holy city (however unrealistic this may seem to be).

Finally, the legislation concerning the skins of animals emphasizes the special nature of the temple city. Since only vessels made from the skins of animals properly slaughtered in the temple could be brought into עיר מקדשי, people coming to the temple on pilgrimage would have had to exchange their ordinary vessels for these special vessels. This would necessitate a certain amount of economic planning.

All of this internal evidence corroborates the thesis that the Temple Scroll does not envision the temple city as an ordinary residential city, but as a special city to which worshippers would go on pilgrimage and then return to their own cities. This special status of the temple city would mean that only those people already ritually pure would go up to עיר המקדש; those who were ritually impure or could anticipate becoming ritually impure (e.g., through menstruation) would stay home.[26] This would include those with corpse impurity and menstruating and postpartum women; hence no quarantine areas were set aside for them. However, for those who became ritually impure after coming to the temple city special procedures and quarantine areas were necessary. Thus, if a man had an involuntary nocturnal emission, he would have to leave the sacred compound and go to the special quarantine area set aside for him outside the city.

Given this entire argument, the meaning of the phrase עיר המקדש and the reason that those impure by reason of sexual intercourse were banned from עיר המקדש becomes clear. The phrase עיר המקדש can be understood in its plain meaning, the city that contains the sanctuary. Those who had had sexual intercourse were banned from the entire city, and that ban did have the effect of interdicting sexual intercourse within the entire city, as the parallel passage in the Damascus Document demonstrates. However,

---

25. The use of בעריכמה here is parallel to the use of עריכמה in 47:15, where it is contrasted with עירי.

26. There is biblical precedent for this idea; after Samuel is born, Hannah does not go up to Shiloh for the yearly sacrifice (1 Sam 1:21–22).

since the holy city was a pilgrimage city, i.e., a city of temporary short-term residence (e.g., the length of a festival), a couple would abstain from sexual relations while on pilgrimage and then resume normal relations upon returning home. Thus, women who were ritually pure were allowed into עיר המקדש, and indeed into the outer court of the temple compound itself.

Cross-Cultural Comparisons

It may be argued that this view of the temple city as only a pilgrimage city and not a residential city is unprecedented in Jewish literature. This is true, but a comparison with other cultures' pilgrimage rites and sacred compounds shows that the kind of legislation found in the Temple Scroll is present in other cultures as well and therefore may be part of a general trend concerning purity and impurity and sacred places.

Dillon, in discussing pilgrims and pilgrimages in ancient Greece, notes the presence of special regulations concerning those participating in the pilgrimage and the site of the pilgrimage itself. He states, "some of these regulations dealt with the need for ritual purity while participating in sacred rites, and these often concerned women, who from the male perspective were a source of impurity because of sexual activity and birth."[27] While these regulations varied from sanctuary to sanctuary and rite to rite, there were often restrictions on diet, clothing, ornaments, sexual behavior, and the avoidance of the impurity of death. There were also rules designed to limit access to the sacred site.[28] A few examples will illustrate the point.

The sacred shrines of Greece such as Olympia and Epidauros had very few building accommodations for pilgrims; most pilgrims pitched tents or used other temporary measures. At the shrine of Isis at Tithorea, the holiest Greek shrine to the Egyptian goddess, no one was allowed to dwell in the vicinity of the shrine.[29]

Death was a source of ritual impurity for the Greeks. At Delos, no one was allowed to be buried on the island: "those who were dying were taken to the nearby island of Rheneia, as were women in childbirth." Dillon notes

---

27. Dillon, *Pilgrims*, xvii.

28. Dillon, *Pilgrims*, 202. Interestingly, none of the regulations have to do with menstruation. However, by the second century BCE inscriptions prohibiting menstruants from sacred sites do appear in the Greek world. It is possible that this is an eastern influence on the Greek world. See Branham, "Blood in Flux," 63.

29. Dillon, *Pilgrims*, 207, 211.

that the restriction on dying was primarily meant for local inhabitants, such as the staff at the shrine.[30] Epidauros, the great healing sanctuary, had no provision for a cemetery. Evidently the dead were removed and buried elsewhere.

The rules of sexual intercourse chiefly concern women by removing them from the sacred site. For example, at Olympia women were barred from the sacred games, although virgins (prepubescent girls) were allowed. Sometimes, however, the rule applied equally to men and women. For example, abstinence from sexual intercourse was called for at the shrine of Oropos in Pergamon, although both men and women were allowed in.[31]

In Islam, chronologically later than Second Temple Judaism but on the same family tree, various regulations exist to maintain purity during the *hajj*, the great pilgrimage to Mecca. Pilgrims to Mecca are considered to be in *ihram*, a state of temporary consecration for one performing the *hajj*. Mecca is surrounded by a special zone within which a pilgrim is expected to maintain a higher degree of purity, and to guard against ritual defilement.[32] A pilgrim wears a special garment, and sexual intercourse is prohibited for the duration of the *hajj*. Access to the pilgrimage sites of Mecca and Medina are limited to Muslims; non-Muslims risk death for violating the prohibition. Hinduism likewise calls for asceticism while on pilgrimage; these ascetic practices (called *niyamas*) include special food laws and abstinence from sexual intercourse.[33]

Conclusion

On internal grounds alone, it seems reasonable to conclude that the Temple Scroll envisages the city in which the ideal temple is located not as an ordinary residential city, but as a city of particular special status, for which special rules of purity apply. Thus, the ritually impure would be barred from the city, and special measures would be taken to safeguard the city's purity.[34]

30. Dillon, *Pilgrims*, 219.
31. Dillon, *Pilgrims*, 187, 194.
32. Peters, *Jerusalem and Mecca*, 68.
33. Haberman, *Journey*, 156.
34. Magness has suggested that the architecture of the settlement at Qumran indicates that the owners of the scrolls found in the surrounding caves organized their space into sacred (pure) and non-sacred (impure) zones, using many of the same criteria as the Temple Scroll. Magness, "Communal Meals," 107–12.

This would have the effect of making Jerusalem indeed the "city of the sanctuary," for it would be only the sanctuary and its activities that would be the purpose of Jerusalem's existence. It would, in effect, become a pilgrimage city. This concept of the temple city, like other concepts concerning the temple's architecture and its cultic practice, is unlike that found elsewhere in Second Temple Judaism, and further confirms the unique nature of the Qumran library.

Bibliography

Adler, Yonatan. "The Distribution of Tefillin Finds among the Judean Desert Caves." In *The Caves of Qumran: Proceedings of the International Conference, Lugano 2014*, edited by Marcello Fidanzio, 161–73. STDJ 118. Leiden: Brill, 2017.

———. *The Origins of Judaism: An Archaeological-Historical Reappraisal*. Anchor Yale Bible Reference Library. New Haven: Yale University Press, 2022.

Alexander, Philip S., and Geza Vermeš. *Qumran Cave 4: XIX: Serekh Ha-Yaḥad and Two Related Texts*. DJD 26. Oxford: Clarendon, 1998.

Allegro, John M. *Qumran Cave 4.1 (4Q158–4Q186)*. DJD 5. Oxford: Clarendon, 1968.

———. "'The Wiles of the Wicked Woman' A Sapiential Work from Qumran's Fourth Cave." *PEQ* 96 (1964) 53–55.

Ariel, Donald T. "Coins from the Renewed Excavations at Qumran." In *Back to Qumran: Final Report (1993–2004)*, edited by Yitzhak Magen and Yuval Peleg, 403–30. JSP 18. Jerusalem: Israel Antiquities Authority, 2018.

Baillet, Maurice. *Qumrân Grotte 4 III (4Q482–4Q520)*. DJD 7. Oxford: Clarendon, 1982.

———. "Textes des Grottes 2Q, 3Q, 6Q, 7Q à 10Q." In *Les "petites grottes" de Qumran: Exploration de la falaise, les grottes 2Q, 3Q, 5Q, 7Q à 10Q, le rouleau de cuivre*, edited by M. Baillet et al., 45–197. DJD 3. Oxford: Clarendon, 1962.

Bar-Adon, Pessach. "Another Settlement of the Judean Desert Sect at 'En el-Ghuweir on the Shores of the Dead Sea." *BASOR* 227 (1977) 1–80.

Bar-Nathan, Rachel. *Masada VII, The Yigael Yadin Excavations 1963–1965, Final Reports: The Pottery of Masada*. Jerusalem: Israel Exploration Society and the Hebrew University of Jerusalem, 2006.

———. "Qumran and the Hasmonaean and Herodian Winter Palaces of Jericho: The Implication of the Pottery Finds for the Interpretation of the Settlement at Qumran." In *Qumran, the Site of the Dead Sea Scrolls: Archaeological Interpretations and Debates; Proceedings of a Conference Held at Brown University, November 17–19, 2002*, edited by Katharina Galor et al., 263–80. STDJ 57. Leiden: Brill, 2006.

Barag, Dan. "'Ein Gedi." In *EDSS* 1:238–40.

Barthélemy, Dominique. "Régle de la Congrégation." In *Qumran Cave I*, edited by Dominique Barthélemy and J. T. Milik, 108–18. DJD 1. Oxford: Clarendon, 1955.

Baumgarten, Joseph M. "4Q502, Marriage or Golden Age Ritual?" *JJS* 34 (1983) 125–35. Reprinted in *Studies in Qumran Law and Thought*, 97–108. STDJ 138. Leiden: Brill, 2022. Pages are cited from this edition.

Bibliography

———. "The Laws of the Damascus Document in Current Research." In *The Damascus Document Reconsidered*, edited by Magen Broshi, 51–62. Jerusalem: Israel Exploration Society and Shrine of the Book, 1992.

———. "On the Nature of the Seductress in 4Q184." *RevQ* 15 (1991) 133–43.

———. "On the Testimony of Women in 1QSa." *JBL* 76 (1957) 266–69.

———. *Qumran Cave 4 XIII: The Damascus Document (4Q266–73)*. DJD 18. Oxford: Clarendon, 1996. Cited as DJD 18.

———. "The Qumran-Essene Restraints on Marriage." In *Archaeology and History in the Dead Sea Scrolls*, edited by Lawrence H. Schiffman, 13–24. Sheffield: Sheffield Academic Press, 1990.

Beall, Todd. *Josephus' Description of the Essenes Illustrated by the Dead Sea Scrolls*. Society for New Testament Studies Monograph Series 58. Cambridge: Cambridge University Press, 1988.

Bélis, Mireille. "The Production of Indigo Dye in the Installations of Ain Feshkha." In *Qumran, the Site of the Dead Sea Scrolls: Archaeological Interpretations and Debates; Proceedings of a Conference Held at Brown University, November 17–19, 2002*, edited by Katharina Galor et al., 253–61. STDJ 57. Leiden: Brill, 2006.

———. "The Unpublished Textiles from the Qumran Caves." In *The Caves of Qumran: Proceedings of the International Conference, Lugano 2014*, edited by Marcello Fidanzio, 123–36. STDJ 118. Leiden: Brill, 2017.

———. "Des textiles, catalogues et commentaries." In *Khirbet Qumrân et 'Aïn Feshkha II: Études d'anthropologie, de physique et de chimie*, edited by Jean-Baptiste Humbert and Jan Gunneweg, 207–76. NTOASA 3. Göttingen: Vandenhoeck & Ruprecht, 2003.

Ben-Dov, Jonathan. "Demonic Deuteronomy? The Ending of Deuteronomy and the Sectarian Debate." In *The Textual History of the Bible from the Dead Sea Scrolls to the Biblical Manuscripts of the Vienna Papyrus Collection*, edited by Ruth A. Clements et al., 253–84. STDJ 137. Leiden: Brill, 2023.

Berlin, Andrea. "Jewish Life Before the Revolt: The Archaeological Evidence." *JSJ* 28 (1997) 417–70.

Bernstein, Moshe J. "Interpretation of Scriptures." In *EDSS* 1:376–83.

———. "Re-Arrangement, Anticipation and Harmonization as Exegetical Features in the Genesis Apocryphon." *DSD* 3 (1996) 37–57.

Branham, Joan R. "Blood in Flux, Sanctity at Issue." *Res* 31 (1997) 53–70.

Brin, Gershon. *The Concept of Time in the Bible and the Dead Sea Scrolls*. STDJ 39. Leiden: Brill, 2001.

Brooke, George J. "4QCommentary on Genesis C." In *Qumran Cave 4, XVII, Parabiblical Texts, Part 3*, edited by George J. Brooke et al., 217–32. DJD 22. Oxford: Clarendon Press, 1996.

———. "Between Qumran and Corinth: Embroidered Allusions to Women's Authority." In *The Dead Sea Scrolls as Background to Postbiblical Judaism and Early Christianity*, edited by James R. Davila, 157–76. STDJ 46. Leiden: Brill, 2003.

———. "A Long-Lost Song of Miriam." *BAR* 20 (1994) 62–65.

———. "The Wisdom of Matthew's Beatitudes (4QBeat and Mt. 5:3–12)." *Scripture Bulletin* 19 (1989) 35–41.

Brooten, Bernadette. "Early Christian Women and Their Cultural Context: Issues of Method in Historical Reconstruction." In *Feminist Perspectives on Biblical Scholarship*, edited by Adele Yarbro Collins, 65–92. Biblical Scholarship in North America 10. Chico, CA: Scholars, 1985.

Bibliography

———. *Women Leaders in the Ancient Synagogue: Inscriptional Evidence and Background Issues.* Brown Judaic Studies 36. Chico, CA: Scholars, 1982.

Broshi, Magen. "Anti-Qumranic Polemics in the Talmud." In *The Madrid Qumran Congress: Proceedings of the International Congress on the Dead Sea Scrolls, Madrid, 18–21 March 1991*, edited by J. Trebolle Barrera and L. Vegas Montaner, 589–600. Vol. 2. STDJ 11. Leiden: Brill, 1992.

———. "Qumran Archaeology." In *EDSS* 1:733–39.

———. "Was Qumran a Crossroads?" *RevQ* 19 (1999) 273–76.

Broshi, Magen, and Hanan Eshel. "Residential Caves at Qumran." *DSD* 6 (1999) 328–48.

———. "Three Seasons of Excavations at Qumran." *Journal of Roman Archaeology* 17 (2004) 321–32.

———. "Was There Agriculture at Qumran?" In *Qumran, the Site of the Dead Sea Scrolls: Archaeological Interpretations and Debates; Proceedings of a Conference Held at Brown University, November 17–19, 2002*, edited by Katharina Galor et al., 249–52. STDJ 57. Leiden: Brill, 2006.

Burchard, C. "Joseph and Aseneth." In *The Old Testament Pseudepigrapha.* Edited by James H. Charlesworth, vol. 2, 177–248. Garden City, NY: Doubleday, 1985.

Camp, Claudia. "What's So Strange about the Strange Woman." In *The Bible and the Politics of Exegesis: Essays in Honor of Norman K. Gottwald on his Sixty-Fifth Birthday*, edited by David Jobling et al., 17–32. Cleveland: Pilgrim, 1991.

Caquot, Andre. "Les testaments qoumrâniens des pères du sacerdoce." *Revue d'histoire et de philosophie religieuses* 78 (1998) 3–26.

Cardman, Francine. "Women, Ministry, and Church Order in Early Christianity." In *Women and Christian Origins*, edited by Ross Shepard Kraemer and Mary Rose D'Angelo, 300–329. New York: Oxford University Press, 1999.

Carswell, J. "Appendix I: Fastenings on the Qumran Manuscripts." In *Qumrân Grotte 4: II*, edited by Roland de Vaux and J. T. Milik, 23–28. DJD 6. Oxford: Clarendon, 1977.

Clark Wire, Antoinette. *The Corinthian Women Prophets.* Minneapolis: Fortress, 1990. Reprint, Eugene, OR: Wipf & Stock, 2003.

Collins, John J. *Beyond the Qumran Community: The Sectarian Movement of the Dead Sea Scrolls.* Grand Rapids: Eerdmans, 2010.

Cotton, Hannah. "4QAccount gr." In *Qumran Cave 4, XXVI*, edited by Stephen J. Pfann et al., 294–95. DJD 36. Oxford: Clarendon, 2000.

Crawford, Sidnie White. "Economic Activity, Trade, and Manufacture at Qumran, with a Special Look at the Inscriptions and Documentary Texts." In *Pushing Sacred Boundaries in Early Judaism and the Ancient Mediterranean: Essays in Honour of Jodi Magness*, edited by Dennis Mizzi et al., 326–48. JSJSup 208. Leiden: Brill, 2023.

———. "The Excerpted Manuscripts from Qumran, with Special Attention to 4QReworked Pentateuch D and 4QReworked Pentateuch E." In *The Text of the Pentateuch: Textual Criticism and the Dead Sea Scrolls*, 261–78. BZAW 493. Berlin: de Gruyter, 2022.

———. "The Meaning of the Phrase עיר המקדש in the Temple Scroll." *DSD* 8 (2001) 1–13.

———. "Qumran: Caves, Scrolls and Buildings." In *A Teacher for All Generations: Essays in Honor of James C. VanderKam*, edited by Eric Mason et al., vol. 1, 253–74. JSJSup 153. Leiden: Brill, 2012.

———. "The Qumran Collection as a Scribal Library." In *The Dead Sea Scrolls at Qumran and the Concept of a Library*, edited by Sidnie White Crawford and Cecilia Wassén, 109–31. STDJ 116. Leiden: Brill, 2016.

Bibliography

———. *Rewriting Scripture in Second Temple Times*. Grand Rapids: Eerdmans, 2008.
———. *Scribes and Scrolls at Qumran*. Grand Rapids: Eerdmans, 2019.
———. "The Single-Copy Literary Manuscripts found in the Qumran Caves." Forthcoming.
———. *The Temple Scroll and Related Texts*. Companion to the Qumran Scrolls 2. Sheffield: Sheffield Academic, 2000.
———. *The Text of the Pentateuch: Textual Criticism and the Dead Sea Scrolls*. BZAW 493. Berlin: de Gruyter, 2022.
Cross, Frank Moore. *The Ancient Library of Qumran and Modern Biblical Studies*. Garden City: Doubleday, 1958. Cited as *Ancient Library*[1]. Rev. ed. Grand Rapids: Baker, 1961. Cited as *Ancient Library*[2]. 3rd ed. Sheffield: Sheffield Academic, 1995. Cited as *Ancient Library*[3].
———. "Reminiscences of the Early Days in the Discovery and Study of the Dead Sea Scrolls." In *The Dead Sea Scrolls Fifty Years after their Discovery, 1947–1997*, edited by Lawrence H. Schiffman et al., 932–43. Jerusalem: Israel Exploration Society, 2000.
Cross, Frank Moore, and Esther Eshel. "Ostraca from Khirbet Qumrân." *IEJ* 47 (1997) 17–28.
———. "Ostraca from Khirbet Qumran." DJD 36: 497–512.
Crowfoot, Grace M. "The Linen Textiles." DJD 1: 18–38.
Crown, Alan D., and Lena Cansdale. "Qumran—Was It an Essene Settlement?" *BAR* 20/5 (1994) 24–35, 73–74, 76–78.
Davies, Philip R., and Joan Taylor. "On the Testimony of Women in 1QSa." *DSD* 3 (1996) 223–35.
Davila, James R. *Liturgical Works*. Eerdmans Commentaries on the Dead Sea Scrolls. Grand Rapids: Eerdmans, 2000.
Dillon, Matthew. *Pilgrims and Pilgrimage in Ancient Greece*. London: Routledge, 1997.
Dimant, Devorah. "The Library of Qumran: Its Content and Character." In *The Dead Sea Scrolls Fifty Years after Their Discovery, 1947–1997*, edited by Lawrence H. Schiffman et al., 170–76. Jerusalem: Israel Exploration Society/Shrine of the Book Israel Museum, 2000.
———. "The Qumran Manuscripts: Contents and Significance." In *History, Ideology and Bible Interpretation in the Dead Sea Scrolls*, 27–56. FAT 90. Tübingen: Mohr Siebeck, 2014.
Donceel, Robert, and Pauline Donceel-Voûte. "The Archaeology of Khirbet Qumran." In *Methods of Investigations of the Dead Sea Scrolls and the Khirbet Qumran Site: Present Realities and Future Prospects*, edited by Michael O. Wise et al., 1–38. New York: New York Academy of Sciences, 1994.
Doudna, Gregory L. "Carbon-14 Dating." In *EDSS* 1:120–21.
———. "The Legacy of an Error in Archaeological Interpretation. The Dating of the Qumran Cave Scroll Deposits." In *Qumran, the Site of the Dead Sea Scrolls: Archaeological Interpretations and Debates; Proceedings of a Conference Held at Brown University, November 17–19, 2002*, edited by Katharina Galor et al., 146–56. STDJ 57. Leiden: Brill, 2006.
Dupont-Sommer, André. *The Essene Writings from Qumran*. Translated by Geza Vermeŝ. Gloucester: Peter Smith, 1973.
Eisen, Ute E. *Women Officeholders in Early Christianity: Epigraphical and Literary Studies*. Translated by Linda M. Maloney. Collegeville, MN: Liturgical, 2000.

Bibliography

Eisenman, Robert, and Michael O. Wise. *The Dead Sea Scrolls Uncovered*. New York: Penguin, 1992.

Elder, Linda B. "The Woman Question and Female Ascetics Among the Essenes." *BA* 57 (1994) 230–32.

Elgvin, Torleif. "4QText Concerning Rachel and Joseph." DJD 36: 456–63.

Elgvin, Torleif, et al., eds. *Gleanings from the Caves: Dead Sea Scrolls and Artefacts from the Schøyen Collection*. London: Bloomsbury T. & T. Clark, 2016.

Elwolde, J. F. "*rwqmh* in the *Damascus Document* and Ps 139:15." In *Diggers at the Well. Proceedings of a Third International Symposium on the Hebrew of the Dead Sea Scrolls and Ben Sira*, edited by T. Muraoka and J. F. Elwolde, 65–83. STDJ 36. Leiden: Brill, 2000.

Eshel, Esther. "4QRebukes Reported by the Overseer." DJD 36: 474–84.

Eshel, Hanan et al. "New Data on the Cemetery East of Khirbet Qumran." *DSD* 9 (2002) 135–54.

Farhi, Yoav. "The Numismatic Finds from the Qumran Plateau Excavations 2004–2006, and 2008 Seasons." *DSD* 17 (2010) 210–25.

Felder, Cain Hope. "Race, Racism, and the Biblical Narratives." In *Stony the Road We Trod: African American Biblical Interpretation*, edited by Cain Hope Felder, 145–64. 30th Anniversary exp. ed. Minneapolis: Fortress, 2021.

Feldman, Ariel. *Tefillin and Mezuzot from Qumran: New Readings and Interpretations*. BZAW 538. Berlin: de Gruyter, 2022.

Fidanzio, Marcello. "The Deposition of the Copper Scroll: New Archaeological Investigations." *EC* 13 (2022) 84–101.

———. "Searching for Cave 6Q." *RevQ* 30 (2018) 2–11.

Fidanzio, Marcello, and Jean-Baptiste Humbert. "Finds from the Qumran Caves: De Vaux's Inventory of the Excavations (1949–1956)." In *The Caves of Qumran: Proceedings of the International Conference, Lugano 2014*, edited by Marcello Fidanzio, 264–97. STDJ 118. Leiden: Brill, 2017.

Fields, Weston W. *The Dead Sea Scrolls: A Full History*. Vol. 1. Leiden: Brill, 2009.

Fitzmyer, Joseph A. "Genesis Apocryphon." In *EDSS* 1:302–4.

———. *The Genesis Apocryphon of Qumran Cave 1 (1Q20), A Commentary*. 3rd ed. Biblica et Orientalia 18/B. Rome: Pontifical Biblical Institute, 2004.

———. "Tobit." In *Qumran Cave 4, XIV, Parabiblical Texts, Part 2*, edited by Magen Broshi et al., 1–76. DJD 19. Oxford: Clarendon, 1995.

Fontaine, Carol R. "Proverbs." In *The Women's Bible Commentary*, edited by Carol Newsom and Sharon Ringe, 145–52. Louisville: Westminster John Knox, 1992.

Galor, Katharina, and Jürgen Zangenberg. "Qumran Archaeology in Search of a Consensus." In *Qumran, the Site of the Dead Sea Scrolls: Archaeological Interpretations and Debates; Proceedings of a Conference Held at Brown University, November 17–19, 2002*, edited by Katharina Galor et al., 1–9. STDJ 57. Leiden: Brill, 2006.

García Martínez, Florentino. *The Dead Sea Scrolls Translated*. Translated by W. G. E. Watson. Leiden: Brill, 1994.

García Martínez, Florentino, and Eibert Tigchelaar. *The Dead Sea Scrolls Study Edition*. 2 vols. Leiden: Brill, 1997.

Gevirtz, Marion. "Abram's Dream in the Genesis Apocryphon: Its Motifs and Their Function." *Maarav* 8 (1992) 229–43.

Ginzberg, Louis. *An Unknown Jewish Sect*. Rev. and translated. Moreshet Series 1. New York: Jewish Theological Seminary, 1976.

Bibliography

Goff, Matthew. "Wisdom." In *T & T Clark Companion to the Dead Sea Scrolls*, edited by George J. Brooke and Charlotte Hempel, 449–56. London: T. & T. Clark, 2019.

Golb, Norman. "Khirbet Qumran and the Manuscripts Finds of the Judaean Wilderness." In *Methods of Investigation of the Dead Sea Scrolls and the Khirbet Qumran Site: Present Realities and Future Prospects*, edited by Michael O. Wise et al., 51–72. New York: New York Academy of Sciences, 1994.

———. "Who Hid the Dead Sea Scrolls?" *BA* 48 (1985) 68–82.

———. *Who Wrote the Dead Sea Scrolls? The Search for the Secret of Qumran*. New York: Scribner, 1995.

Greenfield, Jonas, et al. *The Aramaic Levi Document: Edition, Translation, Commentary*. Studia in Veteris Testamenti Pseudepigrapha 19. Leiden: Brill, 2004.

Gunneweg, Jan, and Marta Balla. "Neutron Activation Analysis Scroll Jars and Common Ware." Pages 3–54 in *Khirbet Qumrân et ʿAïn Feshkha*. Vol. 2: *Études d'anthropologie, de physique et de chimie*. Edited by Jean-Baptiste Humbert and Jan Gunneweg. NTOASA 3. Göttingen: Vandenhoeck & Ruprecht, 2003.

———. "Possible Connection Between the Inscriptions on Pottery, the Ostraca and Scrolls." Pages 389–96 in *Khirbet Qumrân et ʿAïn Feshkha*. Vol. 2: *Études d'anthropologie, de physique et de chimie*. Edited by Jean-Baptiste Humbert and Jan Gunneweg. NTOASA 3. Göttingen: Vandenhoeck & Ruprecht, 2003.

Haberman, D. *Journey through the Twelve Forests*. New York: Oxford University Press, 1994.

Hachlili, Rachel. "The Qumran Cemetery Reassessed." Pages 46–78 in *The Oxford Handbook on the Dead Sea Scrolls*. Edited by Timothy H. Lim and John Collins. Oxford: Oxford University Press, 2010.

Hadas, Gideon. "Where was the Harbour of ʿEn-Gedi Situated?" *IEJ* 43 (1993) 45–49.

———. "Dead Sea Sailing Routes during the Herodian Period." *BAIAS* 26 (2008) 31–36.

———. "Dead Sea Anchorages." *RB* 118 (2011) 161–79.

Halpern-Amaru, Betsy. "Bilhah and Naphtali in Jubilees: A Note on 4QTNaphtali." *DSD* 6 (1999) 1–10.

———. *The Empowerment of Women in the Book of Jubilees*. JSJSup 60. Leiden: Brill, 1999.

Harding, G. Lankester. "Introductory. The Discovery, the Excavation, Minor Finds." DJD 1:3–7.

Har-El, Menashe. "Agriculture." In *EDSS* 1:15.

Harrington, Hannah K. "Purity." In *EDSS* 2: 724–28.

Hempel, Charlotte. "The Earthly Essene Nucleus of 1QSa." *DSD* 3 (1996) 253–69.

———. "'Haskalah' at Qumran: The Eclectic Character of Qumran Cave 4." In *The Qumran Rule Texts in Context: Collected Studies*, 303–38. TSAJ 154. Tübingen: Mohr Siebeck, 2013.

———. *The Laws of the Damascus Document: Sources, Traditions and Redaction*. STDJ 29. Leiden: Brill, 1998.

———. "The Penal Code Reconsidered." In *Legal Texts and Legal Issues. Proceedings of the Second Meeting of the International Organisation for Qumran Studies, Cambridge, 1995*, edited by Moshe J. Bernstein et al., 337–48. STDJ 23. Leiden: Brill, 1997.

Hirschfeld, Yizhar. "Excavations at ʿEin Feshkha, 2001: Final Report." *IEJ* 54 (2004) 37–74.

———. "Qumran in the Second Temple Period." Pages 223–40 in *Qumran, the Site of the Dead Sea Scrolls: Archaeological Interpretations and Debates; Proceedings of a Conference Held at Brown University, November 17–19, 2002*, edited by Katharina Galor et al., 223–40. STDJ 57. Leiden/Boston: Brill, 2006.

Bibliography

Høgenhaven, Jesper. "Copper Scroll." In *T & T Clark Companion to the Dead Sea Scrolls*, edited by George J. Brooke and Charlotte Hempel, 304-5. London: T & T Clark, 2019.

Humbert, Jean-Baptiste. "Cacher et se cacher à Qumrân: Grottes et refuges. Morphologie, fonctions, anthropologie." In *The Caves of Qumran: Proceedings of the International Conference, Lugano 2014*, edited by Marcello Fidanzio, 34-66. STDJ 118. Leiden: Brill, 2017.

———. "Some Remarks on the Archaeology of Qumran." In *Qumran, the Site of the Dead Sea Scrolls: Archaeological Interpretations and Debates; Proceedings of a Conference Held at Brown University, November 17-19, 2002*, edited by Katharina Galor et al., 19-40. STDJ 57. Leiden/Boston: Brill, 2006.

Humbert, Jean-Baptiste, and Alain Chambon, eds. *Fouilles de Khirbet Qumrân et de Aïn Feshkha*. NTOASA 1. Göttingen: Vandenhoeck & Ruprecht, 1994.

Humbert, Jean-Baptiste, and Marcello Fidanzio. *Khirbet Qumrân and Aïn Feshkha IVA: Qumrân Cave 11Q: Archaeology and New Scroll Fragments*. NTOASA 8a. Göttingen: Vandenhoeck & Ruprecht, 2019.

Hutter, Manfred. "Lilith לילית." In *Dictionary of Deities and Demons in the Bible*, edited by Karel van der Toorn et al., 520-21. 2nd ed. Leiden: Brill, 1999.

Ilan, Tal. "The Attraction of Aristocratic Women to Pharisaism During the Second Temple Period." *HTR* 88 (1995) 1-33.

———. *Jewish Women in Greco-Roman Palestine: An Inquiry into Image and Status*. TSAJ 44. Tübingen: Mohr/Siebeck, 1995.

———. "Women in Qumran and the Dead Sea Scrolls." In *The Oxford Handbook of the Dead Sea Scrolls*, edited by John J. Collins and Timothy Lim, 122-47. Oxford: Oxford University Press, 2010.

Isaksson, Abel. *Marriage and Ministry in the New Temple: A Study with Special Reference to Mt. 19.3-12 and 1. Cor. 11.3-16*. Acta Seminarii Neotestamentici Upsaliensis 24. Lund: Gleerup, 1965.

Jacobus, Helen R. "Calendars." In *T & T Clark Companion to the Dead Sea Scrolls*, edited by George J. Brooke and Charlotte Hempel, 433-48. London: T & T Clark, 2019.

Japhet, Sara. "The Prohibition of the Habitation of Women: The Temple Scroll's Attitude toward Sexual Impurity and its Biblical Precedents." In *From the Rivers of Babylon to the Highlands of Judah: Collected Studies on the Restoration Period*, 268-88. Winona Lake, IN: Eisenbrauns, 2006.

Kister, Menahem. "Notes on Some New Texts from Qumran." *JJS* 44 (1993) 280-90.

Knauf, Ernst Axel. "Qôs." In *Dictionary of Deities and Demons in the Bible*, edited by Karel van der Toorn et al., 674-77. 2nd ed. Leiden: Brill, 1999.

Kraemer, Ross. *Maenads, Martyrs, Matrons, Monastics*. Philadelphia: Fortress, 1988.

Kugel, James. *The Bible as It Was*. Cambridge: Harvard University Press, 1997.

Kugler, Robert. *From Patriarch to Priest: The Levi-Priestly Tradition from Aramaic Levi to Testament of Levi*. Early Judaism and Its Literature 9. Atlanta: Scholars, 1996.

Lange, Armin, with Ulrike Mittman-Richert. "Annotated List of the Texts from the Judaean Desert Classified by Content and Genre." Pages 203-38 in *The Texts from the Judaean Desert: Indices and an Introduction to the* Discoveries in the Judaean Desert *Series*. Edited by Emanuel Tov. DJD 39. Oxford: Clarendon, 2002.

Larsen, Eric. "4QNarrative Work and Prayer." DJD 36: 369-86.

Leibner, Uzi. "Arts and Crafts, Manufacture and Production." In *The Oxford Handbook of Jewish Daily Life in Roman Palestine*, edited by Catherine Hezser, 264-96. Oxford: Oxford University Press, 2010.

Bibliography

Lemaire, André. "Inscriptions du khirbeh, des grottes et de 'Ain Feshkha." In *Khirbet Qumrân et 'Aïn Feshkha*. Vol. 2: *Études d'anthropologie, de physique et de chimie*, edited by Jean-Baptiste Humbert and Jan Gunneweg, 341–88. NTOASA 3. Göttingen: Vandenhoeck & Ruprecht, 2003.

Levine, A. J. "Women in the Q Communit(ies) and Traditions." In *Women and Christian Origins*, edited by Ross Kraemer and Mary Rose D'Angelo, 150–70. New York: Oxford University Press, 1999.

Levine, Baruch. "The Temple Scroll: Aspects of Its Historical Provenance and Literary Character." *BASOR* 232 (1978) 5–23.

Lim, Timothy H. *Pesharim*. Companion to the Qumran Scrolls 3. London: Sheffield Academic Press, 2002.

Lönnqvist, Kenneth. *The Report of the Amman Lots of the Qumran Silver Coin Hoards: New Chronological Aspects of the Silver Coin Hoard Evidence from Khirbet Qumran at the Dead Sea*. Amman: National Press, 2007.

Machiela, Daniel A. *The Dead Sea Genesis Apocryphon*. STDJ 79. Leiden: Brill, 2009.

Magen, Yitzhak, and Yuval Peleg. "Back to Qumran: Ten Years of Excavation and Research, 1993–2004." In *Qumran, the Site of the Dead Sea Scrolls: Archaeological Interpretations and Debates; Proceedings of a Conference Held at Brown University, November 17–19, 2002*, edited by Katharina Galor et al., 55–113. STDJ 57. Leiden: Brill, 2006.

———. *Back to Qumran: Final Report (1993–2004)*. JSP 18. Jerusalem: Israel Antiquities Authority, 2018.

Magness, Jodi. *The Archaeology of Qumran and the Dead Sea Scrolls*. SDSSRL. Grand Rapids: Eerdmans, 2002. Cited as *Archaeology*^{1}. 2nd ed., 2021. Cited as *Archaeology*^{2}.

———. "Communal Meals and Sacred Space at Qumran." In *Shaping Community: The Art and Archaeology of Monasticism*, edited by S. McNally, 15–28. BAR International Series 941. Oxford: Archeopress, 2001.

———. "The Community of Qumran in Light of its Pottery." In *Debating Qumran: Collected Essays on Its Archaeology*, 1–15. ISACR 4. Leuven: Peeters, 2004.

———. "The Connection between the Site of Qumran and the Scroll Caves in Light of Ceramic Evidence." In *The Caves of Qumran: Proceedings of the International Conference, Lugano 2014*, edited by Marcello Fidanzio, 184–94. STDJ 118. Leiden: Brill, 2017.

———. "'Ein Feshkha." In *EDSS* 1:237–38.

———. *Masada: From Jewish Revolt to Modern Myth*. Princeton: Princeton University Press, 2019.

———. "Qumran: The Site of the Dead Sea Scrolls: A Review Article." *RevQ* 22 (2006) 641–64.

———. "Qumran Archaeology: Past Perspectives and Future Prospects." In *The Dead Sea Scrolls after Fifty Years: A Comprehensive Assessment*, edited by Peter Flint and James C. VanderKam, Vol. 1, 47–98. Leiden: Brill, 1998.

———. "Were Sacrifices Offered at Qumran? The Animal Bone Deposits Reconsidered." *JAJ* 7 (2016) 5–34.

———. "Why Scroll Jars?" In *Debating Qumran: Collected Essays on its Archaeology*, 151–68. ISACR 4. Leuven: Peeters, 2004.

———. "Women at Qumran?" In *Debating Qumran: Collected Essays on its Archaeology*, 113–50. ISACR 4. Leuven: Peeters, 2004.

Metso, Sarianna. *The Textual Development of the Qumran Community Rule*. STDJ 21. Leiden: Brill, 1997.

Bibliography

Michniewicz, Jacek, and Miroslaw Krzysko. "The Provenance of Scroll Jars in the Light of Archaeometric Investigations." In *Khirbet Qumrân et 'Aïn Feshkha*. Vol 2: *Études d'anthropologie, de physique et de chimie*, edited by Jean-Baptiste Humbert and Jan Gunneweg, 59–100. NTOASA 3. Göttingen: Vandenhoeck & Ruprecht, 2003.

Milgrom, Jacob. "The City of the Temple: A Response to Lawrence H. Schiffman." *JQR* (1994) 125–28.

———. "'Sabbath' and 'Temple City' in the Temple Scroll." *BASOR* 232 (1978) 25–27.

———. "Studies in the Temple Scroll." *JBL* 97 (1978) 501–23.

Milik, J. T. "Appendice: Deux jarres inscrites provenant d'une grotte de Qumrân." DJD 3: 37–41.

———. "Tefillin, Mezuzot et Targums (4Q128–4Q157)." DJD 6: 33–90.

———. *Ten Years of Discovery in the Wilderness of Judaea*. Translated by John Strugnell. SBT 26. Naperville, IL: Allenson, 1959.

Misgav, Haggai. "The Ostraca." In *Back to Qumran: Final Report (1993–2004)*, edited by Yitzhak Magen and Yuval Peleg, 431–42. JSP 18. Jerusalem: Israel Antiquities Authority, 2018.

Mizzi, Dennis. "The Burial of Sealed Jars in the Qumran Cemetery: Disposal of Consecrated Property?" In *Pushing Sacred Boundaries in Early Judaism and the Ancient Mediterranean: Essays in Honor of Jodi Magness*, edited by Dennis Mizzi et al., 349–73. JSJS 208. Leiden: Brill, 2023.

———. "From the Judaean Desert to the Great Sea: Qumran in a Mediterranean Context." *DSD* 24 (2017) 378–406.

———. "The Glass from Khirbet Qumran: What Does It Tell Us about the Qumran Community?" In *The Dead Sea Scrolls: Texts and Contexts*, edited by Charlotte Hempel, 99–198. STDJ 90. Leiden: Brill, 2010.

———. "Miscellaneous Artefacts from the Qumran Caves: An Exploration of their Significance." In *The Caves of Qumran: Proceedings of the International Conference, Lugano 2014*, edited by Marcello Fidanzio, 137–60. STDJ 118. Leiden: Brill, 2017.

———. "'Rome' at Qumran?—What If? Some Remarks on the So-Called Roma Jar from Qumran Cave 7Q." In *The Lure of the Antique: Essays on Malta and Mediterranean Archaeology in Honour of Anthony Bonanno*, edited by Nicholas C. Vella et al., 351–74. ANESSup 5. Leuven: Peeters, 2018.

Mizzi, Dennis, and Jodi Magness. "Was Qumran Abandoned at the End of the First Century BCE?" *JBL* 135 (2016) 301–20.

Mlynarczyk, Jolanta. "Terracotta Oil Lamps (Roland de Vaux's Excavations of the Caves)." In *The Caves of Qumran: Proceedings of the International Conference, Lugano 2014*, edited by Marcello Fidanzio, 109–22. STDJ 118. Leiden: Brill, 2017.

Moore, Rick D. "Personification of the Seduction of Evil: 'The Wiles of the Wicked Woman.'" *RevQ* 10 (1979–81) 505–19.

Murphy, Catherine M. *Wealth in the Dead Sea Scrolls and in the Qumran Community*. STDJ 40. Leiden: Brill, 2002.

Nagar, Yossi, et al. "Conclusive Palaeodemographic Analysis, Based on New Anthropological Data from the Cemetery of Qumran." *RevQ* 34 (2022) 3–70.

Naveh, Joseph. "4QExercitium Calami C." DJD 36: 291–93.

Netzer, Ehud. "Did Any Perfume Industry Exist at 'Ein Feshkha?" *IEJ* 55 (2005) 97–100.

Newsom, Carol. *The Book of Job: A Contest of Moral Imaginations*. Oxford: Oxford University Press, 2003.

Bibliography

———. "'Sectually Explicit' Literature from Qumran." In *The Hebrew Bible and Its Interpreters*, edited by William Propp et al., 167–87. Biblical and Judaic Studies 1. Winona Lake, IN: Eisenbrauns, 1990.

———. "Woman and the Discourse of Patriarchal Wisdom: A Study of Proverbs 1–9." In *Gender and Difference in Ancient Israel*, edited by Peggy L. Day, 142–60. Minneapolis: Fortress, 1989.

Nickelsburg, George. *Jewish Literature Between the Bible and the Mishnah*. Philadelphia: Fortress Press, 1981. 2nd ed., 2005. Referred to as *Jewish Literature*².

Niditch, Susan. "Genesis." In *The Women's Bible Commentary*, edited by Carol A. Newsom et al., 27–45. Rev. and updated ed. Louisville: Westminster John Knox, 2012.

Norton, Jonathan. "Reassessment of Controversial Studies on the Cemetery." In *Khirbet Qumrân et 'Aïn Feshkha. Vol. 2: Études d'anthropologie, de physique et de chimie*, edited by Jean-Baptiste Humbert and Jan Gunneweg, 107–27. NTOASA 3. Göttingen: Vandenhoeck & Ruprecht, 2008.

O'Callaghan, José. "New Testament Papyri in Qumran Cave 7?" *JBL* 91 (1972) 1–14.

Pardes, Ilana. *Countertraditions in the Bible: A Feminist Approach*. Cambridge: Harvard University Press, 1992.

Patrich, Joseph. "Khirbet Qumran in Light of New Archaeological Explorations in the Qumran Caves." In *Methods of Investigations of the Dead Sea Scrolls and the Khirbet Qumran Site: Present Realities and Future Prospects*, edited by Michael O. Wise et al., 73–96. New York: New York Academy of Sciences, 1994.

Peters, F. E. *Jerusalem and Mecca: The Typology of the Holy City in the Near East*. New York: New York University Press, 1986.

Pfann, Stephen J. *The Excavations of Khirbet Qumran and Ain Feshkha: Synthesis of Roland de Vaux's Field Notes*. Eng. ed. Göttingen: Vandenhoeck & Ruprecht, 2003.

———. "Reassessing the Judean Desert Caves: Libraries, Archives, *Genizas* and Hiding Places." *BAIAS* 25 (2007) 147–70.

———. "A Table in the Wilderness: Pantries and Tables, Pure Food and Sacred Space." In *Qumran, the Site of the Dead Sea Scrolls: Archaeological Interpretations and Debates; Proceedings of a Conference Held at Brown University, November 17–19, 2002*, edited by Katharina Galor et al., 159–78. STDJ 57. Leiden: Brill, 2006.

———. "Tithe Jars, Scrolls Jars and Cookie Jars." In *Copper Scroll Studies*, edited by George J. Brooke and Philip R. Davies, 163–79. Journal for the Study of Pseudepigrapha Supplement Series 40. London: Sheffield Academic Press, 2004.

———. "The Wine Press (and *Miqveh*) at Kh. Qumran (loc. 75 and 69)." *RB* 101 (1994) 213–14.

Popović, Mladen. "Qumran as Scroll Storehouse in Times of Crisis? A Comparative Perspective on Judaean Desert Manuscript Collections." *JSJ* 43 (2012) 551–94.

Popović, Mladen, et al. "Dating Ancient Manuscripts Using Radiocarbon and AI-based Writing Style Analysis." *arXiv*:2407.12013v1 (2024) 1–133.

Puech, Émile. "4Q184—Dame Folie." *RevQ* 34 (2022) 241–53.

———. "4Q Béatitudes." In *Qumrân Grotte 4, XVIII: Textes Hébreux (4Q521–4Q528, 4Q576–4Q579)*, 115–78. DJD 25. Oxford: Clarendon, 1998.

———. "The Collection of Beatitudes in Hebrew and in Greek (4Q525 1–4 and MT 5, 3–12)." In *Early Christianity in Context. Monuments and Documents*, edited by F. Manns and E. Alliata, 353–68. Studium Biblicum Franciscanum. Collectio Maior 38. Jerusalem: Franciscan Printing Press, 1993.

———. "Un Hymne Essénien en partie retrouvé et les Béatitudes: '1QH' V 12–VI 18 (= col. XIII–XIV 7) et '4QBéat'." *RevQ* 13 (1988) 57–88.

———. "L'ostracon de Khirbet Qumrân (KhQ1996/1) et une vente de terrain à Jéricho témoin de l'occupation essénienne à Qumrân." In *Flores Florentino: Dead Sea Scrolls and Other Early Jewish Studies in Honour of Florentino García Martínez*, edited by Anthony Hilhorst et al., 1–29. JSJSup 122. Leiden: Brill, 2007.

———. "Visions de 'Amram." In *Qumrân Grotte 4, XXII*, 283–406. DJD 31. Oxford: Clarendon, 2001.

Qimron, Elisha. "Celibacy in the Dead Sea Scrolls and the Two Kinds of Sectarians." In *The Madrid Qumran Congress: Proceedings of the International Congress on the Dead Sea Scrolls Madrid 18–21 March, 1991*, edited by J. Trebolle Barrera and L. Vegas Montaner, Vol. 1, 287–94. Leiden: Brill, 1992.

Qimron, Elisha, and John Strugnell. *Qumran Cave 4, V: Miqṣat Maʿase ha-Torah*. DJD 10. Oxford: Clarendon, 1994.

Rabin, Chaim. *The Zadokite Documents*. Oxford: Clarendon, 1958.

Röhrer-Ertl, Olav, et al. "Über die Graberfelder von Khirbet Qumran, insbesondere die Funde der Campagne 1956, I; Anthropologische Datenvorlage und Erstauswertung aufgrund der Collection Kurth." *RevQ* 19 (1999) 3–46.

Roo, Jacqueline C. R. de. "Is 4Q525 a Qumran Sectarian Document?" In *The Scrolls and the Scriptures: Qumran Fifty Years After*, edited by Stanley E. Porter and Craig A. Evans, 338–67. JSPSup 26. Sheffield: Sheffield Academic Press, 1997.

Sanders, Jack T. "When Sacred Canopies Collide: The Reception of the Torah of Moses in the Wisdom Literature of the Second-Temple Period." *JSJ* 32 (2001) 121–36.

Satlow, Michael L. "4Q502 A New Year Festival?" *DSD* 5 (1998) 57–68.

Schiffman, Lawrence H. "Exclusion from the Sanctuary and the City of the Sanctuary in the Temple Scroll." *HAR* 9 (1986) 301–20.

———. "Laws Pertaining to Women in the Temple Scroll." In *The Dead Sea Scrolls: Forty Years of Research*, edited by Devorah Dimant and Uriel Rappaport, 210–28. STDJ 10. Leiden: Brill, 1992. Reprinted in *The Courtyards of the House of the Lord: Studies on the Temple Scroll*, 519–40. STDJ 75. Leiden: Brill, 2008.

———. "Miqṣat Maʿase Ha-Torah and the Temple Scroll." *RevQ* 14 (1989–90) 435–57.

———. *Reclaiming the Dead Sea Scrolls*. Philadelphia: Jewish Publication Society, 1994.

Schofield, Alison. *From Qumran to the Yaḥad: A New Paradigm of Textual Development for* The Community Rule. STDJ 77. Leiden: Brill, 2009.

Schuller, Eileen. "The Apocrypha." In *The Women's Bible Commentary*, edited by Carol Newsom and Sharon Ringe, 233–43. Louisville: Westminster John Knox, 1992.

———. "Women in the Dead Sea Scrolls." In *Methods of Investigation of the Dead Sea Scrolls and the Khirbet Qumran Site: Present Realities and Future Prospects*, edited by Michael Wise et al., 115–31. New York: New York Academy of Sciences, 1994.

———. "Women in the Dead Sea Scrolls." In *The Dead Sea Scrolls after Fifty Years: A Comprehensive Assessment*, edited by Peter Flint and James C. VanderKam, vol. 2, 117–44. Leiden: Brill, 1999. Cited as "Women[2]."

Schuller, Eileen, and Cecilia Wassén. "Women: Daily Life." In *EDSS* 2: 981–84.

Schüssler Fiorenza, Elisabeth. *In Memory of Her*. New York: Crossroads, 1983.

Segal, Michael. "4QReworked Pentateuch or 4QPentateuch?" In *The Dead Sea Scrolls Fifty Years After Their Discovery 1947–1997*, edited by Lawrence H. Schiffman, Emanuel Tov, and James C. VanderKam, 391–99. Jerusalem: Israel Exploration Society and Shrine of the Book, 2000.

BIBLIOGRAPHY

Setel, Drorah. "Exodus." In *The Women's Bible Commentary*, edited by Carol Newsom and Sharon Ringe, 26–35. Exp. ed. Louisville: Westminster John Knox, 1998.

Shamir, Orit, and Na'ama Sukenik. "Qumran Textiles and the Garments of Qumran's Inhabitants." *DSD* 18 (2011) 206–25.

Shanks, Hershel. *Frank Moore Cross: Conversations with a Bible Scholar*. Washington, DC: Biblical Archaeology Society, 1994.

Shavit, Yaacov. "The 'Qumran Library' in the Light of the Attitude towards Books and Libraries in the Second Temple Period." In *Methods of Investigations of the Dead Sea Scrolls and the Khirbet Qumran Site: Present Realities and Future Prospects*, edited by Michael O. Wise et al., 7–29. New York: New York Academy of Sciences, 1994.

Sheridan, Susan. "Scholars, Soldiers, Craftsmen, Elites?: Analysis of the French Collection of Human Remains from Qumran." *DSD* 9 (2002) 199–248.

Silberman, Neil Asher. "Sukenik, Eleazar L." In *EDSS* 2: 902–3.

Stacey, David. "Seasonal Industries at Qumran." *BAIAS* 26 (2008), 7–29.

Stacey, David, and Gregory Doudna. *Qumran Revisited: A Reassessment of the Archaeology of the Site and Its Texts*. BAR International Series 2520. Oxford: ArcheoPress, 2013.

Steckoll, Solomon. "Preliminary Excavation Report in the Qumran Cemetery." *RevQ* 6 (1968) 323–52.

Stegemann, Hartmut. *The Library of Qumran: On the Essenes, Qumran, John the Baptist, and Jesus*. Grand Rapids: Eerdmans, 1998.

———. "The Qumran Essenes—Local Members of the Main Jewish Union in Late Second Temple Times." In *The Madrid Qumran Congress. Proceedings of the International Congress on the Dead Sea Scrolls, Madrid, 18–21 March, 1991*, edited by J. Trebolle Barrera and L. Vegas Montaner, vol. 1, 83–166. Leiden: Brill, 1992.

Steudel, Annette. *Der Midrasch zur Eschatologie aus der Qumrangemeinde (4QMidrEschat^{a,b}): Materielle Rekonstruktion, Textbestand, Gattung, traditionsgeschichtliche Einordnung des durch 4Q174 ("Florilegium") und 4Q177 ("Catena A") repräsentierten Werkes aus den Qumran funden*. STDJ 13. Leiden: Brill, 1994.

Stökl ben Ezra, Daniel. "Old Caves and Young Caves: A Statistical Reevaluation of a Qumran Consensus." *DSD* 14 (2007) 313–33.

Stone, Michael E. "The Genealogy of Bilhah." *DSD* 3 (1996) 20–36.

———. "Testament of Naphtali." In *Qumran Cave 4, XVII, Parabiblical Texts, Part 3*, edited by George Brooke et al., 73–82. DJD 22. Oxford: Clarendon, 1996.

Strange, James F. "The 1996 Excavations at Qumran and the Context of the New Hebrew Ostracon." In *Qumran, the Site of the Dead Sea Scrolls: Archaeological Interpretation and Debates; Proceedings of a Conference Held at Brown University, November 17–19, 2002*, edited by Katharina Galor et al., 41–54. STDJ 57. Leiden: Brill, 2006.

Strugnell, John. "More on Wives and Marriage in the Dead Sea Scrolls (4Q416 2 ii 21 [Cf. 1 Thess 4:4] and 4QMMT B)." *RevQ* 17 (1996) 537–47.

———. "Notes en marge du volume V des 'Discoveries in the Judaean Desert of Jordan.'" *RevQ* 7 (1970) 163–276.

Sukenik, Eleazar. *Hidden Scrolls from the Genizah Found in the Judaean Desert* [Hebrew]. Vol. 1. Jerusalem: Bialik Institute, 1948–49.

Sukenik, Na'ama. "The *Temple Scroll* Wrapper from Cave 11. MS 5090/2, MS 5095/4, MS 5095/1." In *Gleanings from the Caves: Dead Sea Scrolls and Artefacts from the Schøyen Collection*, edited by Torleif Elgvin et al., 339–49. LSTS 71. London: Bloomsbury T & T Clark, 2016.

Bibliography

Sukenik, Naʾama, et al. "Textiles and Strings from Cave 11Q." In *Khirbet Qumrân and Aïn Feshkha*. Vol 4A: *Qumrân Cave 11Q: Archaeology and New Scroll Fragments*, edited by Jean-Baptiste Humbert and Marcello Fidanzio, 97–118. NTOASA 8a. Göttingen: Vandenhoeck & Ruprecht, 2019.

Tanzer, Sarah J. "Wisdom of Solomon." In *Women's Bible Commentary*, edited by Carol A. Newsom et al., 404–9. Rev. and updated ed. Louisville: Westminster John Knox, 2012.

Taylor, Joan E. "4Q341: A Writing Exercise Remembered." In *Is There a Text in This Cave? Studies in the Textuality of the Dead Sea Scrolls in Honour of George J. Brooke*, edited by Ariel Feldman et al., 133–46. STDJ 119. Leiden: Brill, 2017.

———. "Buried Manuscripts and Empty Tombs: The Qumran *Genizah* Theory Revisited." In *"Go Out and Study the Land" (Judges 18:2): Archaeological, Historical and Textual Studies in Honor of Hanan Eshel*, edited by Aren M. Maier et al., 269–315. JSJSup 148. Leiden: Brill, 2012.

———. "The Cemeteries of Khirbet Qumran and Women's Presence at the Site." *DSD* 6 (1999) 285–323.

———. *The Essenes, the Scrolls, and the Dead Sea*. Oxford: Oxford University Press, 2012.

———. "Kh. Qumran in Period III." In *Qumran, the Site of the Dead Sea Scrolls: Archaeological Interpretations and Debates; Proceedings of a Conference Held at Brown University, November 17–19, 2002*, edited by Katharina Galor et al., 133–46. STDJ 57. Leiden: Brill, 2006.

———. "The Qumran Caves in their Regional Context: A Chronological Review with a Focus on Bar Kokhba Assemblages." In *The Caves of Qumran: Proceedings of the International Conference, Lugano 2014*, edited by Marcello Fidanzio, 9–33. STDJ 118. Leiden: Brill, 2017.

Taylor, Joan, and Philip R. Davies. "The So-Called Therapeutae of *De Vita Contemplativa*: Identity and Character." *HTR* 91 (1998) 3–24.

Taylor, Joan E., and Shimon Gibson. "Qumran Connected: The Qumran Pass and Paths of the North-Western Dead Sea." In *Qumran und die Archäologie: Texte und Kontexte*, edited by Jörg Frey, et al., 163–210. WUNT 278. Tübingen: Mohr Siebeck, 2011.

Taylor, Joan, et al. "Revisiting Qumran Cave 1Q and its Archaeological Assemblage." *PEQ* 149 (2017) 295–325.

Tervanotko, Hanna. *Denying Her Voice: The Figure of Miriam in Ancient Jewish Literature*. Journal of Ancient Judaism Supplements 23. Göttingen: Vandenhoeck & Ruprecht, 2016.

Thiede, Carsten P. *The Earliest Gospel Manuscript? The Qumran Papyrus 7Q5 and Its Significance for New Testament Studies*. Exeter, UK: Paternoster, 1992.

Tigchelaar, Eibert. "Constructing, Deconstructing and Reconstructing Fragmentary Manuscripts. Illustrated by a Study of 4Q184 (4QWiles of the Wicked Woman)." In *Rediscovering the Dead Sea Scrolls: An Assessment of Old and New Approaches and Methods*, edited by Maxine L. Grossman, 26–47. Grand Rapids: Eerdmans, 2010.

———. "In Search of the Scribe of 1QS." In *Emanuel: Studies in Hebrew Bible, Septuagint and Dead Sea Scrolls in Honor of Emanuel Tov*, edited by Shalom Paul et al., 439–52. VTSup 94. Leiden: Brill, 2007.

———. "Lady Folly and Her House in Three Qumran Manuscripts: On the Relation between 4Q525 15, 5Q16, and 4Q184 1." *RevQ* 91 (2008) 371–81.

———. "The Poetry of *The Wiles of the Wicked Woman (4Q184)*." *RevQ* 100 (2012) 621–33.

Bibliography

Tobin, Thomas H. "4Q185 and Jewish Wisdom Literature." In *Of Scribes and Scrolls*, edited by Harold Attridge et al., 145–52. College Theology Society Resources in Religion 5. Lanham, MD: University Press of America, 1990.

Tov, Emanuel. "A Qumran Origin for the Masada Non-Biblical Texts?" *DSD* 7 (2000) 57–73.

———. *Revised Lists of the Texts from the Judaean Desert*. Leiden: Brill, 2010.

———. *Scribal Practices and Approaches Reflected in the Texts Found in the Judean Desert*. STDJ 54. Leiden: Brill, 2004.

Tov, Emanuel, and Sidnie A. White. "4Q364." In *Qumran Cave 4, VIII, Parabiblical Texts, Part I*, edited by Harold Attridge et al., 197–254. DJD 13. Oxford: Clarendon, 1994.

———. "4Q365." In *Qumran Cave 4, VIII, Parabiblical Texts, Part I*, edited by Harold W. Attridge et al., 255–318. DJD 13. Oxford: Clarendon, 1994.

Trever, John C. *The Untold Story of Qumran*. Westwood, NJ: Revell, 1965.

Ullmann-Margalit, Edna. *Out of the Cave: A Philosophical Inquiry into the Dead Sea Scrolls Research*. Cambridge: Harvard University Press, 2006.

Ulrich, Eugene C. "The Qumran Scrolls and the Biblical Text." In *The Dead Sea Scrolls Fifty Years After Their Discovery 1947–1997*, edited by Lawrence H. Schiffman, Emanuel Tov, and James C. VanderKam, 51–59. Jerusalem: Israel Exploration Society and Shrine of the Book, 2000.

Uusimäki, Elisa. *Turning Proverbs Towards Torah: An Analysis of 4Q525*. STDJ 117. Leiden: Brill, 2016.

VanderKam, James C. *The Book of Jubilees*. Corpus Scriptorum Christianorum Orientalium, Scriptores Aethiopici 87–88. Louvain: Peeters, 1989.

———. *The Dead Sea Scrolls Today*. Grand Rapids: Eerdmans, 1994.

———. *Jubilees: A Commentary on the Book of Jubilees*. 2 vols. Hermeneia. Minneapolis: Fortress, 2018. Cited as *Jubilees*².

VanderKam, James C., and Monica Brady. "4Q377." In *Qumran Cave 4, XXVIII, Miscellanea, Part 2*, edited by Moshe J. Bernstein et al., 205–18. DJD 28. Oxford: Clarendon, 2001.

VanderKam, James C. and J. T. Milik. "Jubilees." DJD 13:1–186.

Vaux, Roland de. *Archaeology and the Dead Sea Scrolls: The Schweich Lectures 1959*. Rev. ed. London: Oxford University Press for the British Academy, 1973.

———. "Archéologie." DJD 3: 3–36. Cited as "Archéologie¹."

———. "Archéologie." DJD 6: 3–22. Cited as "Archéologie²."

———. "La Poterie." DJD 1: 8–17.

Vermeš, Geza. *The Complete Dead Sea Scrolls in English*. New York, Penguin, 1998.

———. *The Dead Sea Scrolls: Qumran in Perspective*. Rev. ed. Philadelphia: Fortress, 1977.

———. "Sectarian Matrimonial Halakhah in the Damascus Rule." *JJS* 25–26 (1974–75) 197–202.

Vermeš, Geza, and Martin Goodman. *The Essenes According to the Classical Sources*. Oxford Centre Textbooks 1. Sheffield: JSOT Press, 1989.

Washington, Harold C. "The Strange Woman (אשה זרה/נכריה) of Proverbs 1–9 and post-Exilic Judaean Society." In *A Feminist Companion to Wisdom Literature*, edited by Athalya Brenner-Idan, 157–84. Feminist Companions to the Bible 9. Sheffield: Sheffield Academic, 1995.

Wassén, Cecilia. *Women in the Damascus Document*. Academia Biblica 21. Atlanta: SBL, 2005.

Bibliography

Webster, Brian. "Chronological Index of the Texts from the Judaean Desert." DJD 39: 351–446.
Wilson, Andrew, and Lawrence M. Wills. "Literary Sources of the Temple Scroll." *HTR* 75 (1982) 275–88.
Wilson, Edmund. *The Scrolls from the Dead Sea*. London: Allen, 1955.
Winston, David. *The Wisdom of Solomon*. AB 43. Garden City, NY: Doubleday, 1979.
Wintermute, Orville S. "Jubilees." In *The Old Testament Pseudepigrapha*, edited by James H. Charlesworth, 2:35–142. Garden City, NY: Doubleday, 1985.
Wise, Michael O., et al. *The Dead Sea Scrolls: A New Translation*. San Francisco: Harper-Collins, 1996.
Wright, Benjamin G. III. "Ben Sira on the Sage as Exemplar." In *Praise Israel for Wisdom and Instruction: Essays on Ben Sira and Wisdom, the Letter of Aristeas and the Septuagint*, 165–82. JSJSup 131. Leiden: Brill, 2008.
Yadin, Yigael. *The Finds from the Bar-Kokhba Period in the Cave of Letters*. Jerusalem: Israel Exploration Society, 1963.
―――. *The Temple Scroll*. Rev. English ed. 3 vols. Jerusalem: Israel Exploration Society, 1983.
Yardeni, Ada. "4QExercitium Calami A." In *Cryptic Texts, Part 1: Qumran Cave 4*, edited by Philip Alexander et al., 185–86. DJD 36. Oxford: Clarendon.
―――. "4QExercitium Calami B." DJD 36: 297.
―――. "Appendix: Documentary Texts Alleged to Be from Qumran Cave 4." DJD 27: 283–317.
―――. "A Draft of a Deed on an Ostracon from Khirbet Qumran." *IEJ* 47 (1997) 233–37.
Yee, Gail A. "I Have Perfumed My Bed with Myrrh: The Foreign Woman (*'iššâ zarâ*) in Proverbs 1–9." In *A Feminist Companion to Wisdom Literature*, edited by Athalya Brenner-Idan, 110–26. Feminist Companion to the Bible 9. Sheffield: Sheffield Academic Press, 1995.
Yoder, Christine Roy. "Proverbs." In *Women's Bible Commentary*, edited by Carol A. Newsom et al., 232–42. Rev. and updated ed. Louisville: Westminster John Knox, 2012.
Zahn, Molly M. *Genres of Rewriting in Second Temple Judaism: Scribal Composition and Transmission*. Cambridge: Cambridge University Press, 2020.
Zangenberg, Jürgen. "Bones of Contention. 'New' Bones from Qumran Help Settle Old Questions (and Raise New Ones)—Remarks on Two Recent Conferences." *QC* 9 (2000) 52–76.
Zeuner, Frederick E. "Notes on Qumrân." *PEQ* 92 (1960) 33–36.
Zias, Joseph E. "The Cemeteries of Qumran and Celibacy: Confusion Laid to Rest?" *DSD* 7 (2000) 220–53.

www.ingramcontent.com/pod-product-compliance
Lightning Source LLC
Chambersburg PA
CBHW031433150426
43191CB00006B/497